DUBLIN

THE MINI ROUGH GUIDE

There are more than one hundred Rough
Guide travel, phrasebook, and music titles,
covering destinations from Amsterdam to
Zimbabwe, languages from Czech to Thai,
and musics from World to Opera and Jazz

Forthcoming titles include

Bangkok • Barbados • Japan
Jordan • Syria • Music USA
Country Music

Rough Guides on the Internet

http://www.roughguides.com

Rough Guide Credits

Text editor: Julia Kelly. Series editor: Mark Ellingham
Typesetting: Andy Hilliard.
Cartography: David Callier, Maxine Burke

Publishing Information

This first edition published February 1998 by
Rough Guides Ltd, 1 Mercer St, London WC2H 9QJ.

Distributed by the Penguin Group:

Penguin Books Ltd, 27 Wrights Lane, London W8 5TZ
Penguin Books USA Inc., 375 Hudson Street, New York 10014, USA
Penguin Books Australia Ltd, 487 Maroondah Highway,
PO Box 257, Ringwood, Victoria 3134, Australia
Penguin Books Canada Ltd, 10 Alcorn Avenue,
Toronto, Ontario, Canada M4V 1E4
Penguin Books (NZ) Ltd, 182–190 Wairau Road,
Auckland 10, New Zealand

Typeset in Bembo and Helvetica to an original design by Henry Iles.
Printed in Spain by Graphy Cems.

The publishers and authors have done their best to
ensure the accuracy and currency of all the information
in *The Rough Guide to Dublin*, however, they can accept
no responsibility for any loss, injury or inconvenience
sustained by any traveller as a result of information or
advice contained in the guide.

DUBLIN

THE MINI ROUGH GUIDE

by Dan Richardson

with contributions from Nick Kelly,
Christine Doran and Ray Beggan

We set out to do something different when the first Rough Guide was published in 1982. Mark Ellingham, just out of university, was travelling in Greece. He brought along the popular guides of the day, but found they were all lacking in some way. They were either strong on ruins and museums but went on for pages without mentioning a beach or taverna. Or they were so conscious of the need to save money that they lost sight of Greece's cultural and historical significance. Also, none of the books told him anything about Greece's contemporary life – its politics, its culture, its people, and how they lived.

So with no job in prospect, Mark decided to write his own guidebook, one which aimed to provide practical information that was second to none, detailing the best beaches and the hottest clubs and restaurants, while also giving hard-hitting accounts of every sight, both famous and obscure, and providing up-to-the-minute information on contemporary culture. It was a guide that encouraged independent travellers to find the best of Greece, and was a great success, getting shortlisted for the Thomas Cook travel guide award, and encouraging Mark, along with three friends, to expand the series.

The Rough Guide list grew rapidly and the letters flooded in, indicating a much broader readership than had been anticipated, but one which uniformly appreciated the Rough Guide mix of practical detail and humour, irreverence and enthusiasm. Things haven't changed. The same four friends who began the series are still the caretakers of the Rough Guide mission today: to provide the most reliable, up-to-date and entertaining information to independent-minded travellers of all ages, on all budgets.

We now publish more than 100 titles and have offices in London and New York. The travel guides are written and researched by a dedicated team of more than 100 authors, based in Britain, Europe, the USA and Australia. We have also created a unique series of phrasebooks to accompany the travel series, along with an acclaimed series of music guides, and a best-selling pocket guide to the Internet and World Wide Web. We also publish comprehensive travel information on our web site: **http://www.roughguides.com**

Help Us Update

We've gone to a lot of effort to ensure that this first edition of *The Rough Guide to Dublin* is as up-to-date and accurate as possible. However, if you feel there are places we've under-rated or over-praised, or find we've missed something good or covered something which has now gone, then please write; suggestions, comments or corrections are much appreciated.

We'll credit all contributions, and send a copy of the next edition (or any other Rough Guide if you prefer) for the best letters. Please mark letters: "Rough Guide Dublin Update" and send to:

Rough Guides, 1 Mercer St, London WC2H 9QJ, or
Rough Guides, 375 Hudson St, 9th floor, New York NY 10014.
Or send email to: **mail@roughguides.co.uk**

Online updates about this book can be found on
Rough Guides' Web site (see opposite)

The Author

Dan Richardson was born in England in 1958. Before joining the Rough Guides in 1984, he worked as a sailor on the Red Sea, and as a commodities dealer in Peru. Since then he has travelled extensively in Egypt and Eastern Europe. While in St Petersburg in 1992, he met his wife, Anna; they now have a baby daughter, Sonia.

Acknowledgements

Many thanks to the Kelly family – Delphine, Nick, Bernard and Alexia – for their warm hospitality and insights into Dublin life; and to Eamonn Clarke of the OPW for his help at Dublin Castle and the Government Buildings. In London, thanks are due to Julia Kelly for her patient and painstaking editing, despite many vexations.

CONTENTS

INTRODUCTION

Emphatically the Republic of Ireland's capital, Dublin is the focus of the energy of a country that's now redefining itself as a European nation. It has become a cosmopolitan and youthful place – of the one million people in greater Dublin, more than 50 percent are under 25, and the relative prosperity of many of them is making its impact on a rapidly changing urban landscape. New shops are everywhere, and restaurants, cafés, bars and clubs are opening in abundance, bringing an unmistakeable buzz to the capital, especially at night.

The city's emergence from provincialism is, however, only part of the truth, as Dubliners will be quick to tell you. With the continuing drift of population from the land to the capital, Dublin is bulging at the seams, which, of course, brings its problems – spend just a couple of days here and you'll come upon inner-city deprivation as bad as any in Europe. The spirit of Dublin has its contradictions, too, with youthful enterprise set against a traditionalism that won't relinquish its grip for many years yet: the national divorce referendum in 1995 may have gone in favour of reform, but it was a close-run thing. However, the collision of the old order and the forward-looking younger generations is an essential part of the appeal of this extrovert and dynamic city.

If you approach Dublin by sea, you'll have an opportunity to appreciate its magnificent physical setting, with the fine sweep of Dublin Bay and the weird, conical silhouettes of the Wicklow Mountains providing an exhilarating backdrop to the south. The city centre is so compact that a long weekend will allow you to see all the major sights (for more on its layout, see p.3), but your stay will be a lot richer if you can find time to sample the myriad pubs and thriving nightlife, and to get out into the surrounding countryside. Trains make access easy to the whole curve of Dublin Bay, from the fishing port of Howth in the north to the southern suburbs of Sandycove (with its James Joyce connections); Dalkey, made famous by the comic writer Flann O'Brien; and salubrious Killiney, now colonized by the rich and famous. And Dublin makes a good base for exploring the hills and coastline of Wicklow to the south and the gentler scenery to the north, where the Boyne Valley offers some of Europe's most imposing megalithic monuments.

When to visit

Dublin's warmest months are usually July and August, which are also often the wettest. However, no month is especially hot or cold, and though the climate of Ireland is often damp, this shouldn't be a determining factor in arranging your trip. Obviously the summer is the most popular time, so if you're planning a visit then, you should make sure you've got your accommodation sorted out well before you go – and whatever time you visit, if your stay is going to straddle a weekend, book your room in advance. Before making your decision, you should take a look at the city's calendar of festivals and special events, which range from the parades of St Patrick's Day and the meanderings of Bloomsday (June 16) to blues in Temple Bar in August and the All-Ireland Hurling final in September (see *Sports*, and *Festivals & Events* for more).

Dublin's Climate

| | °F | | °C | | Rainfall | |
| | Average daily | | Average daily | | Average monthly | |
	max	min	max	min	in	mm
Jan	46	34	8	1	2.6	67
Feb	47	35	8	2	2.2	55
March	51	37	10	3	2.0	51
April	55	39	13	4	1.8	45
May	60	43	15	6	2.4	60
June	65	48	18	9	2.2	57
July	67	52	20	11	2.8	70
Aug	67	51	19	11	2.9	74
Sept	63	48	17	9	2.8	72
Oct	57	43	14	6	2.8	70
Nov	51	39	10	4	2.6	67
Dec	47	37	8	3	2.9	74

THE GUIDE

INTRODUCING
THE CITY

entral Dublin is not big, and it's easy to find your way around. One obvious axis is formed by the river, the **Liffey**, running from west to east and dividing the city into two regions of very distinct character – the **northside**, poorer and less developed than its neighbour the **southside** – each of which has a strong allegiance among its inhabitants. The other main axis is the north–south one formed by **Grafton and Westmoreland streets** south of the river, running into **O'Connell Street** in the north.

The majority of the famous attractions are south of the river, and, for many visitors, the city's heart lies around the best of what is left of Georgian Dublin – the grand set pieces of **Fitzwilliam** and **Merrion squares**, with their graceful red-brick houses with ornate, fan-lighted doors and immaculately kept central gardens, and the wide but strangely decorous open space of **St Stephen's Green**. The elegant southside is also the setting for Dublin's august seat of learning, **Trinity College**, and its famous library; **Grafton Street**, the city's upmarket shopping area; **Temple Bar**, the in-place for the arts, alternative shopping and socializing; most of the city's **museums and art galleries**; and the twin cathedrals of **Christ Church** and **St Patrick's**.

North of the Liffey, the main thoroughfare is **O'Connell Street**, whose main monument, the **General Post Office**, was the scene of violent fighting in the Easter Rising of 1916. Further north, among Georgian squares older and seedier than the ones you'll see on the southside, are the **Irish Writers' Museum** and the **Hugh Lane Municipal Museum of Art**. West again, and you come to Dublin's biggest open space – indeed, one of the world's largest city parks – **Phoenix Park**, home of both the President's Residence and the **zoo**.

The telephone code for the Dublin area is ©01.
Calling Dublin from abroad (or Northern Ireland),
dial ©00–353–1, followed by the subscriber's number.

Arrival

The main **points of arrival** are all within easy reach of the city centre, with the bulk of tourist traffic coming in via either the airport, which is just 12km north, or the port at Dún Laoghaire, 16km south.

By air

Dublin Airport arrivals hall has a **tourist office** (daily June–Sept 8am–10pm), a bureau de change (daily 6am–10.30pm), various car rental desks and an ATM. Buses into town leave from outside the departures exit. *Airlink* buses (Mon–Sat 7.30am–11pm, Sun 7.10am–11pm) run directly to the Busáras (central bus station), and the thirty-minute journey costs £2.50, or £3 if travelling on to Heuston Station, twenty minutes further along. You purchase your ticket on board. A cheaper alternative (£1.10) is to catch a regular #41 bus to Lower Abbey Street, near to O'Connell Street. A taxi into the centre should cost about £12.

By bus

Busáras is located off Beresford Place, just behind the Custom House, and is within easy walking distance of O'Connell Street. Buses from all parts of the Republic and Northern Ireland arrive here, along with *Airlink* buses and coaches from Britain. The Busáras has a bureau de change (Mon–Sat 8am–8pm, Sun 10am–6pm) and a left luggage facility (Mon–Sat 8am–8pm, Sun 10am–5.45pm).

By ferry

Arriving by ferry from Britain, you will dock at either **Dublin Harbour**, 3km east of the centre (for Irish Ferries) or **Dún Laoghaire** (for Stena Line). The former is served by bus #53, which is timetabled to meet ferry services and heads directly for the city centre. Dún Laoghaire is twenty minutes from the centre by the DART (£1.10; see p.9 for more). There is a tourist office at Dún Laoghaire (Mon–Sun 10am–9pm, subject to ferry arrivals), plus a bureau de change (daily 8.30am–8.15pm) and an ATM. Note that coach passengers from Britain will be driven directly to the city centre.

By train

Connolly Station, a couple of hundred yards northeast from the Busáras, is the terminus for trains from Belfast and Sligo to the north and Wexford and Rosslare in the south;

ARRIVAL

it is also on the DART line. Facilities are limited, though there is a left luggage office (Mon–Sat 7.40am–9.30pm, Sun 9.15am–1pm & 5–9pm). **Heuston Station**, its counterpart on the south bank of the Liffey, 4km west of the city centre, is the terminus for trains from Cork, Killarney, Tralee, Waterford, Limerick, Galway, Westport and Ballina. Again, there is a left luggage office (Mon–Sat 7.15am–8.35pm, Sun 8am–3pm & 5–9pm). Bus #90 runs between the two termini. **Tara Street** and **Pearse Street** stations are on the south side of the Liffey and serve DART and suburban train services.

Information

Dublin's **main tourism centre** is in a converted church near the western end of Suffolk Street, between Grafton Street and College Green (mid-June to mid-Sept Mon & Wed–Sat 8.30am–7.30pm, Tues 9.30am–5.30pm, Sun 11am–5.30pm; Oct–May Mon–Sat 9am–5.30pm). There are separate desks for information, accommodation, coach trips, bus and rail tickets, theatre bookings, money exchange and car rental. The first two can be incredibly busy and a numbered ticket queueing system operates, so head directly for the dispenser when you enter. You can also book a room through the interactive video unit outside the building (credit cards only). The offices at the **airport**, **Dún Laoghaire** and in *Exclusively Irish*, 14 Upper O'Connell Street (Mon–Sat 10am–5.30pm) provide similar facilities, though they stock a less comprehensive range of printed information. Alternatively, dialling ✆1550 11 22 33 provides access to a 24-hour recorded information rundown, but it's pretty costly, cumbersome and frequently engaged.

Accommodation listings begin on p.169.

All the offices can find you **accommodation** and charge a flat fee of £3 for the service, together with a deposit of ten percent of your hotel or guesthouse bill. For credit card accommodation booking you can ring ℂ605 7777, but it's often difficult to get through.

Eight attractions are run by Dublin Tourism: Malahide Castle, Newbridge House, the James Joyce Museum and Tower, Dublin Writers Museum, the Shaw Birthplace, the Fry Model Railway, and Dublin's Viking Adventure. A SuperSaver card, covering entry to all, costs £16.50 (children £8.50, concessions £12.50, family £37).

A downtown alternative is the **USIT** discount student travel agency on Aston Quay, opposite O'Connell Bridge (Mon–Fri 9am–5.30pm, Sat 10am–1pm; ℂ677 8117). USIT can book you a B&B during the summer, and runs its own hotel and hostel. Their noticeboard is also useful if you're looking for work or a flatshare, and there are flyers for hostels, clubs and other items of interest.

In any of these places you should be able to pick up a copy of the *Dublin Event Guide* which provides concise **listings** of gigs, clubs, exhibitions and tourist sites. You can also pick it up at **Temple Bar Information Centre**, 18 Eustace St (Mon–Fri 9am–5.30pm, Sat & Sun 11am–4pm; ℂ671 5717), a particularly good source of arts scene info. The other major listings guide is *In Dublin* (£1.50), available at most newsagents, with lots on clubs and style and a longer listings section that also covers restaurants. Both the *Event Guide* and *In Dublin* are published fortnightly.

INFORMATION

Daily cinema and theatre listings appear in the *Irish Times* (the best national daily newspaper, though on Sundays the *Sunday Tribune* holds sway) and the *Evening Herald* (Dublin's only evening paper). Music listings are also included in *Hot Press* (£1.95, fortnightly), Ireland's often witty, occasionally scurrilous and usually iconoclastic rock magazine.

While the **maps** in this book should suffice for your visit, long-stayers might invest in a pocket-sized *Dublin Street Plan* (£4) of the inner city and suburbs. Small freebie maps of the centre can also be picked up in tourist offices.

Transport

The only real way to get to know Dublin is to walk, but to visit the farther-flung sights you'll probably want to use the city's public transport. **Travel passes** come in many forms and are obtainable from Dublin Bus at 59 Upper O'Connell Street and at newsagents displaying the Dublin Bus sign. A one-day adult bus pass (£3.30) covers all buses except *Nitelink* and *Airlink*, while the bus and rail short-hop pass (£4.50) also covers the DART and suburban services. The four-day explorer ticket (£10) is valid for travel after 9.45am and all day at weekends on all services.

Buses

Buses are the mainstay of public transport, reaching most parts of Dublin, including places beyond the city limits. Regular services operate from 6am; last buses leave the city centre at 11.30pm. Special *Nitelink* buses run out to the suburbs on Thursdays, Fridays and Saturdays, departing from D'Olier, Westmoreland and College streets at midnight, 1am, 2am and 3am. Travel passes are not valid for *Nitelink* buses, which charge a flat fare of £2.50. The price of tickets on regular buses ranges from 55p to £1.10. It's prudent to hoard coins as some routes are exact-fare only.

DART and suburban trains

The other vital service is the Dublin Area Rapid Transport system, or **DART** (daily 6.55am–11.30pm), whose trains link Howth to the north of the city with Bray to the south, via such places as Dún Laoghaire and Dalkey, and connect with suburban services to even further afield. The maximum single fare is £1.50, but if you're considering taking more than one or two trips a day, it may be worth buying some form of travel pass. This advice also applies to some of the **suburban trains** operated by Iarnród Éireann, which use the same tracks as the DART but make far fewer stops en route (Connolly, Tara and Pearse Street stations in the centre, Howth Junction to the north and Dún Laoghaire and Bray to the south). The Northern Suburban service from Pearse Street to Dundalk is the speediest way to make day excursions to Malahide (see p.151), Castletown (see p.161) and Newgrange (see p.163).

Taxis

Taxis don't generally ply the streets for custom (though it is possible to hail them), but wait in ranks in central locations, such as outside the *Shelbourne Hotel* on St Stephen's Green, Dame Street (opposite the main gate of Trinity College) and Abbey Street Lower (on the right-hand side of O'Connell Street heading north from O'Connell Bridge). If you want to order a taxi by phone, call *National Radio Cabs* (©677 2222) or *City Cabs* (©872 7272); the latter also run a fleet of **wheelchair-accessible** cabs. Other firms with fixed rates, open 24 hours, include *Checkers Cabs*, 4 Bedford Row (©834 3434), *Radiolink Taxis*, 24 Aungier St

TRANSPORT

9

(℃478 1111) and *Ballymun Cabs*, at the bottom end of Parnell Square East (℃834 3333). Finding a taxi after midnight on weekends is difficult, so if you know you'll need one, book it.

Bus and walking tours

If you're only in Dublin for a short time or just want a quick feel for the city's landmarks, you could take one of the many tours on offer, which range from city-centre walks to coach expeditions to outlying attractions like Glendalough and Newgrange. The following selection gives a sense of the variety available – the tourist offices have full details.

Bus Éireann (℃836 6111) runs excursions to Glendalough and the Wicklow Mountains, Newgrange and the Boyne Valley, Russborough House and Powerscourt Gardens.

Dublin Bus (℃873 4222) has a fleet of open-topped buses in green-and-white livery. Their *Dublin City Tour* lasts just over an hour and passes Parnell Square, Trinity College, the National Gallery, St Stephen's Green, Dublin Castle, the cathedrals and the Guinness Brewery. Tours commence outside the Dublin Bus HQ on O'Connell Street and run every fifteen minutes between 9.45am and 5pm with an evening tour at 6.30pm.

Tickets are valid all day and you can hop on or hop off at any of ten different stops. The *Grand Dublin Tour* lasts almost three hours and includes the Custom House, Kilmainham Jail, the Royal Hospital and Phoenix Park, leaving at 10.15am and 2.15pm daily. They also run a *South Coast Tour* down as far as Enniskerry (near Powerscourt Estate) in the Wicklow Mountains, and a *Coast and Castle Tour* to Howth and Malahide.

Grey Line (℃605 7705) goes to Glendalough, Newgrange, Malahide Castle and Powerscourt Estate, running at times of the year not covered by Bus Éireann and at competitive prices.

Historical Walking Tours (℡845 0241) offer a two-hour walking tour of the old city, featuring Trinity, Dublin Castle, Christ Church, St Audoen's and the Norman walls, accompanied by a lecture on Dublin's development and Irish history.

Literary Pub Crawl (℡454 0228) is an amusing tour of literary haunts on the southside, starting at *The Duke* on Duke Street.

Mary Gibbon's Tours (℡283 9973) does half-day city bus tours and excursions to Newgrange or Powerscourt and Glendalough.

Musical Pub Crawl (℡478 0191) provides a chance to learn about Irish music on an evening roam that kicks off at *Oliver St John Gogarty's* in Temple Bar.

Revolutionary Dublin 1916–1923 (℡497 4912) is a walking tour that covers the key sites in Dublin's republican history.

THE GEORGIAN SOUTHSIDE

The **Georgian southside** is the richest and most attractive part of the city centre and the focal point for much of Dublin's cultural life. While replete with institutions like Trinity College, the Irish Parliament and the National Gallery, it also fizzes with restaurants and watering-holes, the latest fashions and music, and a confidence that impresses visitors – and Dubliners. Ireland's economic boom is reflected in the windows of Grafton Street's stores and the shiny new cars parked around Merrion Square, whose elegant terraces are redolent of a previous era of pride and prosperity.

Most visitors gravitate to **College Green**, where the world-famous *Book of Kells* can be seen at **Trinity College**; from here it's a short walk up **Grafton Street** to **St Stephen's Green**, the leafy centrepiece of Georgian town planning, replicated on a lesser scale by

Merrion and Fitzwilliam squares. In and around them you'll find plenty to enjoy, from the prehistoric gold and medieval treasures of the **National Museum** to the cafés and pubs where some of Ireland's greatest writers and musicians have hung out. While the European art in the **National Gallery** is an obvious attraction, there's a lot to admire in the decorative arts of Georgian times, at **Newman House** (where Joyce studied) and **Number 29 Lower Fitzwilliam Street** (a period-piece reconstruction of domestic life) – or in the modern interior of **Government Buildings**.

Historically, the area covered in this chapter constituted a bold solution to the problems of old Dublin, a walled city little changed since Tudor times and battered by the Cromwellian wars. Given carte blanche by the Wide Streets Commission in the eighteenth century, speculators bought up greenfield sites on both sides of the river and created a whole new city of spacious residences for gentry enriched by rising agricultural profits and merchants and manufacturers capitalizing on Dublin's position as the "second city" of the British Empire.

The moment when its fortunes turned can be dated to January 1, 1801, when the Irish Parliament was dissolved by the Act of Union, and the Anglo-Irish Ascendancy turned their attention to London, selling their Dublin townhouses and transferring their revenues to England. The middle-class professionals who bought their houses soon abandoned the northside, which declined into the worst slum in Europe, and moved to the southside, which remained a bastion of gentility through the Great Famine (when famished countryfolk were fed from cauldrons on Merrion Square). Since independence the area has revived and has fared better than anywhere else in Dublin by a long chalk.

TRINITY COLLEGE

Map 4, E5. Grounds Mon–Fri 7am–midnight (Sat & Sun, main gate locked at 6pm; use Nassau Street gate); free. **Old Library** June–Sept Mon–Sat 9.30am–5pm, Sun 9.30am–4.30pm; Oct–May Mon–Sat 9.30am–4.30pm; £3.50, students & under-18s £3, under-12s free. **Dublin Experience** May 19–Sept 28, daily 10am–5pm; £3, students/children £2.50. Combined ticket for both £6, students £5, children £1.50, family £12.

College Green is something of a misnomer for what is today a heavily trafficked junction outside **Trinity College**, where a tiny lawn is about as green as it gets. The name commemorates the fact that when Trinity was founded it stood on open common land outside the walled city, including a flat-topped mound, 12m high and 72m in circumference, that had once been the Viking *Thingmount*, or parliament (otherwise known as the *Haugen*, hence College Green's old name, Hoggen Green). In Georgian times the ground was levelled to provide the foundations of Nassau Street, and College Green became the centre of political life, as power briefly diverted from the viceregal seat in Dublin Castle to the Protestant Irish parliament, established here in 1782.

Ireland's oldest university, Trinity College, was founded in 1592 by Queen Elizabeth I to rectify "the barbarism" of the Irish and prevent them from being "infected with Popery" at foreign universities. Admission was restricted to Protestants, but Catholics could get free education by rejecting their faith. Trinity had a formative influence on the Anglo-Irish tradition, as Protestant families sent their sons to be educated here rather than in England, and its alumni made their mark in politics (Edmund Burke, Wolfe Tone, Robert Emmet, Edward Carson, Douglas Hyde), literature (Jonathan Swift, Oliver Goldsmith, Oscar Wilde, Bram Stoker, J.M. Synge, Samuel Beckett) and other fields.

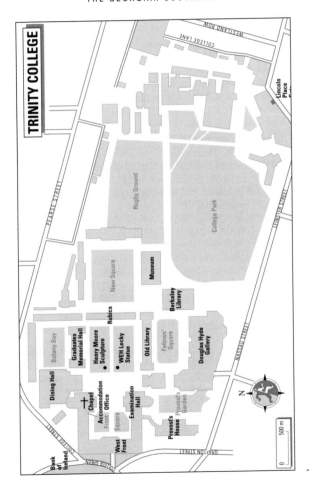

TRINITY COLLEGE

College Lane

Westland Row

Lincoln Place

Pearse Street

Rugby Ground

College Park

New Square

Museum

Botany Bay

Graduates Memorial Hall

Henry Moore Sculpture

WEH Lecky Statue

Rubics

Old Library

Berkeley Library

Fellows' Square

Dining Hall

Chapel

Accommodation

Front Office

Examination Hall

Provost's Garden

Douglas Hyde Gallery

West Front

Provost's House

Nassau Street

Leinster Street

Grafton Street

Bank of Ireland

College Green

College Street

N

0   500 m

Up until the mid-nineteenth century students were notoriously fractious: duelling was so common that few graduated unscarred, and many joined in the affrays of the Liberty and the Ormond Boys (see p.81). During the 1916 Easter Rising, Trinity was held for the Crown by its Officer Training Corps. Although religious restrictions were abolished in 1873, its Protestant bias survived after Irish independence, since as late as the 1970s Catholic archbishops forbade their flocks to study at Trinity without first obtaining special permission, on pain of excommunication.

Today, seventy percent of its students are Catholic and Trinity is one of three universities in the city: Dublin University (of which Trinity is the sole college); University College Dublin, based near Donnybrook; and Dublin City University, in Glasnevin. However, neither of the others can match Trinity as an architectural set piece that looks like a great university should.

The **West Front**, facing College Green, is flanked by statues of two eighteenth-century graduates, the Tory philosopher and statesman Edmund Burke, and the wit and poet Oliver Goldsmith. Both were sculpted by John Foley, who also did Grattan's statue outside the Bank of Ireland, leading to jokes that he cast the legs of all three from the same mould to save money.

Students meet and lounge against the railings by the entrance gates – the point of departure for **walking tours** of Trinity (mid-May to end Sept 9am–5pm; free). Although there's nothing to stop you from wandering around by yourself, the sheer number of visitors over summer makes some shepherding essential. Traffic is steered towards the **Dublin Experience**, an audio-visual flip full of information and images of Dublin's history and some of the most important events of Irish history.

Trinity's main quad is a harmonious composition of eighteenth- and nineteenth-century buildings centred on a thirty-metre-high **Campanile** that's thought to mark the site of the All Hallow's Priory, on whose confiscated land Trinity was built using materials pillaged from other Catholic orders. To the left of the Campanile is a statue of Provost Salmon, who fiercely opposed letting women into Trinity and made good his threat "Over my dead body!" by expiring when they did in 1903.

If you can get inside, it's worth visiting the Examination Hall and the Chapel on either side of Parliament Square. Both were designed in the 1790s by Sir William Chambers, a Scottish architect who never visited Ireland but executed many commissions in Dublin. The **Examination Hall** (or Theatre) contains a chandelier from the old Irish Parliament and an organ reputedly salvaged from a Spanish ship in 1702. Trinity's **Chapel** is the only one in the Republic shared by all denominations. Its main window is dedicated to Archbishop Ussher, one of the first students at Trinity (which he entered at thirteen), who went on to lecture there, devoting years of study to establishing that God created the world on October 23, 4004 BC.

Beyond the Chapel is a grand **Dining Hall** hung with vast portraits of college dignitaries; it has been much altered since it was built by the German architect Richard Cassels in 1742, and was totally restored after a fire in 1989. The oldest surviving building – dating from 1700 – is the red-brick student dormitory called the **Rubrics**, overlooking Liberty Square. Behind the Graduates' Memorial Building is an open area known as Botany Bay, so-called because the unruly students living in the vicinity were considered worthy of transportation to Britain's penal colony.

Most tourists make a beeline for the **Book of Kells** (see p.19) in the **Old Library**, entered from Fellows' Square. On the ground floor is a superb exhibition called "Picturing the Word", which sets the book in the context of Irish Christianity and the art of illumination. Displayed beside the *Book of Kells* in the final room are the *Book of Armagh* (807) and the *Book of Durrow* (675). Upstairs is Thomas Burgh's magnificent library of 1712–32, aptly known as the **Long Room**, to which a second tier of bookcases and a barrel-vaulted ceiling were added in 1852. As a copyright library, Trinity is entitled to a copy of every book published in Ireland and Britain, so its collection of 3.5 million titles grows by 100,000 per year – the bulk of them being kept in a repository in the suburb of Santry. On display in the Long Room are two antique **harps** (one of them is said to have been Brian Ború's, though it post-dates his 1014 victory over the Danes by nearly four centuries), plus an original copy of the 1916 Proclamation of the Irish Republic.

Across Fellows' Square stand the 1960s Brutalist-style **Berkeley Library** and the Arts and Social Sciences Building. The library is named after Kilkenny-born George Berkeley, who studied at Trinity when he was fifteen years old and became a philosopher and educationalist whose influence spread to the American colonies, where he helped found the University of Pennsylvania (California's Berkeley University bears his name). The arts block contains a theatre, a coffee bar and the **Douglas Hyde Gallery** (Mon–Wed & Fri 11am–6pm, Thurs 11am–7pm, Sat 11am–4.45pm; free), an experimental art venue that's usually worth checking out.

Just beyond the Berkeley Library, the School of Engineering occupies a **Museum** designed by Benjamin Woodward (who raised the height of Old Library) and carved with monkeys, owls and parrots by the O'Shea brothers, whom Woodward invited to carve freely like medieval artists, but then fired after the College authorities expressed displeasure with their work. To the north of New Square is Cassels' first building in Dublin, a **Printing House** resembling a Doric temple, which now houses the departments of microelectronics and electrical engineering.

The Book of Kells

Created around 800 AD, the **Book of Kells** probably originated at the monastery on Iona, Saint Columba's first Scottish port of call. In 806, Viking raids forced the Columbine monks to move to the monastery of Kells in County Meath – after which the book is named – whence in 1007 it was stolen. It was later found buried in the ground, but its metal shrine or *cumdach* was subsequently looted by the Vikings (who wouldn't have valued the book itself) and some thirty folios (double-page spreads) disappeared. To prevent a worse fate during the Cromwellian wars, the *Book of Kells* was brought to Dublin and given to Trinity by the Bishop of Meath in 1654. Since then it has been jealously guarded, despite the legend that Queen Victoria autographed it during her first visit to Dublin (she actually signed a parchment that was bound into the volume). In 1953 the folios were rebound in four calfskin volumes, of which two are on display, one showing an illuminated page, the other text. Both are turned to a new page each day.

The 340 folios of the *Book of Kells* contain the four New Testament gospels with prefaces and summaries, all in Latin. Opening letters cover an entire page ornamented with geometric and floral patterns, arcane symbols and images; the text is in rounded Celtic script, with human or animal forms at the margins. The dominant element is the pattern, derived from metalwork such as the Ardagh Chalice and the Tara Brooch in the National Museum.

The shop attached to the exhibition sells *Book of Kells* cards and posters and a range of illustrated books. Insurers value the real *Book of Kells* at $15 million; a limited-edition reproduction costs $18,000, and Thames and Hudson publish an abridged reproduction for about £80.

THE BANK OF IRELAND

Map 4, D5. House of Lords Tues 10.30am, 11.30am & 1.45pm; free. **Story of Banking** Tues–Fri 10am–4pm, Sat 2–5pm, Sun 10am–1pm; £1.50, students £1.

Across the road from Trinity the massive **Bank of Ireland** flanks the curve into Dame Street. It was here that the Anglo–Irish Ascendancy's efforts towards self-government culminated in the **Grattan Parliament** of 1782, where Henry Grattan – whose statue stands outside – declared "Ireland is now a nation." Work on a suitable building began as early as 1729, when Sir Edward Lovett Pearce designed a bi-cameral house with a colonnaded forecourt facing College Green. The Corinthian portico on Westmoreland Street was added by Gandon in 1785, as the Lords' entrance (they objected to sharing a door with MPs). Like the Ionic portico on Foster Place, it is linked to Pearce's building by a curved screen wall.

Grattan's Parliament was short-lived: by patronage and bribery, Britain induced a majority to pass the Act of Union (1801), which subsumed their authority in Westminster. Bereft of a function, the building was sold to the Bank of Ireland for £40,000, after the House of Commons chamber had been demolished to prevent it from being used again as a parliament.

The real attraction is the old **House of Lords**, with its vaulted ceiling, 1233-piece crystal chandelier, and tapestries depicting the Protestant victories of the Siege of Londonderry (1689) and the Battle of the Boyne (1690). Though its long table seems authentic, the Lords actually sat back-to-back around the walls for debates, with the Lord Chancellor on a woolsack. The stuccoed **Cash Hall** looks like part of the House of Commons but is quite unlike the original, which had galleries for some seven hundred spectators; parliamentary debates were a fashionable entertainment at that time. Around the corner on Foster Place, an Armoury added during the Napoleonic wars now serves as an arts centre where concerts are often held and as the venue for the **Story of Banking**, a film "narrated" by David La Touche, the bank's founder (of Huguenot origin), and an exhibition including the silver-gilt **mace** that belonged to the House of Commons. Sold by Speaker Foster's descendants, it was bought back from Christie's in London by the bank in 1937.

GRAFTON STREET AND AROUND

Pedestrianized **Grafton Street**, running uphill to St Stephen's Green, is Dublin's smartest shopping centre and the best place to catch street entertainers, including poets (one of whom claims to be able to recite any Irish poem on request). The famous **Molly Malone statue** (by Jean Rynhart) at the bottom of the street is nicknamed the "tart with the cart" due to its brazen *décolletage* and what Molly reputedly got up to while wheeling her barrow of cockles and mussels through streets broad and narrow. It is thought that she died in 1734 and was buried near St Werburgh's Church (see p.69). At that time, Grafton Street was a fairly rudimentary thoroughfare which led to the execution grounds and common that was then St Stephen's Green. Today it boasts malls and department stores, heaps of places to eat and some famous pubs on its sidestreets (there are none on Grafton Street itself).

Around the corner on Duke Street stands **Davy Byrne's** (for a review of *Davy Byrne's* see p.218), the "moral pub" where Leopold Bloom had a gorgonzola-and-mustard sandwich and a glass of burgundy in *Ulysses*. The *Duke* across the way hosted early concerts by the Hothouse Flowers and is the starting point for *Dublin's Literary Pub Crawl* (see p.10).

Detouring in the other direction off Grafton Street you'll find the **Powerscourt Townhouse** (see *Shopping*) (Mon–Sat 9am–6pm, Thurs till 7pm), an imaginative conversion of an eighteenth-century mansion built for Viscount Powerscourt, using granite from his estate in County Wicklow (see p.156). Its grand entrance on South William Street opens into a hall and a staircase leading to the finest surviving reception room, on the top floor. Like the Georgian Room on the floor below, it was executed by Michael Stapleton, who was responsible for the plasterwork at Trinity. There are **concerts** of light music and jazz in the atrium, which was once the mansion's inner courtyard (see p.227).

While in the vicinity, check out the **Dublin Civic Museum** (Tues–Sat 10am–6pm, Sun 11am–2pm; free) at 58 South William Street. Though it's mainly devoted to temporary exhibitions on anything from barges to coal-hole covers, you can be sure of seeing the head of the statue of Nelson that stood on O'Connell Street till it was blown up in 1966, and the 1877 bylaws of St Stephen's Green, denying entry to persons "in an intoxicated, unclean or verminous condition" and "any dog which may be reasonably suspected to be in a rabid state". Castle Market, the narrow street over the road, leads to the Market Arcade, which comes out on to South Great George's Street (see p.8).

For more on *Bewley's* see p.191.

Returning to Grafton Street, you can't miss the Egyptian mosaic facade of **Bewley's Oriental Café**. *Bewley's* is a Dublin institution where all classes mingle over tea, coffee, all-day fried breakfasts, cakes and sticky buns. Founded by the Quaker Bewley family in the 1840s, it almost folded in 1986, provoking such a national outcry that the government had to step in until a buyer was found. On the top floor is a small **museum** tracing the café's history. There are other branches of *Bewley's* on Westmoreland Street and South Great George's Street.

At the top of Grafton Street looms the **St Stephen's Green Shopping Centre**, a 1980s extravaganza whose frothy white "Mississippi Steamboat" facade mimics the Georgian frontages overlooking the Green. The mall contains a clock face that's six feet six inches larger than Big Ben in London, and a branch of *Dunne's Stores*, whose owners' embroilment in various scandals has titillated the nation in recent years – there's an apt joke doing the rounds at the moment – "Been there, Dunne that, got the Taoiseach."

DAWSON STREET AND MOLESWORTH STREET

There are some quieter streets to the east of Grafton Street that are nice to wander around. **Dawson Street** is notable for its swanky pubs and restaurants, bookshops, and two august institutions. Originally built for the aristocrat Joshua Dawson (after whom the street is named), the **Mansion House** has been the residence of Dublin's Lord Mayor since 1715 – its stucco facade and *porte-cochère* were added in Victorian times. It was here that *Dáil Éireann* (the Irish parliament) adopted the Declaration of Independence in 1919 and where the truce that ended Anglo-Irish hostilities was signed in 1921. Though you can't enter the Mansion House, it's possible to visit the **Royal Irish Academy Library** next door (Mon–Fri 9.30am–5.30pm; closed bank holidays and the last three weeks of Aug), which houses a large collection of ancient Irish manuscripts. Beside the library stands **St Ann's Church**, whose interior dates back to the early 1700s. The shelves behind the altar were used for storing bread to be distributed to the poor of the parish under the terms of a bequest. Past parishioners include Wolfe Tone (who was married here in 1765), Bram Stoker and Douglas Hyde. On Thursday lunchtimes, St Ann's hosts **recitals**. Its graveyard contains the tomb of the poet Felicia Hemans, who wrote "The boy stood on the burning deck . . ." and lived at 21 Dawson Street.

Molesworth Street, running towards Leinster House (see p.31), retains two Huguenot-style gabled houses from the mid-eighteenth century. At no. 17 is **Freemasons' Hall**, the headquarters of Ireland's Grand Lodge, which runs guided tours (June–Aug Mon–Fri 11.30am & 2.30pm). Its interior combines every style of Victorian architecture from Egyptian to Roman and Gothic, all wildly over the top. There's also a museum of Masonic regalia and a library of works on mysticism and secret societies. Visitors are solemnly assured that what little influence the Freemasons have in Irish society is only for the good.

ST STEPHEN'S GREEN

Map 4, E8. Mon–Sat 8am–dusk; Sun & bank holidays 10am–dusk.

St Stephen's Green seems such a tasteful feature of this Georgian city that it's hard to imagine it as anything else. Originally an open common in the vicinity of a lepers' hospital, the Green was surrounded by buildings by the late seventeenth century but nonetheless remained a dangerous spot, with footpads lurking on every corner. Public hangings occurred here until the eighteenth century, and as late as 1800 the Green was surrounded by a fetid ditch clogged with dead cats and dogs. To improve matters, in 1814 railings and locked gates were installed and an annual fee of one guinea was levied on users. True bourgeois respectability was attained later that century, when Lord Ardilaun (Sir

Arthur Guinness) laid out a public garden – complete with bandstand and ornamental waterfowl – and electric lighting came to Dublin's streets. Today, the Green is pleasant enough for a stroll or a rest, but more notable for the buildings around it. Like other Georgian squares, its sides are designated as North, South, East and West.

Once known as "Beaux Walk" after the dandies who promenaded there in the eighteenth century, St Stephen's Green North still reeks of money, with pedestrians gabbling into their mobiles as they stride towards the **Shelbourne Hotel** (see p.173 and p.224). The *Shelbourne* boasts of having "the best address in Dublin" and has been a meeting place for the upper echelons of society since it was founded in 1824. Non-residents can wander in for a drink and something to eat in the lobby at any time of day. Afternoon tea (from 3pm) is popular, but the lobby and bar really come alive in the evening, when the hotel is great for celebrity spotting. Aloys Hitler, the Führer's half-brother (who married an Irishwoman), worked here as a wine-waiter before World War I.

Across the road is a **monument to Wolfe Tone**, nicknamed "Tone-henge" for its granite slabs, and there's another in memory of the Great Famine behind it. A small **Huguenot Graveyard**, established in 1693 for the French Protestant refugees who settled in Dublin's Liberties (see p.80), lies just past the *Shelbourne* at the start of Merrion Row. Only a few simple tombs are left, visible through the railings.

On the northwest corner of the Green, the **Fusiliers' Arch**, honouring the 212 Royal Dublin Fusiliers killed in the Boer War, is still known to some as "Traitor's Gate", enlistment or conscription into the British army being a long-standing *bête noire* of Nationalists. During the Easter Rising, the Green was occupied by insurgents led by Commandant Mallin and Countess Markievicz, who neglected to seize the *Shelbourne* and soon found themselves pinned down by British snipers, forcing them to retreat into the **Royal College of Surgeons** on the western side of the green, whose pillars are still scarred with bullet-marks.

On the edge of the green are statues of Robert Emmet (who was born close by) and Lord Ardilaun; James Joyce, W.B. Yeats (by Henry Moore) and Countess Markievicz are honoured by sculptures further in. Spare a thought for the equestrian statue of George II, blown up in 1937, and a statue of Viceroy Montgomery that was similarly removed in 1958.

Newman House

Map 4, D9. Guided tours only, June–Sept Tues–Fri noon, 2pm, 3pm & 4pm, Sat 2pm, 3pm & 4pm, Sun 11am, noon & 1pm; £2, students & unwaged £1.

On the south side of the Green, nos. 85–86 are collectively known as **Newman House**, named after John Henry Newman, first rector of the Catholic University of Ireland. Founded in 1854 to provide a Catholic equivalent to Trinity College, the institution provided education for generations of Catholics who would otherwise have been obliged to study abroad or submit to the Protestant hegemony of Trinity; James Joyce, Pádraig Pearse and Éamon de Valera were among its alumni. The university later moved out to Belfield, changing its name to University College Dublin (UCD) along the way.

Newman House is fabulously decorative. **Number 85** was originally Clanwilliam House, a miniature Palladian mansion built by Cassels in 1738 for Captain Hugh Montgomery to entertain while in town for the "Season". Off its custard-yellow hall lies the **Apollo Room**, named after a figure of the god above the fireplace, moulded in high-relief like the nine muses on the walls and two *putti* with a rabbit over the doorway – all superb examples of the work of the Swiss-Italian Francini brothers, the foremost stucco artists of the day. Upstairs is the **Saloon**, with its coffered ceiling and allegorical relief of good government and prudent economy. When the Jesuits acquired the building in 1883, they covered the naked female bodies on the ceiling with what look like furry bathing costumes, to protect the morals of their students; the garments were removed when the house was restored in the 1980s, but one was left *in situ* to show how bizarre they appeared. At the back of the house is an extension in the Gothic style, used as a **Physics Theatre**, where Joyce once lectured to the "L & H" (Literary and Historical Society).

Number 86 is a larger house built in 1765 for Richard "Burnchapel" Whaley, a virulent anti-Catholic who earned his sobriquet by torching chapels in County Wicklow. His son, Buck Whaley, was a founder of the Hellfire Club who walked all the way to Jerusalem and played handball against the Wailing Wall to win a bet of £15,000. The saloon has flowing Rococo plasterwork by Robert West and is known as the **Bishop's Room**, having been used for meetings of the university's committee. On the top floor are the **classroom** where Joyce studied from 1899 to 1902 and the **bedroom** of the poet Gerard Manley Hopkins, who was Professor of Classics from 1884 until his death in 1889, a miserable period during which he wrote what are called the "Terrible Sonnets".

Beside Newman House stands the Byzantine-style **University Church**, whose opulent interior is adorned with marble quarried from five different sites in Ireland (definitely worth seeing) and regarded as a chic location for weddings. **Iveagh House**, further along, was the first building that Cassels designed in Dublin, and now houses the Department of Foreign Affairs.

Harcourt Street and the Iveagh Gardens

Harcourt Street, leading off from the southwest corner of the Green, is a well-preserved Georgian street, laid out in 1775. The *Celtic* bookshop at no. 6 was formerly the headquarters of Arthur Griffith's Sinn Féin; Sir Edward Carson, a staunch opponent of Home Rule who founded the Ulster Volunteers, was born next door; and George Bernard Shaw once resided at no. 61. Near the far end is a defunct railway station whose arches are occupied by Dublin's main wine merchants and the exclusive *POD* nightclub (see p.233). **Findlaters** set up in Dublin in 1823 and have a small **museum** in their warehouse (Mon–Fri 9am–6pm, Sat 10.30am–5.30pm; £1.50).

Whilst here, visit the secluded **Iveagh Gardens** (Mon–Sat 8am–dusk, Sun 10am–dusk) off Clonmell Street. One of the least known parks in the centre, with its own grotto, cascade and rosarium (now being restored), it formed the back garden to Clonmell House, which once belonged to a Lord Chief Justice whose jailing of the owner of the *Dublin Evening Post* resulted in a devious act of revenge. The *Post* advertised a "Grand Olympic Pig Hunt" near the judge's country estate in Blackrock, gave whiskey to everyone who turned up and invited them to catch soaped pigs, which fled into the estate pursued by thousands of tipsy Dubliners – causing the judge to rush off to Dublin Castle telling the Viceroy that Blackrock was in a state of insurrection.

The garden's far exit brings you out on to Earlsfort Terrace near the **National Concert Hall** (see p.227), Dublin's premier classical venue. An imposing building constructed for the Great Exhibition of 1865, it subsequently became the centrepiece of University College Dublin, before being inaugurated as the National Concert Hall in 1981.

Georgian squares and houses

The eighteenth century saw the transformation of Dublin into a European-style capital of wide streets and leafy squares, due to the enrichment of the gentry by rising land rents. Besides creating a demand for new residences, they required lawyers, surveyors and tradesmen – who also contributed to the gentrification of Dublin. It's no accident that the leitmotif of Georgian urban planning was the terraced house, which could be executed on a grand scale for the wealthy, or a small and basic version for the petite bourgeoisie.

Many of Dublin's Georgian **squares** were created by two rival families. The *nouveau-riche* Gardiners led the way on the northside before the old-money Fitzwilliams developed the southside around Merrion and Fitzwilliam squares. Economic stagnation soon forced once-prosperous families to move into smaller homes, turning their old houses into tenements, rented out to dozens of people – Mountjoy and Parnell squares have never really recovered. The southside managed to stay in better shape until the property boom of the 1960s, when whole terraces were demolished to erect offices.

Built of mellow Bridgewater brick brought as ballast by ships plying the Bristol route, Georgian houses have flat facades of uniform appearance. What makes them distinctive is their detail, with variations in heights of windows, shapes of doorways and balconies (though the wrought-iron balconies that survive are either Victorian-era additions or replacements) and varieties of door-knockers, boot-scrapers and door fanlights. Inside, the arrangement was standard. The kitchen occupied the basement, with the dining room above. The drawing rooms on the first floor were the house's finest – family bedrooms were more modest affairs. Few houses had gardens but the parks in the middle of the squares were reserved for its residents.

NO. 29 LOWER FITZWILLIAM STREET

Map 4, H8. Tues–Sat 10am–5pm, Sun 2–5pm; closed Dec 11–25; £2.50, students £1, children free.

The painstaking replica of a Georgian household at **no. 29 Lower Fitzwilliam Street** was fabricated by the Electricity Supply Board as a penance for demolishing a row of 26 such houses in the 1960s in order to build their headquarters. Located at the southwest corner of Merrion Square, the house is really a front for the board's offices (the two are linked by an atrium used for concerts over winter). Although an introductory film omits to mention the board's act of vandalism, you can't fault the decor, as many genuine artefacts were used in its creation. There's also a **guided tour** explaining the minutiae of bourgeois life when the house was occupied by the Beatty family.

In the basement water was filtered for drinking and coal and wine were stored in the cellar. The housekeeper slept next door to the pantry, using a small window in her room to keep a close eye on light-fingered servants (who slept in slums elsewhere). Gracious living began upstairs, where you'll see such contraptions as a lead-lined cooler and a pneumatic exercise machine for days when Master hadn't time to go riding. The nursery contains a giant doll's house and a bed for the governess who was hired to instruct daughters (boys went to boarding school) in such ladylike arts as embroidery; the needlework samplers on the wall were the Georgian equivalent of a curriculum vitae.

Continue your tour of the Georgian southside by walking along Fitzwilliam Street to **Fitzwilliam Square**. Laid out between 1791 and 1825, it was the last and smallest square to be developed by the Fitzwilliams.

W.B. Yeats resided at no. 42 between 1928 and 1932, and today the square is largely occupied by private medical practices. A dwindling number of residents still hold keys to the central garden, which is the last private park in Dublin.

LEINSTER HOUSE

Kildare Street, to the north of St Stephen's Green, is the heartland of Dublin's establishment. The area was developed by James Fitzgerald, Earl of Kildare, who in 1745 bought some cheap land on the edge of town and commissioned Richard Cassels to build a great mansion on it. Asked if he regretted leaving the fashionable northside, the Earl replied, "they will follow me wherever I go" – and he was right, for Lord Fitzwilliam then laid out Merrion Square, starting a development boom on the southside. The Earl's mansion was designed so that the facade facing town resembles a town house, and the side on what is now Merrion Square looks like a country residence. Its present name, **Leinster House**, honours the elevation of the Earl to Duke of Leinster. One of his sons, Lord Edward Fitzgerald, escaped arrest here by the British after spies betrayed his preparations for the 1798 Rebellion.

During his lifetime, Daniel O'Connell had dreamt of restoring the former Grattan Parliament but the Free State Provisional Government preferred Leinster House, as it was easier to defend, and in 1922 it was duly converted into the **Irish Parliament**. Beset by enemies at home and abroad, they felt – as Kevin O'Higgins confessed – like "eight young men standing amidst the ruins of one administration with the foundation of another not yet laid, and with wild men screaming through the keyhole".

The Irish Parliament

Few legislatures have been so hard won – and divisive – as the **Irish Parliament** (*Oireachtas na hÉireann*). Its basic form was hammered out in the London negotiations that established the Irish Free State (a title reflecting Britain's objection to the term "Republic"). Under the Anglo–Irish Treaty it had to vow loyalty to the British monarch and accept Ireland's partition into a 26-county Free State and a 6-county Northern Ireland.

Both conditions split the Nationalists down the middle, with the anti-Treaty side initiating a bitter Civil War (1922–24) where both sides claimed to be the rightful heirs of *Dáil Éireann*, the Irish shadow parliament of 1919 to 1921, whose own legitimacy derived from the Proclamation of the Republic during the Easter Rising. Not until 1927 did de Valera and his Fianna Fáil party grudgingly recognize the Free State and enter parliamentary life "with guns under their coats". In 1937, citizens voted to accept a new constitution formulated by de Valera, which is the basis for the present system of government of the Republic of Ireland.

While the president is the head of state, legislative and executive powers are vested in parliament, which has two chambers: *Dáil Éireann* (House of Representatives) and *Seanad Éireann* (Senate). The Dáil (pronounced "Doil") has 166 representatives (*Teachtaí Dála*, TDs), elected by proportional representation, whereas the sixty senators are appointed by various authorities including the Prime Minister or *Taoiseach* (pronounced "Tee-shuck") and the universities. Critics say that the system encourages cronyism and corruption – as evinced by a stream of scandals involving nearly every party and government since the 1970s.

Parliament sits for ninety days a year, from mid-January to Easter, May to June/July and mid-September until two weeks before Christmas, on Tuesdays (2.30–8.30pm), Wednesdays (10.30am–8.30pm) and Thursdays (10.30am–5.30pm). You can observe **debates** by getting an entry ticket from the Kildare Street gates; bring your passport. The sedate Senate meets in a semicircular blue salon in the north wing – the Dáil sits on the other side of the building and is more of a bear-pit. Visitors are guided from one chamber to the other by frock-coated ushers.

THE NATIONAL MUSEUM OF IRELAND

Map 4, F7. Tues–Sat 10am–5pm, Sun 2–5pm; free.

With its prehistoric gold, medieval treasures and Viking exhibits, the **National Museum of Ireland** is one of the city's essential sights. It's next door to Leinster House, occupying part of a building raised in the late 1880s to accommodate both the museum and the National Library. The core of the collection was acquired in 1891, as a donation from the Royal Irish Academy (or Royal Hibernian Academy), a society founded in 1785 by the Earl of Charlemont. Since then it's grown immensely, and with the Irish and Japanese decorative arts collections soon moving to the Collins Barracks (p.121), the remaining sections may expand further in years to come.

Overleaf are listed just the highlights, and by focusing on these you could see the best of the museum in an afternoon. In addition to the exhibits we've singled out, there are also fine displays of glass and silverware, antique dolls, embroidery and an Egyptian Room complete with three female mummies. The numbers in the text correspond to the floor plans on pp.34 and 36.

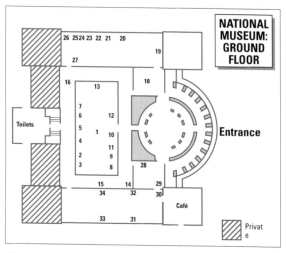

Ór – Ireland's gold

The museum's stunning collection of prehistoric gold (*ór*) occupies the sunken main hall; less glamorous artefacts from the same era are ranged around the raised perimeter. A central display section [1] explains how gold was extracted in ancient times and why peat bogs have yielded so many treasures during turf-cutting or ploughing, when so few have been found at excavations of inhabited sites.

In the Early Bronze Age (c. 2200 BC) goldsmiths created **lunulae** [2] – crescent-shaped collars made from thin sheets of beaten gold – and decorated them with chevrons or stripes, incised on the front or hammered out from behind, by the technique known as repoussé. They applied the same methods and economy of material to sun discs and basket-shaped ear- or hair-rings (it's not known which) [3]. During the Mid-

THE NATIONAL MUSEUM OF IRELAND

Bronze Age, sheet-gold was beaten into armlets, earrings and necklaces – as in the **Derrinboy Hoard [4]** – or twisted into **torcs**; one from County Antrim is as chunky as an industrial drill [5]. From c. 1200 BC, twisting became the favoured technique and torcs grew much larger, suggesting that a new source of gold had been found. Note three for the waist, with different kinds of fasteners [6]. Gold beads were also combined with chunks of amber, to form lustrous necklaces [7].

Despite scant evidence for goldworking at the start of the Late Bronze Age (1000–500 BC), after 850 BC came a period of prolific production using various techniques. Cast or hammered bar goldwork gave rise to bracelets and dress- or sleeve-fasteners with cupped terminals, decorated with incised whorls [8]. Applying gold foil to base metal objects (termed *bullae*) produced purse-shaped artefacts and so-called ring money [9]. The **Tumna Hoard [10]** of nine hollow gold balls the size of doughnuts is flanked by two sunflower pins from County Laois [11] and the **Banagher Hoard [12]** of an amber necklace, a gold bracelet and dress-fastener and two bronze rings – all dating from 800–700 BC.

From the same period come the magnificent **Gleninsheen Gorget** (one of several gold collars with roundel fastenings attached by gold wire) and the **Mooghaun Hoard [13]**. The latter was found by navvies digging the West Clare railway in 1854.

Prehistoric Ireland

The collection of prehistoric material ranges from a lifesize reconstruction of a Late Neolithic (3400–2800 BC) **Passage tomb [14]** and the **Lurgan Longboat**, carved from a trunk of oak c. 2500 BC, to the half-metre-long **Lissan Rapier [15]** and the bronze spearheads and shields of the **Dowris Hoard [16]** from the final phase of the Irish Bronze Age (900–500 BC).

THE NATIONAL MUSEUM OF IRELAND

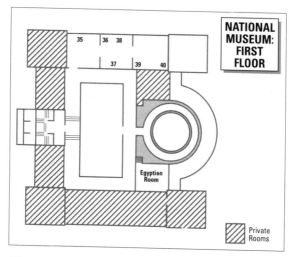

The Treasury

The Treasury is where you'll find the most well-known ecclesiastical objects in the collection, dating from the Iron Age to the late Middle Ages. The **Petrie Crown** gold collar [**17**] and miniature sailing boat with oars [**18**] are beautiful pieces from the **Broighter Hoard** (first century BC) discovered in County Derry in 1896.

The **Derrynaflan Hoard** [**19**] found in 1980 in County Tipperary contains a silver filigreed paten and fine chalice dating from the eighteenth and nineteenth centuries displayed alongside the more elaborate chalice from the **Ardagh Hoard** [**20**], from the tenth century. Perhaps the finest example of Irish metalwork is the **Tara Brooch** [**21**] found on the shore near Bettystown in 1850, both sides of which bear intricate patterns that may have inspired those in manuscripts such as the *Book of Kells*. Such "knot" designs also appear on the shaft of a stone **cross** from County Offaly, depicting a horseman and a stag [22].

During the Middle Ages, elaborate reliquaries were made to hold holy relics or texts. **St Patrick's Bell Shrine** [23] contains a bell reputedly owned by the saint. Adorned with gold wire upon a silver backplate, it was created in the early twelfth century and handed down through generations of the Mulholland family until the late 1770s. In the same case is the bronze **Shrine of St Lachtin's Arm**. Odder still are the **Shrine of St Bridget's Shoe** – the size of a child's foot – and the **fiacail Pádraig**, containing the tooth that fell from St Patrick's head at Killespugbrone, which share a case with the house-shaped shrine called the **Breac Moedóic** [24] and its original leather satchel. Book-shrines decorated with repoussé saints include the **Stowe Missal**, the **Cathach** and the **Soiscél Molaise** [25].

Incongruously surrounded by processional crosses of English manufacture, the ivory **Kavanagh Charter Horn** [26] was for centuries one of the symbols of the Kings of Leinster. Last but not least, you'll find two **Sheela-na-Gigs** [27], enigmatic female figures that appeared on many early Irish churches despite their pagan antecedents and their overt sexuality.

The Road to independence

The final exhibition on the ground floor relates the struggle for Irish independence, but lacks the space to do justice to its subject and will eventually be moved to the Collins Barracks. Meanwhile, the first room covers events in the nineteenth century, from the abortive uprising of Robert Emmet (whose sword and death mask [28] are displayed) to the activities of the Fenians in America, before returning to Ireland and the

THE NATIONAL MUSEUM OF IRELAND

campaigns of O'Connell and Parnell. After both failed to achieve reform through Britain's parliament, a new generation sought to revive and promote Irish culture through the Gaelic League, founded by Douglas Hyde, whose bust shares a display case with the first Gaelic typewriter [**29**].

The main section is devoted to the Easter Rising and the War of Independence. You'll see the uniforms of the Irish Volunteers and the Citizen Army that fought in 1916 [**30**]; Sir Roger Casement's dress suit and a sword-stick and barrister's gown belonging to Pádraig Pearse [**31**]; the pistols fired by Countess Markievicz [**32**]; a uniform of the hated British Black and Tans [**33**]; and one worn by Michael Collins as Commander-in-Chief of the Irish Republican Army [**34**]. There's a video-wall at the far end which gives a brief account of the Easter Rising using contemporary newsreel footage.

Viking age Ireland

Upstairs, the exhibition on Viking-age Ireland (800–1200 AD) overlaps chronologically with the Treasury on the floor below. The early Viking invasions are represented by artefacts from burial grounds at Islandbridge and Kilmainham, including the **skeleton of a warrior** [**35**] with a long sword. It was partly due to the Viking threat that the *crannog* or lake-dwelling persisted for so long in Ireland; one from County Westmeath has yielded a wooden bucket and gaming board, and antler combs [**36**]. While the Vikings appreciated the skills of Irish jewellers – as evinced by penannular and "thistle" **brooches** [**37**] – others were liable to be enslaved or killed, like the man whose hacked-about **skull** was found with an iron slave-chain [**38**].

The next section covers **Viking Dublin**, with **models** of a house and the layout of Fishamble Street [**39**], accompanied

by a host of finds from excavations on Winetavern Street and
Wood Quay, ranging from loom weights to ironworkers'
tools. Notice the finely carved **deer-antler combs [40]** that
the Vikings used as money as well as for taming their hair.

The final room displays Christian artefacts from Viking
times, including some of the museum's most famous possessions. The **Tau Crozier** is the only surviving one with a T-
shaped head, though they were often depicted in early
manuscripts, while the exquisite **Crozier of St Tola** follows the familiar form of a shepherd's crook [41]. Iron and
bronze bells (often hand-held rather than hung in belfries)
presage **St Manchan's Shrine**, a mid-twelfth-century
masterpiece of repoussé saints and a magnificent Celtic cross
[42]. Finally, there's the famous **Cross of Cong [43]**, made
to enshrine a fragment of the True Cross given by Pope
Calixtus II to the King of Connaught in 1123 but later lost.

THE NATIONAL LIBRARY AND HERALDIC MUSEUM

To the north of the museum, the **National Library** (Mon
10am–9pm, Tues & Wed 2–9pm, Thurs & Fri 10am–5pm,
Sat 10am–1pm; free) is less of a crowd-puller, but it's a
handsome building and is worth visiting for its associations
alone – almost every major Irish writer from Joyce onwards
has used it at some time. Temporary exhibitions in the foyer
feature anything from old Irish maps to the diaries of Joseph
Holiday, describing Dublin's theatrical life. Ask for a visitor's pass to enter the stately domed Reading Room on the
first floor, scene of one of the great set pieces of *Ulysses* –
Stephen's extravagant speech on Shakespeare.

Further north by the corner of Nassau Street stands a
Venetian-Gothic red-brick edifice with whimsical figures
carved on its pillars – monkeys with billiard cues and a
mole with a lute hint at the building's former role as the

Kildare Street Club. Once a bastion of Anglo-Irish conservatism, it was described by novelist George Moore in 1886 as "a sort of oyster-bed into which all the eldest sons of the landed gentry fall as a matter of course. There they remain spending their days drinking sherry and cursing Gladstone in a sort of dialect, a dead language which the larva-like stupidity of the club has preserved." Today it houses the *Alliance Française* and Ireland's **Genealogical Office** (Mon–Fri 10am–12.30pm & 2.30–4.30pm), which offers a consultancy service (£25) to help people trace their Irish ancestors. The **Heraldic Museum** (same hours; free) contains such items as Sir Roger Casement's Order of St Michael and George, the Lord Chancellor's purse and mantle, and the insignia of the Order of St Patrick.

MERRION SQUARE

In 1785, Richard Crosbie from County Wicklow, attired in a fur-lined silk robe and a leopard-skin cap, made Ireland's first balloon ascent. Lift-off was from **Merrion Square**, which had been laid out by Lord Fitzwilliam of Merrion in the previous decade and which marks the zenith of Georgian town-planning. Its spacious terraced houses have belonged to diverse famous citizens (commemorated by plaques) and though most now serve as offices, enough people still live here to retain a residential feel. On weekends during the summer, the park railings are used by artists flogging their wares.

Like St Stephen's Green, the north side of the square was once the most fashionable. The Wildes lived at no. 1; their son Oscar was born at nearby 21 Westland Row. However, Merrion Square South has had the longer list of eminent ex-residents. Daniel O'Connell bought no. 58 in 1809, to the dismay of his frugal wife Mary, who lamented, "Where on earth will you be able to get a thousand guineas?". The Austrian physicist Erwin Schrödinger, co-winner of the 1933 Nobel Prize, occupied no. 65; the poet, mystic and painter George Russell (AE) worked at no. 84, and in 1922 W.B. Yeats moved into no. 82, having previously lived at 52 Merrion Square East. There's nothing to recall the British Embassy at no. 39, burnt out in 1972 by a crowd protesting against the Bloody Sunday massacre in Derry. On the Leinster Lawn behind parliament is an obelisk dedicated to Michael Collins, Arthur Griffith and Kevin O'Higgins, the architects of the Free State.

THE NATIONAL GALLERY OF IRELAND

Map 4, G7. Mon–Sat 10am–5.30pm, Thurs 10am–8.30pm, Sun 2–5pm; closed on Good Friday and Dec 24–26; free.

The Irish Industrial Exhibition of 1853 included a Fine Art Hall organized by the railway magnate William Dargan. So enthusiastic was the public response that Dargan donated his profits to fund the **National Gallery of Ireland**, on Merrion Square West. Since its inauguration in 1864, the gallery's collection has grown from 125 paintings to more than 10,000 pictures and sculptures, partly thanks to bequests by the likes of the Countess of Milltown (who gave almost 200 paintings from Russborough House) and George Bernard Shaw (who left one third of his residual estate to the "cherished asylum" of his youth).

Besides free **guided tours** on Saturdays (3pm) and Sundays (2.15pm, 3pm & 4pm), the gallery offers a range of **lectures** and **workshops**, some of them intended for children and the visually impaired (as detailed in the monthly *Gallery News*, available in the foyer). Be warned though, that due to staff shortages a few of the rooms might be closed – this is least likely to occur on Thursdays and Sundays.

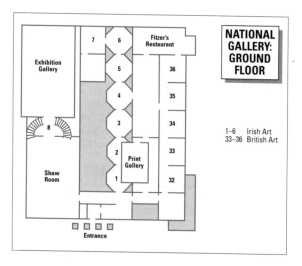

NATIONAL
GALLERY:
GROUND
FLOOR

1–6   Irish Art
33–36 British Art

Irish art

The ground-floor Milltown Rooms (1–6) cover **Irish art**, beginning with the eighteenth century, a period when most Irish painters looked to England for their livelihoods. Notable among the exiles was **Nathaniel Hone** the Elder, who spent most of his life there and became a founder member of the Royal Academy – his most famous painting, *The Conjurer*, is a satire of the Academy's president, Sir Joshua Reynolds. In the late eighteenth and early nineteenth centuries the grandiose gestures of Romanticism emerged in Irish art, as demonstrated by *The Opening of the Sixth Seal* by **Francis Danby**, an apocalyptic vision based on the Book of Revelations (room 3).

Though *The Sick Call*, by **Matthew James Lawless**, makes oblique reference to the misery of the Irish people in the years after the Famine, most artists of the second half of the nineteenth century drew their inspiration from France and Impressionism – a development exemplified by **Walter Osbourne** and **Roderic O'Conner** (the latter is better represented in the Hugh Lane Gallery; see p.102). Ireland's most influential teacher of this period was **William Orpen**, one of whose pupils, **Seán Keating**, is depicted atop the well-house in Orpen's *The Holy Well*. Keating himself painted *An Allegory*, whose ruined house and uniformed figures suggest the chaos of the Civil War. The fervently expressive work of **Jack B. Yeats** (brother of W.B.) is well represented by *The Liffey Swim* and more enigmatic paintings such as *Men of Destiny* and *The Singing Horseman*. Also on show is work by the society painter **Sir John Lavery**, a man now chiefly remembered for his wife, Lady Hazel, who had affairs with Michael Collins and Kevin O'Higgins and appeared on the first Irish banknotes (which Lavery designed) as Erin, the personification of Ireland.

British art, the Print Gallery and the Shaw Room

The North Wing is largely devoted to **British art**, mostly of the eighteenth century, including a dozen paintings by **Sir Joshua Reynolds**, whose *Parody of Raphael's "School of Athens"* is a caricature of the Earl of Charlemont (see p.8) and his circle and their obsession with ancient Rome and Greece. There are ten works by Reynolds's great rival, **Gainsborough**, ranging from a *View of Suffolk* that reveals his debt to the Dutch landscape tradition, to sentimental images like *The Cottage Girl*. Portraits of the aristocracy

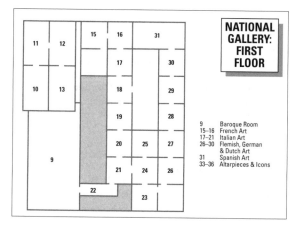

NATIONAL
GALLERY:
FIRST
FLOOR

9   Baroque Room
15–16   French Art
17–21   Italian Art
26–30   Flemish, German
        & Dutch Art
31   Spanish Art
33–36   Altarpieces & Icons

constituted the bread-and-butter of **Francis Wheatley**, until debts and a scandalous love affair forced him to seek refuge in Ireland, where he painted *The Dublin Volunteers on College Green*, which shows how much College Green has changed since then. There's also a charming portrait of *The Mackinen Children* by **Hogarth**.

Room 35 gives access to an atrium with stairs ascending to the **Print Gallery**, which holds various temporary exhibitions throughout the year and exhibits watercolours by **Turner** every January, including views of Rhineland castles and the Doge's Palace in Venice. On weekdays, by prior arrangement, you can also view works in the **Print Room**, such as **James Malton**'s original watercolours of Georgian Dublin.

On the other side of the foyer lies the grandiose **Shaw Room**. Here you'll find the gigantic *Marriage of Princess Aoife of Leinster and Richard de Clare* by **Daniel Maclise**, an

Irishman who made his name as a historical painter in England with scenes such as *The Death of Nelson* (in the House of Lords). It depicts the consummation of the alliance between the King of Leinster and the Norman warlord Strongbow, which took place on the battlefield after the capture of Waterford in 1170 (hence the corpses in the foreground). The double staircase at the far end leads upstairs to a gallery used for temporary exhibitions, for which there is sometimes an admission charge.

French art

The **upper floor** of the gallery has a convoluted layout – this is particularly true of the **French art** section, which occupies two separate areas. Basically, rooms 15 and 16 take you up to the Barbizon school, while rooms 10–13 are given over to the Impressionists, Post-Impressionists and Cubists.

The oldest French painting is a fifteenth-century *Annunciation* by **Jacques Yverni**, an artist of the Avignon school that developed around the papal court during the Great Schism. Once the papacy returned to Italy in 1429, Rome developed into one of the artistic centres of Europe. **Poussin** spent most of his career in the city and it was there that he painted *Acis and Galatea*, *The Entombment* and *The Holy Family*. **Claude Lorraine**, Poussin's contemporary and compatriot, also mainly worked in Italy, and is represented here by *Hagar and the Angel* and *Juno Confiding Io to the Care of Argus*. With the exception of Watteau, the gallery owns something by every major French artist of the eighteenth century, two especially fine examples being *Venus and Cupid* by **Fragonard** and *The Funeral of Patroclus* by **David**.

The major Barbizon painters – **Corot**, **Millet** and **Courbet** – are all here, but nowadays they can't match the popularity of the Impressionists and Post-Impressionists. The gallery owns fine works by the pivotal Impressionists **Sisley** (*The Canal du Loing at Saint Mammes*), **Pissarro** (*A Bouquet of Flowers in a Chinese Vase*) and **Monet** (*A River Scene, Autumn*), as well as pictures by **Degas**, **Bonnard** and **Signac**.

There are also two Cubist collages by expatriate Spaniards **Picasso** and **Gris**, more of whose work can be found in the Spanish section.

Italian art

The **Italian art** collection in rooms 17–21 kicks off with *Allegory of the Immaculate Conception and the Redemption* by **Tiepolo**, Canaletto-like vistas of Rome by **Giovanni Paolo Panini**, and two fine views of eighteenth-century Dresden by **Bernardo Belloto**. However, the most notable paintings are in the rooms that follow. *The Taking of Christ* by **Caravaggio**, in room 19, had hung for decades in the dining hall of the Jesuit House on Leeson Street until a visiting member of the National Art Gallery recognized it as a Caravaggio original in 1990. Once it was authenticated, the Jesuit Order gave the painting to the gallery, where it was restored and eventually put on display. How the masterpiece ended up in this country has baffled art experts for years; some believe it was bought by a Scottish family in Italy in the last century and eventually made its way to Ireland.

Titian's stupendous *Ecce Homo* shares room 20 with a couple of other Venetian masterpieces: a *Portrait of an Elderly Senator* by **Tintoretto** and *Saints Philip and James the Lesser* by **Paolo Veronese**. The highlight of room 21 is a small monochrome *Judith with the Head of Holofernes* by **Mantegna** – notice the feet of the decapitated Philistine chieftain protruding from the tent.

Altarpieces and icons

The Italian section is succeeded by three rooms (23–25) devoted to **altarpieces and icons**. One of the gallery's earliest acquisitions was *Saints Cosmas and Damian*, a panel by **Fra Angelico**, the fifteenth-century Florentine master, which hangs near his *Portrait of a Musician*. The collection of **icons** features *The Virgin and Child Hodigitria, with John the Baptist and Twelve Prophets*, an excellent example of the Byzantine style. The quite different conventions of Russian iconography are displayed in *St George and the Dragon*, from the powerful Russian city-state of Novgorod, whose independence was crushed by Ivan the Terrible. Ivan then brought the finest icon-painters to work in the Kremlin, giving rise to the Moscow School, represented here by *The Entry into Jerusalem*.

Flemish, German and Dutch art

Rooms 26–30 of the North Wing contain **Flemish, German and Dutch art** from the fifteenth century onwards. Some of the finest works are in room 26, such as the lively *Peasant Wedding* by **Brueghel the Younger**, *St Dominic and St Francis of Assisi* by **Rubens**, and a couple of pieces by his most talented pupil, **van Dyck**. Room 27 features two works by **Conrad Faber**, who specialized in portraiture during the first half of the sixteenth century, when it was rare for a German painter to do so, plus *The Descent into Limbo* by an anonymous follower of Hieronymous Bosch. From the twentieth century there's *Two Women in a Garden* by the Expressionist **Emil Nolde**.

Rest on the Flight into Egypt* by **Rembrandt** hangs in room 29, along with a *Portrait of a Lady* and *David's Dying Charge to Solomon* by his leading pupil, **Ferdinand Bol**, and *The Castle of Bentheim* by **Jacob van Ruisdael**. *A Young Fisherman* by **Frans**

Hals and **Vermeer**'s *Lady Writing a Letter* can be found in room 30. This painting has been stolen and recovered twice – first by Bridget Rose Dugdale in 1974, in order to raise money for the IRA, and again in 1986 from Russborough House.

Spanish art

Room 31 holds the gallery's collection of **Spanish art**. *St Francis Receiving the Stigmata* is a typically emotive painting by **El Greco**, while **Murillo** is represented by *The Holy Family* and *The Penitent Magdalene*. Another highlight is the *Kitchen Maid with the Supper at Emmaus*, by **Velázquez**, which relegates the revelation of the resurrected Christ to a detail in the background. Three works by **Goya** – *Sleep*, and his portraits of *Dona Antonia Zárate* and a *Lady in a Black Mantilla* – are also on show, close to **Picasso**'s *Still Life with a Mandolin*, and *Pierrot* by **Juan Gris**.

The Baroque Room

The **Baroque Room** in the Dargan Wing is a slightly less opulent counterpart to the Shaw Room on the floor below, hung with enormous paintings chiefly by artists who are little known today. However, there are four by famous masters that are too large to include in their respective national sections – *The Annunciation* and *Peter Finding the Tribute Money* by **Rubens**, *The Meeting of Jacob and Rachel at the Well* by **Murillo**, and *The Finding of Cyrus* by **Castiglione**.

THE NATURAL HISTORY MUSEUM

Map 4, G7. Tues–Sat 10am–5pm, Sun 2–5pm; free.

Across the Leinster Lawn from the National Gallery stands the **Natural History Museum**, which preserves the essence of Victorian museums like a fly in amber, being virtually unchanged since the explorer and missionary Dr David Livingstone delivered its inaugural lecture in 1857. A statue of a rifle-toting naturalist on the lawn presages an orgy of the taxidermy and taxonomy within. The ground-floor Irish Room opens with three skeletons of the giant Irish deer, which became extinct 10,000 years ago, and ends with a section on endangered wildlife, so the mood is sombre. Upstairs, the World Collection has rhinoceroses, pandas and other appealing creatures, plus the skeletons of two humpback whales stranded on Irish shores. Sadly, due to lack of funds, the top gallery is closed, so you can't see the amazing Blaschka collection of glass models of marine plants, masterpieces of the glassmaker's art.

The museum's annexe at nos. 7–9 Merrion Row (same hours) has an ongoing dinosaurs exhibition, including a video narrated by Richard Attenborough.

THE GOVERNMENT BUILDINGS

Map 4, F8. Sat 10am–12.30pm & 1.30–4.30pm; guided tours only (maximum 16 people). Free tickets from the National Gallery.

Beyond the National History Museum, the Edwardian colossus of the **Government Buildings** looms. The last great edifice erected by the British, its domed centrepiece was inaugurated by George V as the Royal College of Science in 1911, and lectures proceeded despite eleven more years of noisy construction work. No sooner was it finished than the north wing was occupied by the Free State government, whose ministers lived and worked there during the Civil War, for fear of assassination. (Kevin O'Higgins was nearly killed by a sniper when he went onto the roof at night to smoke.) After the Royal College vacated in 1989 the whole complex was refurbished to suit the

THE GOVERNMENT BUILDINGS

government. Besides the stylish decor, it's fascinating to see the lair of the powers-that-be, with their odd perks and quirks, in a forty-minute **guided tour** shadowed by a gimlet-eyed security man.

You'll start by mounting the **Ceremonial Staircase** – the square holes in the balustrades are a trademark of Angela Rolf, who designed much of the furniture. Though Charles Haughey vetoed moving Cabinet meetings into the **Sycamore Room**, he was happy with the **Taoiseach's Office**, complete with a private lift to a rooftop helipad and a basement limo. The historic **Cabinet Room** is the only part of the building that's still in old-fashioned style, hung with portraits of Wolfe Tone, Parnell and other Irish heroes including Countess Markievicz, who led troops in the Easter Rising and was the first woman MP elected to Westminster, and the first woman Cabinet minister in Ireland.

That most English of Irishmen, Arthur Wellesley, Duke of Wellington, may have been born across the road at no. 24 Merrion Street Upper (now a hotel) – though evidence also points towards Trim in County Meath. The Duke was reticent about his Irish origins – on one occasion when reminded, he retorted, "Being born in a stable doesn't make one a horse."

TEMPLE BAR AND THE OLD CITY

N owhere is Dublin's economic transformation over the last decade more evident than in **Temple Bar**, the area sandwiched between Dame Street and the Liffey. Locals and visitors gravitate here to enjoy the city's greatest concentration of restaurants, galleries, pubs, clubs and esoteric shops.

You'll see building work everywhere in Temple Bar – swanky new cyber cafés, spartan coffee houses, shops and restaurants seem to be opening on a daily basis and apartments are being built or refurbished in old warehouses all over the place in an effort to bring people back to the city centre. As property prices soar and its cobbled streets become ever more crowded, the tide of development has begun to sweep westwards towards Wood Quay, where the hugely controversial civic offices stand, locally known as "the bunkers". Underneath its concrete slabs rests the origins of **Viking Dublin**. There are ongoing excavations into Dublin's past along Essex Street West, and across the road from these **Dublin's Viking Adventure** attempts to recreate Viking-age Dyflin.

The **historic core** of the city lies to the west and south of Temple Bar and is roughly triangulated by Dublin Castle and the cathedrals of Christ Church and St Patrick's. Although few old buildings remain, many streets in this area follow contours as staked out by the Vikings in the ninth century, when a main axis ran east-west along the ridge (now Castle Street, Christchurch Place and High Street) and lanes divided by wattle fences descended to the quays. The Anglo-Normans took and fortified this area in the early thirteenth century, building the castle and enclosing Dublin with walls, towers and gateways and founding both **Christ Church** and **St Patrick's Cathedral.**

From nearby Cook Street you can see a massive section of the Norman city walls, and, if you can get inside, there are curios to be found in **St Werburgh's** and **St Audoen's** churches. **Marsh's Library**, near St Patrick's, is a wonderfully archaic scholar's den from the time of Jonathan Swift, who was dean of the cathedral for many years. If pubs, restaurants and market stalls are more your thing, head for South Great George's Street, running 100m or so from Dame Street.

Near the end of Dame Street stands **Dublin Castle**, the former centre and symbol of British authority and the seat of the viceroy. Only since independence have Dubliners been able to enjoy its architecture and tour the State Apartments where the viceroys once held court. Today the castle is still used for state ceremonies and diplomatic summits.

TEMPLE BAR

Until the dissolution of the monasteries in 1537, the land on which Temple Bar stands was the property of the Augustinian order. It owes its names not to the friars, however, but to Sir William Temple, who bought the plot in the late sixteenth century. During the eighteenth century, this area was a centre for Dublin's low life, while in the nineteenth it attracted small businesses and traders.

The land was bought up in the 1960s by CIE (the state transport company at the time), which wanted to build a new central bus terminal to replace the one on the other side of the river. This idea was abandoned in the 1980s, and a decision was taken to develop Temple Bar as an entertainment centre. Today its streets are full of restaurants, second-hand bookshops, art galleries and bric-a-brac stores.

In this section are highlighted some of the major galleries and exhibitions in the area, but for a comprehensive list of what's on where, check the listings section of this guide. It's also worth dropping in to the **Temple Bar information centre** (see p.54) at no. 18 Eustace Street; their free quarterly *Temple Bar Guide* comes with a useful map.

For details of the best places to drink in Temple Bar, see *Pubs & Bars*; for restaurants see *Cafés & Restaurants*; for music venues see *Live Music*.

If you're approaching Temple Bar from the Ha'penny Bridge, you enter through **Merchant's Arch**, a dark alleyway that gives you an idea of how Dickensian Temple Bar must have looked a century ago, when many of the streets beside the quays had such archways. Straight ahead of you is **Crown Alley**, which leads to Central Bank on Dame Street. About halfway down on the alley to your right is the *Bad Ass Café*, where Sinéad O'Connor once worked as a waitress while singing with Ton Ton Macoute.

Dublin's financial centre since the eighteenth century, **Dame Street**, named after a dam which linked the hilltop Viking settlement to the outlying *Thingmount* (see p.14), has a flush of Victorian banking houses now trumped by the **Central Bank**. Designed by controversial architect Sam

TEMPLE BAR

Stephenson in 1978, it's an outsized stack of concrete slabs whose plaza has been colonized by roller-bladers. In a recent survey of Dublin's most loved and hated buildings it came among the top five of both lists.

The heart of Temple Bar

You won't have to wander far to find an arts centre of some kind in Temple Bar. Ultra-modern **Curved Street**, off Temple Lane (once known as Dirty Lane), is flanked by the Arthouse Artists Association of Ireland (AAI), the representative body for professional visual artists in Ireland, and the state-of-the-art **Temple Bar Music Centre**, home to recording and television studios and organizations supporting the development of the Irish music industry. A passageway links to **Eustace Street**, where you'll find the Information Centre and, further up, the coolly minimalist **Irish Film Centre** (see p.221 and p.239). Its two screens show art-house and special-interest films, and its bar and restaurant attract a trendy crowd.

On the corner opposite Temple Bar Square stand Temple Bar Gallery and Studios, the largest of its kind in Ireland with thirty artist studios and two exhibition spaces. Next door, you can see a wide selection of the best work of emerging and established Irish and international printmakers at the Original Print Gallery.

Dublin's unique outdoor performance venue, **Meeting House Square** (named after a former Quaker meeting-hall), hosts a wide variety of events throughout the summer, including outdoor screenings of films and concerts and, during the summer, an outdoor food market; see *Shopping*. Nearby are the **Gallery of Photography** and Ireland's premier drama school, the Gaiety School of Acting. Facing the stage at Meeting House Square is the **Ark**, which is dedicated to artwork by and for children.

TEMPLE BAR

The Eagle Tavern
and the Hellfire Club

Before it was demolished by the Wide Streets Commission in
1757, the **Eagle Tavern** was among the foremost roistering
spots of Georgian Dublin. Standing beside the equally popular
Lucas Coffee Shop, it allowed gentlemen-about-town to spend
day and night in dissipation without having to walk far. It was
at the **Eagle** that the notorious **Hellfire Club** was founded in
1735 by the Earl of Rosse, Buck Whaley, Colonel St Leger and
the artist James Worsdale. Dedicated to gambling, whoring
and profanity rather than black magic *per se* – though the Devil
is said to have appeared at one of their parties – their main
meeting place was outside Dublin at Speaker Conolly's hunting lodge on Montpelier Hill. Because of the scandal they
caused, they eventually had to quit Ireland, but in 1755 the
Club was re-established in England by Sir Francis Dashwood,
at Medmenham Abbey. He later became Chancellor of the
Exchequer but made such a hash of it that he was retired to
the Lords, while the Hellfire Club languished as its members
succumbed to bankruptcy or cirrhosis.

Sadly, for those seeking any relic of the Club in Dublin, the
location of the tavern is uncertain, due to a missing portion of
the original surveyor's map. Although a plaque on the wall of Eustace
Street states that it occupied the site of the Quaker meeting-hall
where Wolfe Tone later founded the Dublin United Irishmen, most
sources place the tavern on Cork Hill, where much was levelled
to create Parliament Street and City Hall, so *Thomas Read* pub or
Da Pino restaurant may be closer to the mark.

Along Essex Street East there's a showcase for contemporary Irish jewellery, furniture and interior design in the
DesignYARD (see p.245). Further up on the same side of

the street, U2 spent millions on *The Clarence Hotel* (see p.171*)* and have turned it into Dublin's coolest establishment, with a rooftop penthouse used by the likes of Björk and Jack Nicholson. Before the Custom House moved downriver in the 1780s, this was the site where a crane used to unload ships – hence Crane Lane, nearby.

Broad **Parliament Street** was the first of the new roads cut through the old city after the formation of the Wide Streets Commission in 1757. Despite the results it achieved within a decade, the Commission was widely hated at the time, since tenants who ignored its compulsory purchase orders had their roofs removed overnight to force them to quit. Fortunately, it spared what is now Dublin's oldest shop, at no. 4. *Thomas Read* has been a cutlers since 1670 and contains its original display cabinets and furniture.

On the corner of Parliament Street which faces Grattan Bridge stands the Sunlight Chambers, whose filthy exterior has a beautiful bas-relief frieze of men making their clothes dirty through honest toil, and women washing them. Its unusual theme is explained by the fact that Sunlight was the brand of soap manufactured by Lever Brothers, who commissioned the building at the turn of the century. Their family business has since grown into the Unilever conglomerate, producing everything from washing powder to breakfast cereals.

CITY HALL AND THE OLYMPIA

Parliament Street slopes slightly uphill towards the **City Hall** on Dame Street. Built in 1769 as the Royal Exchange, it's been occupied by Dublin Corporation since 1825. You can walk in to view its Rotunda, which contains statues of O'Connell and other worthies in Roman garb; among the murals is one depicting Lambert Simnel being carried through the streets (see p.68). The civic coat of arms on the floor shows three burning bastions, symbolizing resistance to invaders, but the motto *Obedientia Civium Urbis Felicitas* (Happy the City whose Citizens Obey) suggests that rebellion was a greater worry for Dublin's rulers. During the Easter Rising, City Hall was seized by the insurgents, who sniped at British forces in the castle from its roof.

Opposite the City Hall, behind a stained-glass *porte cochère,* is the **Olympia Theatre** (see p.237). Since opening as the "Star of Erin Music Hall" in 1749, it has played host to many great Irish and international entertainers and features gigs by local bands on Friday and Saturday nights.

DUBLIN CASTLE

Map 6, C6. Mon–Fri 10am–5pm, Sat, Sun & bank holidays 2–5pm; £2, students/children £1, family £5.

For seven hundred years, **Dublin Castle** embodied English rule as the headquarters of the viceroy. Built by the Anglo-Normans in the early thirteenth century, it was the key element of their walled city and served their successors well, withstanding all attempts to take it by force.

Its gravest test was in 1534, when besieged by Silken Thomas Fitzgerald Henry VIII's Lord Deputy, who had renounced his allegiance to the English crown. The castle was formally handed over to Michael Collins and the Irish Free State on January 16, 1922. According to legend, the last viceroy complained, "You're seven minutes late, Mr Collins", to which he replied, "We've been waiting 700 years, you can have the seven minutes." Today, denuded of menace, it could be mistaken for a private college. Its palatial interior is revealed only on guided **tours** of the State Apartments, though you can look around the courtyards and the Chapel Royal for free.

DUBLIN CASTLE

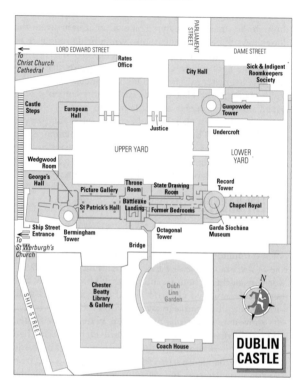

DUBLIN CASTLE

Above the main gate is a **figure of Justice** that turns her back on Dublin – an apt symbol of British justice, Dubliners said. Moreover, the scales of Justice tilted whenever it rained, till the authorities ensured even-handedness by drilling holes in the scale-pans. The nearby **Bedford Tower** is an eighteenth-century clocktower built upon the base of a Norman gate-tower from where the Irish "Crown Jewels"– a diamond St Patrick Star and Badge, together with other insignia – were stolen shortly before the state visit of Edward VII in 1907. Nobody was ever caught and the jewels have never been recovered.

The **Upper Yard** marks the extent of the medieval castle, which was ravaged by fire in 1684. Surveyor-General Sir William Robinson took the opportunity of creating a larger complex of residential and administrative buildings, the arcaded appearance of which closely resembles his design for the Royal Hospital, Kilmainham (see p.87). It's hard to imagine it heaped with the bodies of rebels brought into the city on carts after the British crushed the Rebellion of 1798 – or the castle's defenders being slain and buried here in shallow graves during the Easter Rising.

The State Apartments

You'll begin your tour of the **State Apartments** by ascending a grand staircase leading to the Battleaxe Landing, where the viceroy's ceremonial bodyguards stood. During World War I the **bedrooms** served as a Red Cross hospital – the wounded James Connolly was held here before his execution at Kilmainham Jail. Famous names like Nelson Mandela, Chancellor Kohl and Mrs Thatcher (who insisted cable TV be installed) have slept in Her Majesty's Bedroom. Across the corridor, the **Apollo Room** has a gorgeous ceiling from another house, featuring symbols of hunting, farming, war and music. The Drawing Room was also reconstructed after a fire in 1941, and contains a mirror bought for £5 by a farmer who used it for a headboard for 25 years; it's now valued at £100,000.

In the **Throne Room**, the Act of Union is embodied in a chandelier combining the rose, shamrock and thistle and in a throne belonging to William of Orange. Viceregal portraits line the gallery-cum-dining room, with Cornwallis (who lost the American colonies) hung in disgrace behind the door. After dinner, men would play billiards in the **Wedgwood Room**, which is decorated with four plaques in that style and roundels of Day and Night. The circular **Birmingham Tower Room** is an eighteenth-century conversion of a medieval prison tower. Off an anteroom opens George's Hall, built in 1911 for the visit of George V and Queen Mary – the last British monarchs to visit Dublin. Best of all is the blue, white and gold **St Patrick's Hall**, which once hosted ceremonies of the Knights of St Patrick (an order created in 1738) and is now used for presidential inaugurations and funerals. Ceiling paintings depict George III's coronation, Henry II receiving the surrender of the Irish chieftains, and St Patrick lighting the Paschal Fire on the Hill of Slane, watched by suspicious Druids.

The Lower Yard and Grounds

In the **Lower Yard**, the dramatic juxtaposition of the Record Tower and the Chapel Royal is marred by a hideous modern tax office. Beefed up with battlements in Victorian times, the **Record Tower**, a rough-hewn mass dating back to 1258, originally served as a prison. In 1592, Red Hugh O'Donnell made two celebrated escapes from here; first by climbing down a rope, and then via a privy. The adjoining **Chapel Royal** is a neo-Gothic gem by Francis Johnston. Mindful of the underground river that had undermined two earlier chapels, Johnston made it as light as possible by using plaster-coated brick rather than stone.

Tours currently finish at an **undercroft** exposing a wall and corner tower of the Norman castle and part of the original Viking ramparts. Only regular pumping stops it being submerged by the River Poddle, which originally flowed above ground into the "Dark Pool" (*Dubh Linn*) in the area of what is now the castle **garden**, around the back of the chapel, facing a side of the castle unexpectedly painted terracotta, grey and yellow. A small door at the rear of the Record Tower gives access to the **Garda Síochána Museum**, relating the history of Ireland's police force, which is due to open in late 1997 and will form the last stop on guided tours.

Another attraction, opening in 1998, is the **Chester Beatty Library and Gallery** based on the bequest of Sir Alfred Chester Beatty, an Irish-American mining magnate who settled in Dublin in 1950 and later gave his entire collection of oriental art to the nation. Its superbly crafted *objets* range from Japanese *netsuke* and Chinese rhino-horn cups (over 200 of them – the largest collection in the world) to lifesize Burmese Buddhas, while the books and manuscripts include the oldest surviving examples of Egyptian love poetry and illustrated miniatures of Persian and Moghul poetry. Opening hours will be as for the castle, with no admission charge.

DUBLIN'S VIKING ADVENTURE

Map 6, B4. March–Dec Mon & Thurs–Sun 9.30am–4pm; £4.75, students, under 18s and OAPs £3.95, children £2.95, family £13.

North of the castle, in Essex Street West, is the site of ongoing excavations into Dublin's past. Though much was lost at Wood Quay (see p.64) and other sites, archeologists have been lucky to find a stratum of Viking dwellings from the tenth century, which may overlie the remains of an earlier Celtic settlement at the mouth of the Poddle. Unfortunately, though notices on the fence explain the basics of archeology, you're not told what's been found so far, and to the untrained eye there's little to see but a lot of people poking about in muddy pits.

The Vikings

The **Vikings** (from the Norse *vik*, meaning "creek" or "bay") were Scandinavian pirates who pillaged the European seaboard, and sometimes beyond, between the eighth and twelfth centuries, establishing kingdoms as far afield as Ireland and Russia. Sea-power was the key to their success. Their oak "dragon ships" could sail more than 120 miles in a day with the wind behind them; could be rowed against headwinds in either direction, as the prow and stern were the same shape; and could even be rolled across ground to the next river by an average crew of sixty warriors. Viking fleets of up to one hundred ships ranged as far south as Constantinople and Tangiers, and their settlement of Greenland led them to plant a colony on Labrador five centuries before Columbus "discovered" America.

The Vikings who raided Ireland came from Norway and over-ran the Picts in the Hebrides, which, with the Isle of Man, formed a base for future attacks upon Scotland and Ireland. Their first recorded raid in Ireland was in 795, and in 837 sixty longships sailed up the Liffey to raid inland; four years later they created a fortified port which became an important trading post and eventually the town of **Dyflin**. Though their first settlement was plundered by Danish Vikings, and the Norsemen were forced out by the King of Leinster in 902, they returned fifteen years later to build timber and mud defences at the base of the high ground around the "Dark Pool" and houses on the hillside above the quays.

There was much intermarriage with the Irish (the name Doyle, for example, derives from *Dubh Gaill*, meaning "dark-haired foreigners") and the Norse trading links were valued by Brian Bóru, king of Munster. Although credited with "driving out the Danes" at the battle of Clontarf in 1014, Bóru let the Norse king, Sitric IV, remain in Dyflin where his conversion to

Christianity encouraged the growth of a **Hiberno-Norse culture**. Meanwhile, Danish Vikings forged the Duchy of Normandy into a formidable power bent on expansion. Having conquered England in 1066 (their longships appear on the Bayeux Tapestry), the **Normans** were later invited by Diarmuid Mac Murchada to invade Ireland and restore him to the throne of Leinster, in return for making it subject to the king of England and marrying his daughter to the Norman leader, Richard de Clare (Strongbow). The Anglo-Normans' archers and chainmail proved irresistible, and by 1170 they had routed the Hiberno-Norsemen from Dyflin, obliging those that remained to live in Oxmantown, across the river, where they gradually lost their ethnic identity and merged into the general population.

Across the road from the excavations, **Dublin's Viking Adventure** offers an "experience" of Viking-age Dyflin that's short on facts but fun in its own way. You start by boarding a "boat" that sails through a cinematic storm to reach Dyflin, to be greeted by actors in wigs and homespun wit with the best joke of the tour: "It's been a long journey; does anyone want to use the cesspit?" The pole-and-wattle houses, ponds and ramshackle fences are quite convincing (apart from the lack of foul smells), and catwalks zig-zag up past a cross-section of the Wood Quay site, showing the layers of homes and graves that accumulated there over a thousand years. You end up in the hall used for Viking feasts, containing a lifesize model of a longship whose "sail" is the screen for another film, full of stormy seas and majestic Scandinavian landscapes, which imparts a few facts about the Vikings' voyages.

To partake of the "Viking Feast" it's essential to book ahead, as the event is popular with coach parties (nightly, except Tues & Wed). Since Viking food seems gross to modern tastes, the menu is a mixture of Irish and Olde

DUBLIN'S VIKING ADVENTURE

Medieval dishes, served at long tables. Axe- and knife-throwing were ruled out by the safety inspectors, and nobody knows what Viking music sounded like, so the entertainment is based around the development of music and dance from traditional Irish to *Riverdance*. It'll set you back £31.50 (£20 per child), and that doesn't cover the drinks bill.

WOOD QUAY AND FISHAMBLE STREET

The most populous part of Viking Dyflin covered the hillside by **Wood Quay** – a site now occupied by the gigantic **Civic Offices** of Dublin Corporation, a much-loathed lump known as "the bunkers". As layers of medieval timber structures were being destroyed by mechanical diggers, archeologists won an injunction allowing them to conduct an excavation of the site before these finds on show in the National Museum and the remains of tenth-century houses and quay walls were lost forever. As a token apology, the bunkers are surrounded by ornamental references to the Vikings, with a wooden longship and brass images of axe-heads and other artefacts embedded on Wood Quay, and the outlines of a Viking house picked out on the slope behind Christ Church.

Twisting uphill towards the cathedral, **Fishamble Street** has followed the same route for a millennium. A fish market for much of that time, it was the birthplace of Archbishop Ussher (of Trinity fame) and Henry Grattan, the founder of the Irish Parliament. A plaque outside the derelict Kennan's engineering works marks the site of the Musick Hall where the combined choirs of Christ Church and St Patrick's first performed Handel's *Messiah* in 1742. Ladies were asked not to wear hoops in their crinolines so that more people could attend, as proceeds went to charity. Swift's verdict was,

"Oh, a German, a genius, a prodigy". Excerpts from the *Messiah* are performed here on the anniversary of the event (April 13).

DUBLINIA

Map 6, A5. Oct–March Mon–Fri 10am–7pm, Sat 11am–4pm & Sun 10am–4.30pm; £3.95; students/children £2.90; family £10. A visit to Christ Church Cathedral is included in the price.

As "a bridge to the medieval past", **Dublinia** falls short of virtual reality but conveys lots of impressions and facts with a light touch. The exhibition occupies the ex-**Synod Hall** of the Church of Ireland, which is connected to Christ Church Cathedral by an elegant bridge. Though both were created in Victorian times, the Hall incorporates a medieval tower and stands on the site of the palace of the last Viking ruler, Hasculf, who was chased out by the Normans in 1170.

Dublinia opens with a panoramic **model** of Dublin c.1500, by which time its wooden suburbs had been burned and its population decimated by the Black Death, leaving the walled Norman city amid tracts of open land, with just one bridge across the Liffey. Wall-maps trace Dublin's subsequent evolution well into Georgian times, and humble **medieval artefacts** found at Wood Quay are displayed in two rooms offside.

Equipped with a guide-tape, you move on through lifesize **tableaux** of events such as the crowning of Lambert Simnel and the rebellion of Silken Thomas. A timber-framed merchant's house and a quayside give a sanitized view of medieval life, which the captions admit was anything but salubrious.

After a plug for its sponsor, *Baileys*, Dublinia concludes in the Great Hall with a half-hour **audiovisual show** on the

DUBLINIA

Normans, trade, the "riding of the franchises", and the "Liberties of Dublin". After five minutes of this you'll probably want to make your getaway – it's worth climbing **St Michael's Tower**, a lofty relic of the fifteenth-century Church of St Michael and All Angels, for a great view of Dublin and the Wicklow Mountains on fine days. Finally, the coffee shop in the **Malton Room** was named after the English artist James Malton (c.1760–1803), whose water-colours (see p.44) were the basis for *A Picturesque and Descriptive View of the City of Dublin* – a set of 25 prints depicting buildings and streetlife during its Georgian hey-day.

CHRIST CHURCH CATHEDRAL

Map 6, A5. Daily: 10am–5pm; £1, students/children 50p.

In medieval times, Church of Ireland **Christ Church Cathedral** would have soared above the city's wooden houses from its commanding site on the brow of Dublin Hill. Today, the view is generally obscured by buildings till you get near by, and the cathedral has been isolated from its surroundings by the traffic system.

A small Celtic church, Cill Céle Christ, may have stood on this site as early as 600 – long before the coming of the Vikings, who probably pillaged it. In 1028 their ruler Sitric IV ("Silkenbeard") converted to Christianity and requested that Bishop Dúnán found a cathedral on these grounds. Judging by Viking churches in Norway, Sitric's Christ Church was made of wood and probably decorated with pagan as well as Christian symbols, since both faiths co-existed for decades. When the Normans ousted the Vikings, their leader, Richard de Clare "Strongbow", made an agreement with Archbishop Laurence O'Toole to demolish the old cathedral and replace it with one symbolizing their joint

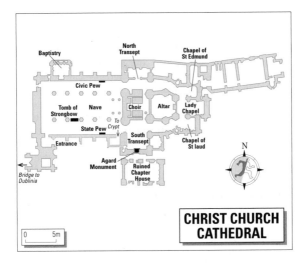

North Transept

Chapel of St Edmund

Baptistry

Civic Pew

Tomb of Strongbow

Nave

Choir

Altar

Lady Chapel

To Crypt

State Pew

South Transept

Entrance

Chapel of St Iaud

Agard Monument

Ruined Chapter House

N

Bridge to Dublinia

0   5m

CHRIST CHURCH CATHEDRAL

glory. Work began in 1172 but was not completed until 1240. Unfortunately, the structure had been built on a bog, and in 1562 the south wall collapsed, pulling down half the cathedral. The rest continued as a church (and a tavern and market) but steadily deteriorated until the distiller Henry Roe donated £230,000 (worth £23 million today) to finance its restoration in the 1870s. Architect George Street then refaced the exterior and transformed the cathedral's outward appearance by adding flying buttresses.

The interior was also renovated, but it preserves more of its original character: the choir and transepts belong to Strongbow's cathedral, to which the nave was added in 1234.

Close to the entrance lies the curious **tomb of Strongbow**. The original was destroyed by the collapse of the south wall, but was substituted with an effigy of an earl

CHRIST CHURCH CATHEDRAL

so that Dublin landlords could resume their practice of collecting rents around it. Depending on which version you want to believe, the smaller figure alongside is a fragment of the original tomb which may contain Strongbow's bowels – or an effigy of one of his sons, whom he cut in two for cowardice on the battlefield.

In Norman and Tudor times Christ Church was used for swearing in the viceroy, until the building of the Chapel Royal in Dublin Castle usurped its role. In 1487, the cathedral witnessed the pseudo-coronation of ten-year-old Lambert Simnel as "Edward VI"; within a month his revolt was crushed by Henry VII, who amused himself by sparing Simnel's life to employ him as a kitchen-scullion. At one side of the nave the Civic Pew for Dublin's Lord Mayor has brass supports for his Great Sword and Mace (rarely used today), and the State Pew, used by the Irish president, still bears the royal arms of the Stuarts.

The area behind the **choir** contains oak stalls for the canons and choristers and the archbishop's throne. Turning back to face the nave, you'll be startled by the "**leaning wall of Dublin**" – ever since the south wall collapsed, the north wall has leaned half a metre outwards.

In the north transept, notice the Romanesque carvings on the capitals of the archways: a troupe of musicians as you go in, and two human faces being absorbed by griffins (symbolizing wealth) at the exit into the aisle of the choir. The south transept is notable for its tiered **tomb** of the nineteenth earl of Kildare. There are also two medieval effigies of women, one of whom is reputed to be the wife or sister of Strongbow.

The right-hand chapel extending off the choir is the Chapel of St Laud, named after the fifth-century bishop of Coutances in Normandy. On the wall of Laud's chapel is a heart-shaped iron casket containing the **heart of**

Archbishop O'Toole, the patron saint of Dublin, canonized after his death in Normandy. The original medieval floor tiles in the chapel were copied by the Victorians throughout the cathedral.

Finally, visit the **crypt**, the purest remnant of the twelfth-century cathedral (you can still see parts of the timber frame used during construction), now a repository for effigies and curios. The grumpy-looking Charles I and II statues came from the city hall that stood opposite the cathedral until 1806, and the punishment-stocks remained in use in Christchurch Yard till 1870. One vault displays a tabernacle and a pair of candlesticks used by James II in 1689 (when, for three months only, Latin mass was again used at Christ Church), and a mummified cat and rat known to generations of Dublin kids – the cat chased the rat into an organ pipe, where both perished.

To hear Christ Church's excellent choir, come along for Choral Evensong (Thurs 6pm, Sat 5pm, Sun 3.30pm).

ST WERBURGH'S AND ST AUDOEN'S

There are various reminders of past religious and political upheavals along the meandering route from Christ Church to St Patrick's Cathedral, via St Werburgh's, St Audoen's and the city walls.

Across Christchurch Place, on Werburgh Street, **St Werburgh's** has been lacking its spire since it was removed after Emmet's rising of 1803 for fear that future rebels would use it as a sniper's nest. Founded by the Normans in 1178, it was named after the daughter of the king of Mercia, the Abbess Werburgh. One of the leaders of the

1798 Rebellion, Lord Edward Fitzgerald, who was betrayed by spies and died of wounds sustained during his arrest, lies in the Fitzgerald vault. His captor, Major Henry Sirr, is buried in the yard. "Mrs Molly Malone, fishmonger" is listed in the parish records as having died in 1734. Rebuilt in 1715 and again mid-century, the church has an elegant Georgian interior that comes as a surprise should you manage to gain entry (Sun 11am–noon for services).

....

If you're hungry after all that walking, *Leo Burdock's*, just across the road, serves the best fish and chips in town (see p.192).

....

To the west of Christ Church stand two churches dedicated to St Audoen (the Norman saint, Ouen of Rouen). The Protestant **St Audoen's**, built around 1190, has been reduced to a nave that can only be entered on Sunday mornings; for centuries, its bells were tolled during storms to remind citizens to pray for those at sea. After the Catholics were displaced by the Reformation, they used a chapel on Bridge Street until the Emancipation enabled them to build their own St Audoen's on the hilltop in 1846. As Maurice Craig wrote, "It looks like some impregnable fortress of the faith, its rugged calp masonry battened like a medieval castle to its base, pierced only by windows at the very top and crowned with the cross which breaks up the silhouette against the sky." The door is flanked by two giant turtle shells from the South Pacific, given by a sea captain to his brother, the parish priest. Catholic St Audoen's celebrates Latin Mass at 11am on Sundays.

Behind the Protestant church, mossy steps descend to **St Audoen's Arch**, the only remaining gate in the **Norman city walls** – a dramatic remnant stretching for 200m along Cook Street, 7m high and tipped with battlements.

To reach St Patrick's Cathedral cross High Street and head down Nicholas Street. The slums in this area were considered among the worst in Europe prior to their demolition in the 1890s, when they were replaced by the **Iveagh Buildings**, a model housing estate built by the Guinness family. Its decorative main block faces **St Patrick's Park**, once the cathedral green, where Cromwell's troops planted cabbages and thereby introduced them to Ireland.

ST PATRICK'S CATHEDRAL

Map 4, A7. April–Oct Mon–Fri 9am–6pm, Sat 9am–5pm;
Nov–March Mon–Fri 9am–4pm, Sun 10–11am & 12.45–3pm; £1.

Like Christ Church, **St Patrick's** was restored by the Victorians, though it seems closer to its origins than Christ Church and is altogether quirkier, thanks to its array of odd memorials. The cathedral stands on one of Dublin's earliest Christian sites, where St Patrick is said to have baptized converts in a well (c.450). Bishop John Comyn founded St Patrick's in 1191 in order to create his own diocese beyond the city walls. However, it was Archbishop Henry de Londres who raised it to cathedral status and entirely rebuilt it (1220–70) at the same time as completing Christ Church. In 1544 the vaulting of the nave collapsed, and in 1649 it was used as a stable by Cromwell's cavalry, hastening St Patrick's decline into separate chapels serving different communities. Eventually, in the 1860s, Sir Benjamin Guinness commissioned Thomas Drew to reconstruct the cathedral, setting a precedent for the restoration of Christ Church.

The sombre exterior is dominated by the fourteenth-century **Minot tower**. Oddly misaligned with the rest of the cathedral, the tower seems to have been built for defence, a precaution necessitated by St Patrick's exposed location outside the city walls.

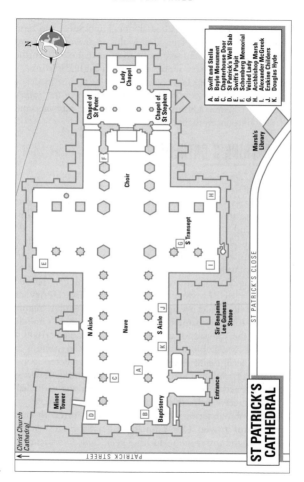

ST PATRICK'S
CATHEDRAL

N

Christ Church Cathedral

Minot Tower

Baptistery

N Aisle

Nave

S Aisle

Choir

Chapel of St Peter

Lady Chapel

Chapel of St Stephen

S Transept

Sir Benjamin Lee Guiness Statue

Entrance

ST PATRICK'S CLOSE

Marsh's Library

PATRICK STREET

A. Swift and Stella
B. Boyle Monument
C. Chapterhouse Door
D. St Patrick's Well Slab
E. Swift's Pulpit
F. Schomberg Memorial
G. Veiled Lady
H. Archbishop Marsh
I. Alexander McGreek
J. Erskine Childers
K. Douglas Hyde

This is the longest medieval church in Ireland and its interior is majestically proportioned, its nave and transepts scrutinized by enigmatic **figures** carved on the pillars of the aisles. (Don't miss the Veiled Lady in the south transept or the bestiary of monsters in the nave.) Most visitors make a beeline for the **graves of Jonathan Swift and Stella**, Swift's long-term partner, beneath brass tablets in the nave. On the wall of the south aisle are a bust of Swift and two plaques bearing their epitaphs, penned by him. His reads:

Here is laid the body of
Jonathan Swift, Doctor of Divinity,
Dean of this Cathedral Church,
Where fierce indignation can no longer
Rend the heart.
Go, traveller, and imitate, if you can
This earnest and dedicated
Champion of liberty.

She is merely "Mrs Hester Johnson, better known to the world as Stella, under which she is celebrated in the writings of Dr Jonathan Swift, Dean of this cathedral". To add injury to insult, her body was exhumed by Victorian phrenologists, studying the skulls of the famous. There is also a tribute to Swift by his friend Alexander Pope, with whom he planned to share a home in retirement.

The gigantic **Boyle monument** teems with painted figures of the fifteen children borne by Catherine Fenton, the "dearest, dear wife" of Richard Boyle, earl of Cork. Erected in 1632, it originally stood near the altar but was moved after the viceroy objected to churchgoers being forced to pray "crouching to an Earl of Cork and his lady. . . or to those sea nymphs his daughters, with coronets upon their heads, their hair dishevelled, down upon their shoulders". The earl got his revenge by engineering Viceroy Wentworth's execution, years later.

ST PATRICK'S CATHEDRAL

73

Jonathan Swift

Born at Hoey's Court near Dublin Castle in 1667, **Jonathan Swift** could read by the age of three, and at fifteen was accepted as a student at Trinity College. On graduating, he worked for the diplomat Sir William Temple and subsequently for the Church of England, hoping to secure "a fat deanery or a lean bishopric". This ambition clashed with his activities as a political pamphleteer, from 1704 onwards. As his pen had been deployed on behalf of the Tories, the incoming Whig administration of 1714 bore a grudge against Swift, who felt it wise to return to Dublin and take up the post of Dean of St Patrick's, which he had accepted the previous year.

Back home his commitment to Ireland and his social conscience grew, as expressed in a series of anonymous **tracts** during the 1720s. An early advocate of economic independence, Swift's *Proposal for the Universal Use of Irish Manufactures* argued that the Irish should burn all English imports, except coal. *The Drapier's Letters* exposed shady business deals, and *A Modest Proposal* bitterly suggested that the Irish poor could solve their problems by selling their babies to the rich, as food. He is now chiefly known for *Gulliver's Travels* (1726), a dazzlingly diverse satire now too often misperceived as a children's story.

Besides his increasingly vitriolic writings, Swift was famous for his eccentricities and his mysterious relationship with **Esther Johnson**, known as "**Stella**". The daughter of Sir William Temple's housekeeper was variously rumoured to have been Swift's niece or sister, his secret bride or his platonic companion. Whatever the truth, Swift was heartbroken by her death, finishing his *Journal to Stella* in the darkened cathedral on the nights following her burial.

His final years were overshadowed by a malady causing gid-
diness, which Swift mistook for symptoms of insanity.
Eventually he *did* go mad, hailing the viceroy as "you fellow
with the Blue String" and assaulting two clergymen in a carriage. As soon as Swift's death became public, admirers burst
into the Deanery and cut off all his hair, carrying the locks away
as souvenirs. In his will, he left money to build a mental hospital, which opened in 1749 and was one of the first in Europe.

Given Swift's reputation as a Dubliner and a patriot, he was
astonishingly rude about both, calling Dublin "the most dis-
agreeable place in Europe, at least to any but those who have
been accustomed to it from their youth", in which case "a jail
might be preferable"; and averring that "no man is thoroughly
miserable unless he be condemned to live in Ireland".

His heir, Robert Boyle, is given a niche of his own on the
monument. Boyle is famous above all for formulating Boyle's
Law on the relationship between the pressure, volume and
temperature of gases. He is less well known for leaving a
legacy to fund eight sermons a year, refuting "Atheists,
Theists, Pagans, Jews and Mohammedans".

Another curiosity is the **wooden door** leaning against a
pier, once belonging to the cathedral's chapter house. In 1492,
so the story goes, a quarrel arose between soldiers of the earls
of Kildare and Ormond. Ormond barricaded himself in the
chapter house, whereupon Kildare, eager to end hostilities, cut
a hole in the door and stuck his arm through, inviting
Ormond to shake hands. Peace was restored, and so the
expression "chancing your arm" entered the English language.

In the northwest corner of the nave lies a stone **slab** with a
Celtic cross that once marked the site of St Patrick's well.
Marble statues and plaques commemorating such luminaries
as the Marquis of Buckingham (the first Grand Master of the

ST PATRICK'S CATHEDRAL |

Knights of St Patrick) and the harpist Turlough Carolan, the "last of the Irish bards", are ranged along the north aisle.

The **north transept** is hung with flags of the Irish Regiments of the British army; 49,400 Irishmen died in World War I alone. In one corner are Swift's pulpit, chair and table.

Until 1869 the **choir** was used for investitures of the Knights of St Patrick – hence the helmets, swords and banners above the pews, scathingly described by Thackeray as "tawdry old rags and gimcracks" representing a "humbug of chivalry". A plain slab in the north aisle of the choir honours Duke Frederick Schomberg, slain at the battle of the Boyne. As the tablet above relates, his heirs didn't care to erect a memorial, so his admirers had to make amends; in Swift's words, "The renown of his valour had greater power among strangers than had ties of blood among his kith and kin." Peering through the grille into the Chapel of St Stephen, you'll see the armchair used by William III at the thanksgiving service after his victory at Boyne. Also note the statue of Sir Benjamin Guinness's daughter, beneath a window inscribed "I was thirsty and ye gave me a drink".

The **south transept** (once the chapter house where Kildare chanced his arm) contains a magnificent stained-glass **window** and various opulent funerary monuments – that of Archbishop Marsh (see opposite) is the finest surviving carving by Grinling Gibbons in Ireland. In one corner is a small tablet dedicated by Swift to his manservant, Alexander McGeek, "in memory of his discretion, fidelity and diligence in that humble station". McGeek's discretion in the libel case arising from *The Drapier's Letters* (purportedly written by a humble tailor) saved Swift from financial ruin.

Eminent Irish Protestants of the twentieth century are commemorated in the **south aisle**, starting with Erskine Childers (Irish President 1973–74), whose father was executed by the Free State during the Civil War. The plaque in

Irish honours Douglas Hyde, the founder of the Gaelic League, who became Ireland's first president. At his funeral service in 1949, former government colleagues waited outside St Patrick's in their cars, as their Catholic faith forbade them to enter a Protestant cathedral.

MARSH'S LIBRARY

Map 4, A8. Mon & Wed–Fri 10am–12.45pm & 2–5pm, Sat 10.30am–12.45pm; donation £1.

Almost right beside St Patrick's Cathedral, a crenellated wall with an arched gateway surrounds a Georgian edifice half faced in stone to match the cathedral. This is **Marsh's Library**, the oldest public library in Ireland, opened to "All Graduates and Gentlemen" in 1707. Its founder, Archbishop Narcissus Marsh, was a scholar and scientist who translated the Old Testament into Irish and first used the word "microphone" in his own works on acoustics. The core of the library is the collection of Edward Stillingfleet, archbishop of Worcester, whose entire collection of 10,000 books Marsh bought for £2,500; donations by other clerics and bibliophiles have boosted the tally to 25,000 books.

Built by Sir William Robertson (the architect of Dublin Castle), it's a charming example of an eighteenth-century scholar's library, consisting of two L-shaped rooms whose oak bookcases have carved and lettered gables crowned by a bishop's mitre, and three alcoves or "cages" where readers were locked in with rare books. The middle one contains a cast of Stella's skull, and a case displays books owned by Swift, including a *History of the Great Rebellion*, with pencilled notations disparaging the Scots. The bindery for the conservation and repair of antique books (featured in *Ulysses*) has had the odd task of treating bullet-marks, as Marsh's Library was peppered by shots aimed at Jacob's Biscuit Factory in 1916 (see p.79).

SOUTH GREAT GEORGE'S STREET AND AUNGIER STREET

Between Marsh's Library and St Stephen's Green is an area of rundown flats bisected by a lively thoroughfare whose initial stretch, **South Great George's Street**, is lined with restaurants, pubs and the red-brick Gothic facade of the **Market Arcade** (Mon–Sat 10am–6pm). A Victorian market hall leading through to Drury Street, it sells jewellery, secondhand books and clothes.

Exchequer Street, running parallel to the arcade, is one of the nicest small streets in Dublin. Its name recalls the Exchequer that stood here in Tudor times; the word itself derives from a chequered tablecloth that was used to make and demonstrate tax calculations to illiterates.

Aungier Street, South Great George's Street's seedier continuation, is named after Francis Aungier, who developed this area on land seized from the Whitefrairs Priory in 1537. An anonymous pamphlet of 1725 (possibly written by Swift) describes a throng of "Bawds with band-boxes, borrowed smocks, and scoured manteaus", apothecaries carrying "purges and potions" and "lap-dogs cleaning and dressing to go to church with their ladies". Today there are massage parlours and martial arts shops.

Raised on the site of the bygone Carmelite priory in 1827, **Whitefriar Street Carmelite Church** (Mon–Fri 8am–3.15pm, Sun 8am–7pm, holidays 10am–1pm) was blessed eight years later by Pope Gregory XVI's gift of the heart of St Valentine, patron saint of lovers. **Our Lady of Dublin**, a life-sized, sixteenth-century Flemish oak statue of the Virgin and Child standing near the altar, is the only such image to have survived the sack of Ireland's monasteries. Hollowed-out and used as a cattle trough, it was rescued by a priest from a junk shop near St Mary's Abbey, whence it probably came.

Easter Rising buffs may be curious about **Jacob's Biscuit Factory**, a fortress-like complex where 150 rebels blocked a British advance from the Portobello Barracks for five days, as its walls proved impervious to rifle-fire and the narrow streets made it hard to use artillery. A crumbling wall bearing the Jacob's name links remnants of the factory incorporated into the Dublin Institute of Technology and the National Archives on Bishop Street.

SOUTH GREAT GEORGE'S STREET AND AUNGIER STREET

THE LIBERTIES AND KILMAINHAM

To the west of St Patrick's Cathedral lies the sprawling district of the **Liberties**, so called after the patchwork of parishes with charters giving its residents "freedom from toll, passage, portage, lestage, pavage, quayage and carriage". Originally the area was known as Meath's Liberty, after the earl of Meath who invited Huguenot refugees from France to settle in the quarter known as the Coombe in 1650. Over the following sixty years the 10,000 Huguenots who settled here had a profound effect on the small and undeveloped city, introducing poplin- and silk-weaving, founding a horticultural society and encouraging the wine trade. However, in the 1770s industry in the Liberties was hit by competition from imported fabrics, unemployment soared and the area became a slum. As an American doctor wrote sarcastically: "Winds and rain have *liberty* to enter freely through the windows of half the houses – the pigs have *liberty* to ramble about – the landlord has *liberty* to take possession of most of his tenements – the silk-weaver has *liberty* to starve or beg."

The Liberty and the Ormond Boys

Until the early nineteenth century, rivalry between the Liberty Boys (tailor- and weaver-apprentices of the Coombe) and the Ormond Boys (butchers from Ormond Market on the quays) frequently erupted into pitched battles of up to a thousand men. Captives were sometimes hamstrung and impaled on the hooks of their own butchers' stalls.

The harshness of working-class life was partly to blame for this sort of brutality. In the late eighteenth century landlords charged one to two shillings a week for a single room, so two or even four families would cohabitate to lighten the rent. At the same time, over 19,000 weavers faced unemployment due to the import of Indian muslin and French silks. To protect their jobs they formed gangs who went around cutting "every foreign dress worn by man or woman, no matter of what rank", and kidnapping haberdashers, dragging them through the mud to Weaver's Square, where they were tarred and feathered.

Although the Liberties have maintained their traditional self-sufficiency and many families are able to trace their local roots back for generations, there is little in the way of "sights" to attract tourists beyond the **markets** and **antique shops** on Back Lane and Francis Street.

Conversely, the area further west – Kilmainham – has less atmosphere but several *bona fide* attractions. The **Guinness Hop Store** on Crane Street reveals all you might wish to know about the famous stout produced at the nearby Guinness Brewery. Further out, the former Royal Hospital Kilmainham houses the **Irish Museum of Modern Art**, a venue for temporary exhibitions of contemporary art. Nearby is **Kilmainham Jail**, a prison indelibly associated with the struggle for Irish freedom and now a fascinating museum of penal and revolutionary history.

Wolfe Tone, the United Irishmen and the Rebellion of 1798

The French Revolution of 1789 had a profound effect on Ireland, where the credo "Liberty, Equality, Fraternity" inspired a Protestant barrister, **Theobald Wolfe Tone**, to issue *An Argument on Behalf of the Catholics in Ireland* (1791), urging all denominations to unite in the cause of Irish freedom. Within months of its publication, societies of **United Irishmen** were formed in Dublin and Belfast, aiming to achieve the emancipation of Catholics and Dissenters. Though their "Back Lane Parliament" avowed change by constitutional means, the movement turned towards revolution after Wolfe Tone, exiled in 1794, travelled to the new republics of the USA and France trying to win support for an insurrection.

The **Rebellion of 1798** was the first major rising against British rule since the seventeenth century, and set a precedent for future attempts. The revolt in Dublin ended prematurely in May of that year, when Lord Edward Fitzgerald was arrested. Martial law was imposed and local uprisings in County Dublin and County Mayo were virtually over when an 1100-strong French invasion force landed near Killala in County Sligo in August. After some successes, the Franco-Irish army was defeated in County Longford on September 8. More than 11,000 Irish fell in battle and 2000 were hanged or deported; the British lost 1600 men. In November a second French force, with Wolfe Tone on board, was intercepted off Donegal. Sentenced to death and denied the honour of a firing squad, Wolfe Tone cut his throat with a penknife to avoid being hanged, drawn and quartered as a traitor.

Henceforth revered as the founder of Irish Republicanism, Wolfe Tone was buried at Bodenstown in County Kildare – a

THE LIBERTIES AND KILMAINHAM

place of pilgrimage for many Nationalists. On the anniversary
of his birth (June 20, 1763), members of the Fianna Fáil party
travel here to pay their respects.

Conversely, a few critics of Wolfe Tone argue that his actions
destroyed any chance of the Anglo-Irish ruling class conceding
reforms, for in response to the 1798 Rebellion Britain engi-
neered the Act of Union, which dissolved the Irish Parliament
and fettered Ireland to Britain more strongly than ever.

While the most interesting parts of the Liberties are close to
Christ Church or St Patrick's Cathedral, and the Guinness
Hop Store is within walking distance, the Museum of
Modern Art and Kilmainham Jail are best reached by bus.

FROM TAILORS' HALL TO ST CATHERINE'S CHURCH

On Back Lane, near Christchurch Place, stands Dublin's last
surviving guildhall, **Tailors' Hall**, a modest brick structure
that was rescued from demolition when *An Taisce* (Ireland's
National Trust) bought the building and restored it as their
headquarters. Its assembly hall contains a plaque listing the
masters of the tailors' guild from 1491 to 1841 and a gallery
from which Wolfe Tone and Napper Tandy addressed the
"Back Lane Parliament" in 1792 (see box opposite).

Directly opposite Tailor's Hall are **Mother Redcap's
Market** (Fri–Sun 11am–5pm) and pub, both modern sub-
stitutes for their predecessors in an area that was bulldozed
away in the 1960s. The market sells kitsch and household
goods and the pub has live music at weekends.

Christ Church flea market is held outside the hall at
weekends, and Francis Street, to the west, is the centre of
Dublin's **antiques** trade, with numerous shops down the
road from the **Iveagh Market Hall** (Tues–Sat 9am–5pm).
As its name suggests, this was another bequest by Lord

FROM TAILORS' HALL TO ST CATHERINE'S CHURCH

Iveagh of the Guinness family, who is said to have been used as the model for the winking face that's among the stone heads carved above the arches of the hall.

At the bottom of Francis Street you'll find the **Coombe**, an ancient route and one of the Liberties' main thoroughfares. Slum clearances have spared the **gateway** of the old Coombe Maternity Hospital, founded in 1826 as a result of the plight of two poor women and their newborn babies, who died in a blizzard while attempting to reach the Rotunda Hospital on the northside. Inscribed in concrete behind the gateway is an odd **list of nicknames** of well-known Dublin characters such as Bang Bang, a shell-shocked veteran famous for "shooting" people with an imaginary gun, who died in 1981. Other intriguing names include Johnny Wet Bread, Nancy Needle Balls, Stab the Rasher and Harry Wank. **Meath Street**, across the road, is the site of an indoor market for cut-price clothes and tat – nothing to get excited about, but a good place to imbibe the atmosphere of the Liberties.

On the middle section of **West Thomas Street**, leading from High Street to the Guinness Brewery, stands the **Church of Saints Augustine and John,** possessor of Dublin's tallest spire; it was designed by Edward Pugin, whose father, Augustus, played a leading role in Britain's Gothic Revival. A discreet plaque about 200m away on *Laws Pub* commemorates the arrest of Lord Edward Fitzgerald, a leader of the 1798 Rebellion, who died of wounds received in the struggle.

Thomas Street was the starting point of a brief insurrection in 1803, led by 24-year-old Robert Emmet, who led his men towards Dublin Castle, only to find that when the crunch came "he had hardly fifty to sustain him in his reckless attempt". Many were drunk and began looting despite his efforts to control them, and it turned into a fiasco. Captured some weeks later, Emmet was hanged and decapitated outside **St Catherine's Church** on Meath Street; "Let no man write my epitaph . . . " is one of the classic orations of Irish history.

THE GUINNESS BREWERY AND HOP STORE

Thomas Street becomes James's Street as it passes the **Guinness Brewery**, whose chimneys, tanks and wonderful aroma dominate the neighbourhood. The St James's Gate Brewery covers 64 acres on both sides of the road, making it one of the largest in the world. However, when 34-year-old Arthur Guinness leased the derelict brewery in 1759, the industry in Dublin was at a low ebb; ale was notoriously bad, and whiskey, gin or poteen were preferred throughout rural Ireland. Although he began by brewing ale, Guinness soon switched to producing a new black brew called "porter" (because of its popularity with the porters at London's Covent Garden and Billingsgate markets). His new formula proved so successful that it was being exported to England within a decade; by the nineteenth century brewing had become such a major industry that brewers were elevated to the House of Lords. An old joke has an outraged peer of ancient lineage asking, "Who is this fellow Moyne, anyway?", the reply being "Moyne's a Guinness". Today, the Guinness Brewery produces about sixty percent of all the beer consumed in Ireland (2,500,000 pints a day) and is the world's largest exporter of beer, exporting some 300 million pints a year.

Sadly the brewery is not open to the public, but you can learn all about the company and its products at the **Hop Store** (Mon–Fri 10am–4pm; £2, students £1.50, children 50p; bus #68A or #78A from Aston Quay) on Crane Street, which has been converted into an exhibition centre. You'll end the tour by tasting what is arguably the best

Guinness in Dublin – arguably because the honours traditionally went to *Mulligan's* pub in Poolbeg Street, which still has its supporters (see p.222).

To the west of the Hop Store rises the fifty-metre-high **St Patrick's Tower**, the tallest smock windmill (ie with a revolving top) in the British Isles. Originally used to facilitate work at Roe's Distillery on the other side of Watling Street from the Guinness Brewery, it's topped with a St Patrick's weathervane, but no longer has any sails.

If you feel like walking off the effects of a pint, it shouldn't take more than twenty minutes to reach the Irish Museum of Modern Art. Near the point where James's Street forks at an obelisk with four sundials, off Steven's Lane, is St Patrick's Hospital, known as **"Swift's Hospital"**, having been founded for the care of the mentally ill by Jonathan Swift (see pp.74–75), whose bequest included a witty explanation: "He gave the little wealth he had, to build a house for fools and mad: And shew'd by one satiric touch, No nation wanted it so much." The larger St James's Hospital, off nearby James's Street, incorporates part of the old South Dublin Union, a nineteenth-century workhouse that was a rebel stronghold during the Easter Rising. Before becoming a workhouse it had been a foundling's hospital, where conditions were so wretched that 41,524 babies died in thirty years.

IRISH MUSEUM OF MODERN ART

Map 3, B5. Tues–Sat 10am–5pm, Sun noon–5.30pm; free. Bus #79 or #90 from Aston Quay.

Much criticized when it opened in 1991, the **Irish Museum of Modern Art** (IMMA) is now acknowledged to have proved its worth. The project was backed by the government of Charles Haughey but many felt that the £20 million spent on converting a derelict hospital into a gallery could have been better used for buying artworks, and the end result was reviled as a blank space which denied the character of the building. Criticism has faded as IMMA has increased its holdings through bequests and loans and asserted its stature with bold exhibitions. There is no permanent display, only temporary shows, often two or three at a time.

You can usually expect to find one exhibition of stuff on loan, and another selected from IMMA's holdings. Items on long loan from other galleries include works by Picasso, Miró and Modigliani, and contemporary artists such as Gilbert and George, Damien Hirst, Richard Long, Julian Schnabel and Rachel Whiteread. The Madden-Arnholtz Collection includes works by Dürer, Goya, Hogarth and Rembrandt. There's a good bookshop by the lobby and a fine restaurant in the basement of the north wing.

IMMA occupies the former **Royal Hospital Kilmainham**. Built by Sir William Robinson (who restored Dublin Castle) in 1680–87, this was one of the first Classical-style public buildings in Ireland. Austerely elegant in shades of grey, it was modelled on Les Invalides in Paris and served as a home for retired veterans. Its rules decreed that if any inmate "presumed to marry, he be immediately turned out of the house and the hospital clothes taken from him". On Sundays there are **guided tours** (2–4.30pm) of the north wing, whose lofty chapel has a magnificent Baroque ceiling and woodcarvings by the Huguenot master James Tarbery. You'll also see the panelled Great Hall, hung with portraits of monarchs and viceroys, and the Master's Residence.

When leaving the IMMA, depart by the arch in the west wing and aim for the **Kilmainham Gate** at the end of a tree-lined avenue. Formerly the Richmond Tower and sited at Watling Street Bridge near the Guinness Brewery, it was moved here in 1846 to improve access to Heuston Station. The avenue passes by **Bully's Acre**, one of Dublin's oldest cemeteries, and brings you out across the main road from Kilmainham Jail – the greatest attraction in this part of town.

KILMAINHAM JAIL

Map 3, A6. May–Sept 10am–6pm; Oct–April Mon–Fri 1–4pm, Sun 1–6pm; £2, students/children £1, family £5. Bus #51, #51B, #78A or #79 from the city centre.

A forbidding hulk on Inchicore Road, **Kilmainham Jail** is enshrined in Irish history as a symbol of political martyrdom and oppression.

Opened in 1796, Kilmainham replaced an earlier prison that epitomized the evils criticized by the English penal reformer John Howard, whose remedies were first applied in Ireland. Howard advocated the separation of prisoners to prevent criminal associations and encourage individuals to repent in solitude. In accordance with his stress on hygiene, the new jail was sited on a hill to ensure good ventilation. Unfortunately, it was built from a limestone that weeps in wet weather, so perennial damp and cold took a heavy toll on prisoners' health. Over the 128 years of Kilmainham's existence, some 100,000 men and women passed through its gates. Between 1845 and 1847, at the height of the Great Famine, it was swamped with destitute folk jailed for stealing food or begging, resulting in wretched conditions that made a mockery of Howard's intentions. Only after the Famine had abated did reformers build a new East Wing. Turned into a military detention barracks in 1911, Kilmainham later held insurgents from the 1916 Easter Rising. Even the end of British rule brought no respite, for 150 Republican women were interned here during the

Civil War, including the daughter and the widow of two of the martyrs of 1916. The last prisoner to be released by the Free State in 1924 was Éamon de Valera – subsequently elected prime minister, then president, of Ireland.

Shut down after the Civil War, Kilmainham was left to rot till 1960, when volunteers (many of them ex-inmates) began to restore it as a memorial. Now one of Dublin's best museums, it can be visited only on **guided tours** (every 45min; the last one begins 1hr 15min before closing).

While waiting to start the tour, visit the **exhibition** on conditions at Kilmainham and the development of hanging. It was a Dublin surgeon, Samuel Haughton, who devised the "long drop" method, which the Victorians saw as an improvement on the old "short drop" technique which slowly asphyxiated victims. Altogether, over 140 hangings took place at Kilmainham, 24 of them involving political prisoners. Upstairs covers the struggle for independence, with numerous items relating to the Fenians, the Easter Rising and the IRA, including Countess Markievicz's dispatch-bag and Michael Collins's walking stick.

The tour begins in the **East Wing**, a lofty hall flanked by tiers of cells and walkways. Like many Victorian prisons it was based on philosopher Jeremy Bentham's "Panopticon", a layout that maximized light (thought to be morally uplifting) and enabled constant surveillance of prisoners. Its architect, John McCurdy, had previously refurbished the *Shelbourne Hotel*.

In the Catholic **chapel** you'll hear the moving story of Joseph Plunkett and Grace Gifford, who were married here on the eve of Plunkett's execution. British soldiers stood by with fixed bayonets as the vows were read. Immediately afterwards the newlyweds were separated; later they were granted ten minutes together – timed by a stopwatch – before Plunkett was taken out and shot. A short, emotive

film on the history of Kilmainham and the struggle for independence leaves you in no doubt as to who the heroes and villains were, gliding over the moral and political ambiguities of the Civil War.

In the crumbling **West Wing** a chill seeps into your bones as the guide describes conditions at the prison: there was no glass in the windows nor any heating (there still isn't); an hour of candlelight each evening was the sole concession to comfort. Occasionally, certain prisoners were accorded privileges – when Parnell was jailed for sedition, he had a room with a fireplace and armchairs and was allowed to give interviews. Most, however, were obliged to do hard labour, oakum-picking or stone-beaking; the practice of "shot-drill" – passing cannonballs from one man to another – ceased after a prisoner threw one at the governor. Among those held here were Robert Emmet, the "Invincibles", and fourteen leaders of the Easter Rising on the night before their executions.

You will also see the **yacht** *Asgard*, used by Erskine Childers and his sister Molly to run guns into Ireland in 1914. Despite being half-English, Childers was a staunch Republican; in 1923 he was executed at Beggar's Bush Barracks (see p.130) for the possession of a revolver given to him by Collins, when the two were still allies.

THE INNER NORTHSIDE

Much of the **inner northside** was developed in the eighteenth century by Luke Gardiner, a banker who married into the Mountjoys and Blessingtons and bought land – which had once belonged to St Mary's Abbey – from families who had fallen on hard times. Profits from commercial premises near the quays were used to finance **Henrietta Street**, a luxury development on Constitution Hill (then open country), followed by Gardiners Mall (now **O'Connell Street**). With the establishment of the Wide Streets Commission in 1757, Gardiner's schemes became the blueprint for a whole new city of elegant terraces and squares for society's élite. Soon, however, rival developments on the southside began to entice them away, and the Act of Union sunk the property market after Gardiner's grandson had invested heavily in Mountjoy Square. This proved to be the swansong of the dynasty, and of the northside too.

Now a poor relation to the fashionable southside, this area can be noisy, dirty and in places a little rough, but don't be put off by first impressions – there's a lot that is worth exploring on this side of the city. Although it may not be as well preserved as its southern counterpart, the northside's significance lies more in its associations with events and movements central to Dublin and Ireland's history – the **GPO**, which played a seminal role in the history of independent Ireland, is probably its most important landmark. And as home to the **Abbey Theatre**, **Dublin Writers' Museum** and the **Municipal Gallery of Modern Art**, it offers plenty of cultural interest too.

O'CONNELL STREET AND AROUND

The commercial hub of the northside and Dublin's main axis, **O'Connell Street**, was laid out by Luke Gardiner in the 1740s. Originally envisaged as an exclusive residential square, it became a public highway following the completion of Gandon's Carlisle Bridge (1794), causing Dublin's centre of gravity to shift eastwards from the old axis of Capel Street. Renamed Sackville Street after the British viceroy, the avenue was 45m wide (one of the widest in Europe) and lined with grand edifices that anticipated the Parisian boulevards of Haussmann by a century. Today the street's facades are marred by neon and plastic, particularly near the Liffey where buildings were destroyed in the Easter Rising of 1916.

An imposing statue of "The Liberator", **Daniel O'Connell**, stands smack in the centre of the street on a plinth flanked by winged figures symbolizing his patriotism, courage, eloquence and fidelity. Born in 1775 in County Kerry, O'Connell was elected MP for Clare in 1828 and barred from entering parliament on the grounds of his Catholicism. He was re-elected in 1830 after Emancipation and became the first Catholic Lord Mayor of Dublin in 1841. Having secured the backing of Dublin for the repeal of the Union in 1843, he then organized mass rallies to put presssure on Westminster. These scared the British so much that they jailed him for sedition. Though he was released after a few months, O'Connell's health was failing; the Famine decimated his rural following, and in 1847 he died. His statue (financed by subscription) was unveiled in 1882, and his name was bestowed upon the new, wider bridge that replaced the Carlisle. Soon, Dubliners began to call Sackville Street "O'Connell Street", though its name was not officially changed until 1924.

Further north, where the street is crossed by Abbey Street, the central strip is graced by smaller statues of two lesser nineteenth-century figures: William Smith O'Brien, leader of the Young Ireland Party, and Sir John Gray, the publisher of the influential *Freeman's Journal*. More arresting is the **statue of Jim Larkin**, the trade unionist who led Dublin's workers during the Lock-Out Strike of 1913. It shows Larkin haranguing a crowd, as he did from a window of the *Imperial Hotel* across the road, shortly before mounted police charged the demonstrators, killing two and injuring hundreds. After the hotel was gutted during the Easter Rising, the site was redeveloped as **Clery's** department store (see p.253), a scaled-down replica of London's *Selfridges*.

Looming beyond Larkin's statue is the **General Post Office** (GPO) designed by Francis Johnston, whose huge Ionic portico is still scarred by gunfire from the Easter Rising (see box overleaf), when the building was used as the insurgents' headquarters. From its porch, Pádraig Pearse read the Proclamation of the Irish Republic to onlookers bemused by the sight of his men smashing windows and sandbagging them with mailbags. For six days they held out against

The Easter Rising

The heroic **Easter Rising** of April 1916 was one of the key events leading to Irish self-government. At the time, however, most Dubliners saw it as a calamity; many Nationalists regarded it as a botched and futile attempt, while Loyalists reckoned it high treason, fermented by Imperial Germany.

The Rising was conceived by the **Irish Republican Brotherhood** (IRB) or "Fenians", a revolutionary organization dating back to 1858, led by a new generation of activists including **Pádraig Pearse** and **Joseph Plunkett.** For manpower and arms they relied on support from two legal militias: the **Citizen Army** under **James Connolly**, who helped in drawing up the battle plan and was given operational command; and the **Irish Volunteers** headed by Éoin MacNeill, who only agreed to commit his forces after Pearse showed him a forged document from Dublin Castle, ordering the suppression of the Volunteers. The final element was a shipment of arms from Germany, whose delivery was to be arranged by Sir **Roger Casement**, an ex-British diplomat turned Irish rebel.

Things started to go wrong quickly. The ship arrived prematurely and left without delivering its cargo and Casement was caught by the British. MacNeill, on learning that he had been duped, revoked the mobilization order by placing notices in the Sunday papers, which resulted in only a minority of the 10,000 Volunteers turning up the next day. Though both mishaps foredoomed the Rising, its strategy was already flawed by Connolly's belief that "a capitalist government would never use artillery against private property". While the exact number of insurgents is uncertain (somewhere between 700 and 1750), the British ultimately committed over 20,000 troops to crush them.

The first shots were fired at noon on **Easter Monday**. A group of insurgents assaulted the castle, other units seized the

GPO, the Four Courts and sites such as Jacob's Biscuit Factory and Jameson's Distillery, which overlooked the routes from British barracks into the centre. As Pearse emerged from the GPO to read the Proclamation of the Irish Republic, his comrades were fortifying their positions against a British response. Initial attacks were beaten back, but the tide turned once reinforcements arrived from England with artillery. After six days of bitter fighting which destroyed Sackville Street and other areas, the insurgents surrendered and were led away through jeering crowds.

This reaction was only to be expected, since the Rising left 1351 people dead or gravely wounded, 179 buildings smouldering, and much of Dublin's population needing aid. It occurred on the first anniversary of the battle of Gallipoli, when many Dublin families were in mourning for their menfolk who had perished there.

British attacks, until the GPO was set ablaze and survivors retreated to nearby Moore Street, where Pearse and Connolly agreed to surrender. Their subsequent martyrdom conferred iconic status on the Rising and the GPO itself, which is still a focal point for political protests. In the front window stands a bronze statue of *The Death of Cuchulainn*, the mythical Irish warrior who tied himself to a tree to confront his enemies even in death. Totally gutted in the fighting, the GPO reopened in 1929 after complete restoration.

When you reach the intersection with Henry Street and North Earl Street, try to imagine how O'Connell Street looked when it was dominated by **Nelson's Pillar**, execrated by W.B. Yeats as "that monstrosity that destroys the view of the finest street in Europe". Erected 32 years before Nelson's Column in London's Trafalgar Square, this symbol of British imperialism survived several attempts to destroy

O'CONNELL STREET AND AROUND

it, until a bomb on the fiftieth anniversary of the Rising left it so damaged that it had to be demolished. Nelson's head now lies in the Civic Museum (see p.22). The monument's demise put paid to an old joke that O'Connell Street had statues honouring three notorious adulterers: O'Connell, Nelson, and Parnell (see pp.100–101).

In the 1980s the Corporation commissioned two additional monuments along more whimsical lines. The **James Joyce statue** outside *Café Kylemore* on the corner of North Earl Street has the rakish insouciance of a boulevardier, but its dishevelment is quite unlike Joyce, who was always dapper. Further up O'Connell Street is the recumbent **Anna Livia Fountain,** representing Joyce's female personification of the River Liffey – nicknamed "the floozie in the jacuzzi" or "the whore in the sewer" (which rhymes in a Dublin accent), she's treated as a rubbish bin.

Many bus tours start at the offices of Bus Éireann and Dublin Bus, at no. 59 (see pp.9–11).

On the central strip is a **statue of Father Matthew** (1790–1856), the "Apostle of Temperance", whose Pioneer Total Abstinence Movement, founded in 1838, persuaded five million Irish (out of eight million) to take a pledge of teetotalism, and reduced the production of whiskey by half. Father Matthew is also honoured by a bridge named after him, upriver from the Four Courts.

The **Gresham Hotel** (see p.172) is Dublin's finest after the *Shelbourne* and surpasses it for nostalgia. This was where Michael Collins often met his agents during the War of Independence. After the Nationalists split over the Anglo-Irish Treaty, the anti-Treaty "Irregulars" led by Cathal Brugha and de Valera made it their headquarters during the insurrection of July 1922. Following a week of fighting that left central Dublin in ruins for the second time in six years, Brugha ordered his men to surrender but refused to do so himself and was mortally wounded outside the hotel. A nearby sidestreet now bears his name.

O'Connell Street ends at a crossroads, where the **Parnell Monument** proclaims in gold letters: "No man has a right to fix the boundary to the march of a nation. No man has a right to say to his country, Thus far shalt thou go and no further. . . "

The Abbey Theatre

Map 5, I5.
Located on the corner of Lower Abbey Street, the **Abbey** is in effect Ireland's national theatre, but the building itself is a replacement for the old Abbey, which was burned down in 1951. Its genesis was the Irish Literary Society founded by **W.B. Yeats** and **Douglas Hyde**, which became the Irish Literary Theatre in 1899. An English tea heiress bought the site on Abbey Street (formerly a morgue), where the playhouse opened in 1904, with Yeats and Lady Gregory as its first directors. Their 1907 production of John Millington Synge's tragi-comedy *The Playboy of the Western World* caused outrage – one critic called it "the outpouring of a morbid, unhealthy mind ever seeking on the dunghill of life for the nastiness that lies concealed there". There were nightly affrays needing up to 500 policemen to pre-vent bloodshed; in 1926 there was an equally fierce reaction to Séan O'Casey's *The Plough and the Stars*, which took a cynical view of the Easter Rising and displayed the Free State flag in a pub frequented by prostitutes. As the audi-ence booed on opening night, Yeats rebuked them, "You have disgraced yourselves again. Is this to be an ever-recur-ring celebration of the arrival of an Irish genius?"

O'CONNELL STREET AND AROUND

For more on the Abbey, see p.236.

As time went on, a general uneasiness about one theatre receiving the lion's share of state subsidies became widespread – a conviction that would lead to the establishment of the Gate Theatre (see opposite). The Abbey still produces dazzling drama, with two auditoriums and companies on the premises: the Abbey, devoted to the Irish classics and contemporary dramatists like Brian Friel and Frank McGuinness; and the **Peacock Theatre** (see p.238), which shows new experimental drama.

Moore Street Market and St Mary's Pro-Cathedral

To the left of the GPO, Henry Street, an earthier version of upmarket Grafton Street, is lined with department stores outside which black-market cigarettes are openly touted. Just off Henry Street is the colourful **Moore Street Market** (see p.251). At no. 16 Moore Street there's a small plaque commemorating the site where survivors from the GPO laid up in the back of a fish and chip shop and decided against a fighting retreat through Henry Street and Ormond market, to avoid further civilian casualties. This shop is now a butchers, aptly called *Plunkett's*. Apropos of names, Moore Street, Henry Street and North Earl Street are all named after Henry Moore, earl of Drogheda, who even squeezed in an "Of lane", leading into Drogheda Street so that his name and title would be blazoned across maps of Dublin.

In 1814, Dublin's Protestants were up in arms about the plan to build a Catholic cathedral on O'Connell Street (where the GPO now stands), so the castle decreed that **St Mary's Pro-Cathedral** (daily 8am–7pm) be tucked away down a side road, where its facade, based on the Temple of Theseus in Athens, can be seen from Marlborough Street. It was here in 1847 that funeral rites were performed over the body of Daniel O'Connell, brought back from Genoa for burial; crowds lined the way from the Custom House to the Marlborough Street Chapel (as it then was). St Mary's is the premier Catholic church in Dublin, and every Sunday at 11am you can hear Latin Mass sung by the famous **Palestrina Choir**, where the tenor John McCormack began his career in 1904.

PARNELL SQUARE

Parnell Square is one of the few on the northside which wasn't begun by Luke Gardiner. The credit goes to Sir Benjamin Mosse, the surgeon who founded the **Rotunda Maternity Hospital**, which when it opened in 1748 was the first purpose-built maternity hospital in Europe. Designed by Cassels, the architect of Leinster House, it retains a gorgeous Baroque chapel which, with the tarnished glory of the west facade, suggest how fine it must have once looked. Mosse funded the project by laying out a pleasure garden and organizing fancy dress balls and concerts, including the premiere of Handel's *Messiah*. While the gardens fell out of fashion as the northside declined, the Rotunda on the corner remained a concert hall until it became the *Ambassador* cinema. The Rotunda had previously witnessed the birth of Sinn Féin, founded by Arthur Griffiths at a public meeting in 1905.

Since 1930 the Assembly Rooms have been home to the **Gate Theatre**. It was founded by Hilton Edwards and Micheál MacLiammóir, and the latter continued to perform here until 1975, retiring at the age of 76 after the 1384th performance of his one-man show, *The Importance of Being Oscar*.

For more on the Gate, see p.237.

PARNELL SQUARE

Charles Parnell

"There is something vulgar in all success. The greatest men fail, or seem to have failed." So said Oscar Wilde of Charles Stewart Parnell, the "uncrowned king of Ireland".

Parnell was born into the Anglo-Irish Protestant hierarchy in Avondale, County Wicklow, in 1846. His family had originated in Cheshire and purchased an estate in Wicklow in the seventeenth century. His great-grandfather, John Parnell, was Chancellor of the Irish Exchequer. Parnell's mother was the daughter of an American admiral, a connection that would subsequently bring financial rewards.

Despite his background, Parnell became committed to the cause of land reform, recognizing that Ireland would never prosper while the rights of tenant-farmers lay unprotected. In April 1875 he was elected to parliament on the Home Rule ticket and from 1878 he wholeheartedly devoted himself to agrarian reform, becoming president of the Irish National Land League in that year. He sought support for its efforts in the USA and raised the colossal sum of £70,000. In the election of 1880 Parnell stood and was returned in no fewer than three seats, choosing to sit for the city of Cork, and was elected leader of the Irish Home Rule Party.

The Phoenix Park murders in 1882 (see p.124) marked a major turning point in the affairs of the Home Rule movement. Parnell had already been jailed in Kilmainham that year for sedition, and attempts were made to implicate him in the murders. Parnell denounced the crime in parliament and, in so doing, revived his own popularity at home. However, Gladstone's Liberal government reacted by hurrying through parliament a Prevention of Crimes Act which temporarily abolished trial by jury and increased police powers, despite the Home Rulers' opposition.

The Land League was declared illegal after urging tenants to withhold payments of rent to absentee landlords, but it was revived in 1884 with Parnell as president. After attempting to strike deals with the Conservatives, Parnell flung the Irish vote behind Gladstone and, in so doing, brought about the fall of the short-lived first Salisbury administration. Gladstone was returned to power, now committed to Home Rule, but when the bill was put to parliament, his own party members defected and it was defeated. A consequent appeal to the country was overwhelmingly rejected and a new Tory government was elected in 1886 with a Unionist majority of more than 100. Parnell and the Irish Party no longer held the balance of power.

The reason for Parnell's increasingly frequent absences from parliament became clear in 1890 when he was named as co-respondent in a divorce case brought by Captain William O'Shea against his wife Katherine (Kitty). The decree was granted with costs against Parnell, and public disgrace followed. The Liberals demanded his resignation as leader of his party and, after some wrangling, the majority elected Justin McCarty chairman. Parnell now carried what was left of the fight back into Ireland but his credibility was destroyed, and the party formed by his supporters was to collapse at the 1892 general election. Before then, however, Parnell had died suddenly in Brighton, five months after his marriage to Kitty O'Shea.

Despite the notoriety of his latter years, 200,000 people jammed Dublin for his funeral.

But the prize for longevity goes to **Conway's Pub**: established in 1745, it's the oldest on the northside and has been a haven for nervous fathers-to-be since the hospital opened. Originally named *Doyle's*, it was another of Collins's local haunts – having survived the Easter Rising, he surrendered to the British on the corner right outside the pub. Today, a

Sinn Féin Bookshop (Mon–Sat 11am–4pm) is sited at 44 Parnell Square West, just uphill from no. 46, whose basement was once used by Collins to brief his hit-team, "The Apostles". In January 1922, the infant Free State was distracted when the Maternity Hospital was seized by a band of dockers and the writer Liam O'Flaherty, protesting against unemployment. Their "Irish Soviet Republic" fell in three days without a shot being fired.

Parnell Square slopes up to a **Garden of Remembrance** established to commemorate all who died in the struggle for Irish freedom. There's also a memorial to the Dubliners killed by Loyalist car-bombs between 1973 and 1975.

During the 1760s and 1770s, Parnell Square North was Dublin's poshest address, nicknamed "Palace Row" and inhabited by the earls of Ormond and Charlemont. The needle-spired **Abbey Presbyterian Church** on the corner is known as "Findlater's Church" after the grocer and brewer Alex Findlater, who financed its construction in 1864.

Hugh Lane Municipal Art Gallery

Map 5, G3. Tues–Fri 9.30am–6pm, Sat 9.30am–5pm, Sun 11am–5pm; free. Buses #10, #11, #13, #16 and #22.

Former residence to the earl of Charlemont, the **Hugh Lane Municipal Art Gallery** occupies a grey-stone town house on Parnell Square designed by the Scottish architect Sir William Chambers. The gallery was founded in 1908 by Sir Hugh Lane (a nephew of Lady Gregory), who had intended to bequeath his entire collection, but – piqued by the Corporation's refusal to build a special gallery – added a codicil leaving just 39 works to "the nation", before dying aboard the SS *Lusitania* when it was sunk by a German U-boat in 1915. With Ireland's independence, the question of *which* nation arose, and an unseemly wrangle began that wasn't resolved till the 1980s, when the Irish and British governments agreed that half of Lane's bequest should remain in Dublin.

Though the mansion works well as a gallery, its modest size means that well-known pictures often disappear to make room for temporary exhibitions. Don't miss the **Stained Glass Room** of panels by Evie Hone, Wilhelmina Geddes, James Scanlon and Harry Clarke. Room 1 kicks off with **French art**, including Manet's *Le Concert aux Tuileries*, Monet's *Waterloo Bridge*, Degas's *On the Beach*, and Vlaminck's *Opium*. Their plein-air progenitors, Corot and Courbet, can be found in Room 9. **Irish art** is spread over several rooms. Room 5 is devoted to Roderic O'Conner, whose oeuvre runs the gamut from Seurat to Gauguin. The works of Jack B. Yeats flit between Rooms 3 and 6, while Room 2 brings together such disparate artists as William Orpen, Sir John Lavery and Nathaniel Hone the younger.

The Hugh Lane Gallery also hosts free classical music concerts at noon on Sundays during the winter, and offers lectures throughout the year.

Room 8 contains works by the **Pre-Raphaelites** Edward Burne-Jones and Augustus John. **Contemporary art** is exhibited in the remaining rooms – most of it is on loan, but there are also works from the gallery's own collection, including *Blackboards* by Josef Beuys and Christo's *Wrapping of St Stephen's Green*.

Dublin Writers Museum

Map 5, G3. Mon–Sat 10am–5pm, Sun & bank holidays 11.30am–6pm; July & August Mon–Fri till 7pm; £2.90, students £2.40, children £1.20, family £7.75.

PARNELL SQUARE

Two doors along from the gallery, 18 Parnell Square houses the **Dublin Writers Museum**, a combination of tourist crowd-puller and serious literary venue, in a lovely Georgian mansion. The ground-floor rooms constitute a whistle-stop tour of Irish literature from the first Gaelic rendition of the Old Testament (1645) to twentieth-century greats such as Shaw, Joyce and Beckett. Though the exhibits are fairly dull (Brendan Behan's typewriter – which he once threw through a pub window in a fit of rage – is as good as it gets), an accompanying guide tape canters through literary fashions and the lives of the writers in a light-hearted way.

Upstairs, the house itself is the main attraction. A staircase with stained-glass windows of the Muses and allegories of art, science, literature and music leads to a resplendent white-and-gold salon, called the **Gallery of Writers**. The ceiling is by Michael Stapleton, Dublin's finest stuccoist, who learnt his art from the Swiss-Italian Francini brothers. On the door panels are figures representing the months of the year and the quarters of the day, accompanied by aphorisms such as "Work is the great reality, Beauty is the great aim." Another room contains the **Gorham Library** of books by writers featured in the museum, and downstairs there's a well-stocked **bookshop** and a pleasant **café**. There's also a Zen garden in summertime, and the *Chapter One* **restaurant** in the basement.

Next door is the **Living Writers Centre**, with an ongoing programme of lectures and seminars.

If you're planning to visit other literary shrines in Dublin, it's worth buying a **combined ticket** (£4.50, student £3.80) for the Writers Museum and the Shaw Birthplace (see p.131) or the Joyce Tower at Sandycove (see p.141).

THE JAMES JOYCE CENTRE

Map 5, H3. April–Sept Mon–Sat 9.30am–5pm, Sun noon–5pm;
Oct–March Tues–Sat 10am–4.30pm, Sun 12.30–4.30pm; £2.50,
students £1.75, children 70p, family £6.

The **James Joyce Centre**, 35 North Great George's Street,
taps deeper into the life of Dublin's most celebrated author,
whose formative years were spent on the northside. His life
and genius are the subject of guided tours of this beautifully
restored Georgian townhouse – which has a regular programme of films and lectures, runs walking tours of Joyce's
haunts, and organizes the Bloomsday celebrations (see
pp.257–259). One of the directors, Ken Monaghan, is a
nephew of Joyce and gives talks on their family life by
arrangement.

Copies of Joyce's cherished **family portraits** are on display (the ones in the centre are copies, the originals are at
Buffalo university), while on the top floor is a **Ulysses
portrait gallery** featuring some of the 300 characters who
appear in the novel. In the tea room at the back of the
house you can see the front door of **7 Eccles Street**, home
of Leopold Bloom. The **Guinness Library** of Joycean literature is available to visitors, along with audio-readings of
his works, so aficionados can really get stuck in.

The **house** itself, with its superlative stucco mouldings by
Stapelton, was restored following a campaign led by the
Joyce scholar Senator David Norris to save it from demolition in the 1980s. The house was built for the earl of
Kenmare's annual visits to Dublin to attend parliament, but
promptly sold after the Act of Union. At the turn of this
century, the ground floor was leased by Denis Maginni, a
well-known dancing teacher (really named Maginnis; he
dropped the "s" to sound sophisticated) who makes six
appearances in *Ulysses*. After his departure it continued as a

A Joycean walk on the northside

Having been reared by governesses and sent to an exclusive Jesuit boarding school when he was six, Joyce was unprepared for the misfortunes that struck him at the age of eleven. Shortly after he was withdrawn from school with his fees unpaid, the family quit their last fashionable address in Blackrock, and two caravans transported all their possessions across the "gloomy foggy city" to the impoverished northside. As an adult, Joyce occupied several flats in the neighbourhood before leaving Ireland for good in 1912.

The James Joyce Centre is only a few doors downhill from no. 38, the last residence of the Trinity Provost John Pentland Mahaffy, who loathed Joyce, describing him as "a living argument in favour of my contention that it was a mistake to establish a separate university for the aborigines of this island – for the corner-boys who spit into the Liffey".

Were it not for the intervention of a Jesuit priest, Joyce might not have gone to university at all. Initially, he and his brother Stanislaus attended a local Christian Brothers school, before his old teacher, Father Conmee, arranged for them to study for free at **Belvedere College** – one of the most prestigious schools in Ireland. The college is on Great Denmark Street, at the top of North Great George's Street.

The Joyce family occupied a series of properties, moving on as they fell behind with the rent. One of the first was a boarding-house at **no. 29 Hardwicke Street**, recalled as "a kip" run by Mrs Mooney, who connived to pimp her daughter in *Dubliners*. At the end of the street, **St George's Church** (now deconsecrated) is a frequent landmark in Joyce's stories.

On nearby Eccles Street Joyce confided to his friend J.F. Byrne about his fears that Nora had been unfaithful. Byrne assured him that it was untrue, and in gratitude Joyce honoured her fidelity by making no. 7 Eccles Street the fictional abode of Leopold and Molly Bloom. *Ulysses* fans must be satisfied with a plaque, as the house was demolished in 1982 to build an annexe to the Mater Hospital.

Following Lower Dorset Street downhill turn right into Upper Gardiner Street and you'll pass the **Jesuit House** where Stephen Dedalus "wondered vaguely which window would be his if he joined the order"; it's beside the Church of St Francis Xavier, where Father Conmee was a priest.

Finally, turn off the northeast corner of Parnell Square to find **14 Fitzgibbon Street**, the "bare cheerless house" that was the Joyces' first home on the northside in 1894. There is nothing to mark their stay, for the house lay derelict until 1997, but it is now being renovated and may eventually sport a plaque.

ballroom run by Dickie Graham (whose grandson is a director of the Centre), which was popular with British officers who never suspected that the basement was an arms dump for a Nationalist group that secretly met upstairs. It's said that de Valera was once smuggled into the house disguised as a woman.

THE WAX MUSEUM AND THE BLACK CHURCH

To the northwest of Parnell Square, on the corner of Granby Row and Dorset Street, Dublin's **Wax Museum** (Mon–Sat 10am–5.30pm, Sun noon–5.30pm; £3.50, students £2.50, children £2, family £10) is a good way to while away a wet afternoon if you have children to entertain. There are over 300 exhibits, from Irish writers and rock stars to Power Rangers and the Flintstones. Young children will enjoy the tunnels to crawl through and the hall of mirrors, while older kids will get a kick out of the chamber of horrors. There are tableaux of historic events and a roomful of Irish presidents plus the actual Popemobile used by John Paul II on his visit to Ireland in 1979. While happily juxtaposing Hitler, Stalin and Churchill, they have yet to add Gerry Adams to the Northern Ireland duo of John Hume and Ian Paisley.

Across Dorset Street, the spiky finials of the **Black Church** brood over St Mary's Place on the brow of the hill. Built of black Dublin calp, the former St Mary's Chapel of Ease is associated with two legends. One holds that it was designed to be turned into a redoubt should the Catholics rise up (as the Protestants feared in the 1820s); the other is that you can summon up the Devil by walking three times around the outside of the church. It has now been deconsecrated and serves as an office.

TO KING'S INNS AND BEYOND

Head downhill into Bolton Street and everything speaks of deprivation: rubbish blowing in the gutters, broken glass, barred shop windows. The Corporation estates which replaced the worst of the old tenements in the 1960s and 1970s have themselves become a blighted area, where **Henrietta Street**, dowdy as it is, comes as a pleasant respite. Laid out by Gardiner between 1730 and 1740, it was the first street in Dublin to contain aristocratic mansions, and it remained a most fashionable address until the 1800s. Its residents included three earls, the primate of Ireland and the Speaker of the House of Commons; Gardiner himself lived at no. 10. In 1908, many houses were stripped and turned into tenements by Alderman Meade, who managed to squeeze seventy tenants into the huge four-bay house at no. 7 alone. As Joyce recalled in *Dubliners*, a "horde of grimy children . . . stood or ran in the roadway, or crawled up the steps before the gaping doors, or squatted like mice upon the thresholds".

Mountjoy Prison

Built in 1847 as a holding centre for transportees to the Australian penal colonies, **Mountjoy Prison** off the North Circular road is the oldest working jail in Dublin, and the most notorious. Early this century its notoriety was due to the political prisoners held here, first by the British (1916–21) and then by the Free State (1922–23). It was here that the IRB leader Thomas Ashe died after forced-feeding during a hunger-strike in 1917 – one of the first instances of what would become a favoured method of protest by imprisoned Republicans. In 1939, Mountjoy also saw the first strike by IRA men demanding to be recognized as political prisoners, a status that the Free State refused to concede as the British would later refuse in Northern Ireland. After the IRA sprung three prisoners by landing a hijacked helicopter in the yard in 1973, most Republican inmates were moved to the high-security jail at Portlaoise. Nowadays, Mountjoy is Dublin's main jail for remand prisoners and convicted felons, and such is the scale of drug-related crime that you don't have to spend long on the northside to meet people who've served time or have friends or relatives in "The Joy". Its most famous inmate was Brendan Behan, who was sentenced to fourteen years for shooting a policeman but amnestied after five years in 1946. His play *The Quare Fellow* is set here.

The street ends at the rear gate of **King's Inns**, crowned by the British lion and unicorn. The third of James Gandon's great edifices, it was designed in 1795 but work on it was delayed for seven years due to residents' objections that it would spoil their view; when completed in 1817 it was unanimously praised. The Inns are the home of Irish Bar, where Ireland's barristers are trained. During daylight hours you can walk through the courtyard to see the allegorical reliefs out front and the view of Dublin from **Constitution Hill**. It was at Glasmanogue (as the hill was anciently called) that St Patrick is said to have stopped on his way north after converting Dubliners to Christianity and, looking back on the settlement, prophesied, "Although it's small and miserable now, there'll be a big town here in time to come. It will be spoken of far and near and will keep increasing until it becomes the chief town of the kingdom."

Having come this far, there are two routes back to the river and the centre of town, with a few sights along the way. The easiest and most obvious route to take is down Church Street past St Michan's Church to the Four Courts – for details of both, see the next chapter. Alternatively, you could take a more easterly route via North King Street and Halston Street, where the former **Black Dog Debtors Prison** is due to open as a museum in 1998. Built in 1760, it had a window on the pavement where prisoners could beg for alms, and stood right beside the Green Street Court where Robert Emmet, the Young Irelanders and the "Invincibles" were later tried. On the corner of Little Britain Street are the boarded-up remains of *Barney Kiernan's* pub, the setting for the "Cyclops" chapter of *Ulysses*.

THE QUAYS: THE CUSTOM HOUSE TO PHOENIX PARK

Although parts of the quays on the northside are still grubby and rundown, this is another section of the city that's beginning to reflect the general boom in Ireland's economy. This is especially true of areas such as Smithfield and nearby Stoneybatter – traditionally working-class pockets which are gradually emerging as the northside alternative to Temple Bar. Beggars and barristers, Georgian piles and Corporation sink-estates stand cheek-by-jowl along the quays, where monumental buildings like the **Custom House** and the **Four Courts** epitomize the heyday of Georgian Dublin. There are plenty of interesting places for detours – like **St Michan's Church** for its ghoulish mummies, **Smithfield** for its monthly horse sales, the **Irish Whiskey Store** for booze enthusiasts, or a walk eastward for the Custom House.

The Liffey, its bridges and its quays

From the source of the **Liffey** in the Wicklow Hills to its outlet in Dublin Bay is a distance of just 20km as the crow flies, but the river meanders for over 128km, remaining quite bucolic till it enters the city. Over the thousand years of Dublin's history, the Liffey has become narrower and deeper as channels have been dredged and land reclaimed and the harbour has moved eastwards. The River Poddle, which once joined the Liffey at the Dark Pool which gave Dublin its name, now runs underground for 5km, to trickle from a grating on the south bank, downstream from the Grattan Bridge.

Dublin's early settlements grew around the river and from it the city derives its Gaelic name *Baile Ath Cliath* (Ford of the Hurdles). The oldest bridge still standing dates from 1764; formerly Queen's Bridge, it is now known as Mellowes Bridge, named after the IRA "Irregular" Liam Mellowes (other Nationalists so honoured are Sean Heuston, Rory O'Moore and O'Donovan Rossa). While each bridge had localized effects, the Carlisle (now O'Connell) Bridge changed Dublin's axis from east–west to north–south, which had profound consequences for the city's development. Today fourteen bridges of varying shapes and sizes cross the Liffey, from the universally loved Ha'penny Bridge (1816) – which derives its name from the halfpenny toll that was levied on pedestrians wishing to cross until early this century – to the ugly railway Loop Line Bridge that ruins the view of Gandon's Custom House.

Explore further west by catching a bus (#25, #67 or #67A from Middle Abbey Street) along the quays to Dublin's latest museum space, the **Collins Barracks**, home to the decorative arts collection of the National Museum of Ireland. Further out lies the huge expanse of **Phoenix Park**, one of Europe's largest urban parks and home to the Irish president, Ashtown Castle and Dublin Zoo.

THE CUSTOM HOUSE

Map 4, F3.

The majestic **Custom House**, just beyond Eden Quay, has surveyed Dublin's waterfront for the past two hundred years. James Gandon, an English architect of Huguenot extraction, was considering going to work in St Petersburg when he received the commission for the Custom House in 1781. Gandon went on to create the Four Courts and the Carlisle Bridge, and spent the rest of his life in Ireland, dying at his home in Lucan at the age of eighty.

Plans for the building were opposed by dockers and merchants, who resented moving from the old customs point near Crane Lane, and by the genteel residents of Lower Gardiner Street, who feared contagion by a "low and vulgar crowd with the manners of Billingsgate". When petitions failed, objectors resorted to violence (Gandon wore a sword to work) and took heart that the proposed site was on a submerged mudflat where it seemed impossible to lay foundations. Gandon, however, confounded everyone by building atop a layer of four-inch-thick pine planks. The Custom House took ten years to build and cost the unheard-of sum of £500,000; nine years later the Act of Union made it redundant by transferring customs and excise to London. In 1921 the building was set alight by Sinn Féiners and totally gutted. Since being restored, it has housed government offices; a visitors' centre is due to open soon.

Its 114-metre-long embankment facade is flanked by arcades culminating in pavilions crowned with the arms of Ireland. Around the building are fourteen heads representing Ireland's rivers (only the Liffey is a goddess, above the main door), and cattle heads symbolizing the beef trade. The Four Continents decorate the rear portico, and the 38-metre-high dome is topped by a figure of Commerce.

Other landmarks in the vicinity are **Busáras** (Dublin's central bus station), the city's first unashamedly modern building, and the **Liberty Hall**, Dublin's only high-rise building. The latter is the headquarters of the Irish Transport and General Workers Union founded by Jim Larkin, whose deputy James Connolly led the Citizen Army in the 1916 Easter Rising, when the old Liberty Hall was pulverized by a British gunboat on the Liffey. A statue of Connolly gestures from the traffic island, affirming that "The cause of labour is the cause of Ireland. The cause of Ireland is the cause of labour."

Monto

The fears of residents of Lower Gardiner Street proved justified when the docks moved east and the area to the west of where Connolly Station now stands declined into "one of the most dreadful dens of immorality in Europe". Known as **Monto**, after Montgomery (now Foley) Street, its seedy terraces were once inhabited by 1600 prostitutes, who were tolerated by the police, provided they kept within the quarter. Among the "flash houses" on Railway Street were Mrs Arnott's, Mrs Meehan's and Mrs Cohen's – all of which feature in the "Nighttown" section of *Ulysses*.

Although the departure of British troops in 1922 hit trade badly, Monto was dealt its fatal blow during Lent in 1925, when Catholic vigilantes and the Garda raided the area, resulting in 120 arrests (including a member of the Dáil). The following morning the Legion of Mary arrrived on the scene, pinning holy pictures on brothel doors and offering succour to penitent prostitutes.

During the 1930s much of the area was swept away and replaced by Corporation flats, now among the most run down in Dublin. Bloomsday tours skip "Nighttown", and you'd be wise to do the same.

FROM O'CONNELL BRIDGE TO THE FOUR COURTS

O'Connell Bridge marks the point to the west of which the quays really come alive. Thundering traffic and run-down buildings make them far from elegant, but the views across the river and the cross-section of Dublin society that you'll encounter here are always stimulating.

Bachelors Walk was laid out in 1678 as an extension of the Ormond Quay, ending at Bagino Slip, where a ferry crossed the Liffey. It's chiefly associated with a violent clash in 1914, when British troops fired on a crowd, killing four of them and wounding thirty-eight. Near the corner of Liffey Street are *The Winding Stair Bookshop* (with a laid-back café where you can sit and gaze over the Ha'penny Bridge; see p.197) and a pair of lifesize **statues** of two housewives taking a rest from shopping, irreverently known as the "Hags with the Bags".

Ormond Quay bears the name of one of the few viceroys who actually liked Dublin and is well remembered here. James Butler, the duke of Ormond, served two terms (1662–69 and 1677–85) and did much to restore Dublin's pride after a century of intermittent war. Exiled in France when Cromwell was in power, Ormond was inspired by continental city planning and he longed to tear down the old city and build anew. He then took advantage of the new Essex Bridge and laid out three quays along the north bank, which was to become the east–west axis of the city. This development spurred the growth of an extensive **market quarter** behind the quays. The infamous Ormond Boys (see p.81) used to meet in the lanes backing onto Chancery Street (near the Four Courts).

Between Ormond's terms of office, the job was held by Arthur Capel, earl of Essex, who gave his name to a new bridge (1676). Further downstream than the others,

Capel Street Bridge became the main crossing point where all routes converged and was to remain Dublin's north–south axis till the Carlisle Bridge was built, and its role was usurped by Sackville (now O'Connell) Street. The well-to-do left the area, which soon assumed a more proletarian character owing to the nearby Ormond market. It still caters for tradesmen, with dozens of tool shops, builders' merchants and cafés in the neighbourhood.

Two blocks inland, the former **St Mary's Church** on Mary Street is now home to *Ryan's Decorating Centre*. Here, Richard Brinsley Sheridan and Seán O'Casey were baptized, Arthur Guinness got married, John Wesley preached his first sermon in Ireland and Lord Norbury, the Hanging Judge of 1798, was buried. Wolfe Tone, the leader of the 1798 Rebellion, was born opposite the church, where the *Guardian Life Assurance* building now stands. It's also strange to imagine that Joyce opened Ireland's first cinema at 45 Mary Street in 1909 – the *Volta's* diet of Continental films was not to Dubliners' tastes, however, and his Italian backers sold out after a few months.

Just west of Capel Street, a tiny cul-de-sac, Meetinghouse Lane, harbours what's left of **St Mary's Abbey** (mid-June to mid-Sept Wed 10am–5pm; £1). All that remains is the vaulted chamber of its chapter house, with a model of how the complex once looked. Founded by the Benedictines in 1139 and transferred to the Cistercians eight years later, St Mary's was one of the most important monasteries in the country until the Reformation, when meetings of the Council of Ireland were held here. It was during such a meeting in 1534 that Silken Thomas Fitzgerald renounced his allegiance to Henry VIII and stormed out to raise a rebellion, only to be captured and executed the following year. The monastery was dissolved in 1539 and turned into a quarry in the seventeenth century, when its stones were used to build the Essex Bridge.

Returning to the quays you'll find the *Ormond Hotel* (see p.173*)*, whose barmaids were likened to the Sirens by Joyce in *Ulysses*. The hotel is slightly shabby but surviving thanks to the *Temple of Sound* nightclub next door and a guaranteed supply of out-of-town lawyers and witnesses getting some sleep before appearing at the nearby Four Courts.

THE FOUR COURTS

Map 5, E6.

The second of Gandon's masterpieces on the northside, the **Four Courts** would be a perfect foil to the Custom House were it not for a slight bend in the river making it impossible to view both buildings together from O'Connell Bridge. Built between 1786 and 1802 at a cost of £200,000, the courts provoked criticism of lawyers' "contemptible vanity" for having "the grandest building in Europe, in the world, to plead in". This failed to stop Gandon from undertaking another commission for the legal profession, King's Inns (see p.109). The courts and inns were originally located south of the river, but the latter moved to the site of the present-day Four Courts after Henry VIII gave the legal society land stolen from a Dominican convent; the courts moved north in the seventeenth century, whereupon the society of lawyers got their own premises on nearby Constitution Hill.

....

If you're curious to observe a trial, the courts are open to the public (Mon–Fri 11am–1pm & 2–4pm).

....

Like the GPO, the building is virtually synonymous with a specific event that was to have momentous consequences for

Ireland – not the Easter Rising (when it fell to the insurgents without a shot being fired), but the seizure of the Four Courts by anti-Treaty Republicans in July 1921, an event that marked the onset of hostilities that led to the Civil War. Michael Collins saw it as a direct challenge to the Free State and shelled the rebels into submission. Before surrendering, they blew up the Public Records Office with two lorry-loads of gelignite, sending scraps of historic documents floating above Dublin. In an unwelcome message of congratulation to Collins, Churchill wrote: "The archives of the Four Courts may be scattered, but the title deeds of Ireland are safe."

ST MICHAN'S CHURCH

Map 5, E6. Mon–Fri 10am–1pm & 2–5pm, Sat 10am–1pm; £1.50. Bus #34 from Middle Abbey Street.

Standing since 1095, **St Michan's Church**, in Church Street, is named after Danish Saint Michan and is the oldest surviving building on the northside. For five hundred years it was also the only church on the northside, ensuring it the largest parish in Dublin and funds for a complete rebuild in 1685. Since then its fortunes have declined and its roof has long required costly repairs – hence the exploitation of the "mummies" in its vaults.

Strictly speaking, the dozen **bodies** have not been mummified – they've been preserved by the constant temperature, the limestone masonry that absorbs moisture from the air, and methane gas secreted by rotting vegetation beneath the church. The "best" ones are 300–700 years old – a man thought to have been a Crusader, a woman who may have been a nun, and a man missing a hand, possibly a thief-turned-monk. Later burials are better accounted for, with the brass-studded coffins of a hated family of landlords in one vault, and the Sheares brothers, who were executed for their part in the 1798 Rebellion, in another. It's said that Robert Emmet, the leader of the 1803 rising, is buried in an unmarked grave at the back of the cemetery; a priest from St Michan's attended him on the scaffold.

Outwardly dour, the church is dominated by a grim tower from medieval times. Its much-remodelled interior contains an early eighteenth-century **organ** which was played by Handel. On the organ gallery is a superb carving of seventeen musical instruments cut from a single piece of wood, made by an unknown apprentice as his examination piece. St Michan's font was used to baptize Edmund Burke, who was born nearby at 12 Arran Quay, and the **skull** on the floor near the altar is said to symbolize Cromwell's crimes against Ireland. At one time, erring parishioners confessed their sins to the congregation while kneeling at the **Penitent's Pew** in the corner. All the windows of the church were shattered during the shelling of the Four Courts; the beautiful one based on the Book of Kells wasn't installed until 1958.

IRISH WHISKEY CORNER

Map 5, D6. May–Oct Mon–Fri 11am, 2.30pm & 3pm; Nov–April Mon–Fri 3pm; £3, students £2.50, children £1.50.

Though it's a blatant plug for Ireland's distillers, you'd have to be a vehement teetotaller not to enjoy the **Irish Whiskey Corner**, which currently occupies the former Bow Street Distillery on May Lane but is due to move into a new building just across the road.

The oriental art of distillation was probably brought to Ireland by Phoenician traders or missionary monks in the sixth century. Taking its name from the Irish *uisce beatha* (water of life), whiskey differs from Scotch whisky by not having a peaty taste and by being distilled not twice but three times (bourbon is only distilled once). Exhibits explain the malting, fermenting, distilling and maturing processes, how proof value is assessed and mature whiskeys are blended ("nosed" and left to "marry", as they say in the trade). An audio-visual show fills you in on the pioneering whiskey families – the Jamesons and the Powers in Dublin, the Murphys of Midleton and the Bushmills in the North – now amalgamated as the Irish Distillers Group, which produces all the well-known brands at its ultra-modern Midleton distillery.

Tours finish with a ritual **tasting** of five types of whiskey, Scotch and bourbon, poured out by the *Shelbourne's* former head barman, and the presentation of a "taster's certificate". Tots are watered down as the Irish believe that this brings out the flavour, but neat refills are available on request and connoisseurs are rewarded with a dram or two of vintage stuff. To sober up, read the rules of the lodging house for distillery workers; their minutely detailed laundry allowance ends, "and once every fortnight, one night-shirt".

SMITHFIELD HORSE SALES AND THE COLLINS BARRACKS

The cobbled expanse of **Smithfield**, just west of Bow Street, appears to be an open space without purpose – but on the first Sunday of every month, when the **horse sales** take place, the area is transformed. Horse-boxes start arriving from 9am and by midday the market's buzzing, and stays busy until around 4pm. Though there's nothing glamorous about the event, there's plenty to watch; blacksmiths shoeing horses at mobile forges, kids riding bareback on ponies, and weather-beaten farmers spitting into their palms and clapping their hands together to seal agreements.

After the sales you'll see ragged ponies being ridden away towards the northern suburbs, where impromptu races are held. Whether the horse sales will remain here is another matter, for the inhabitants of the new Smithfield Apartments aren't likely to appreciate them, and the Dáil has recently introduced a law restricting the ownership of "urban ponies".

Further out towards Phoenix Park, the imposing grey stone **Collins Barracks** are an annexe of the National Museum (Mon–Wed & Fri–Sat 10am–5.30pm, Thurs 10am–8.30pm, Sun 2–5pm; free), exhibiting Irish silver, glassware, china and textiles, musical instruments and Japanese art, as well as mounting special shows. The Barracks themselves date from 1701 and until being decommissioned in 1997 claimed to be the oldest continuously inhabited barracks in the world, with the largest drill square in Europe – it could hold six regiments.

Between the barracks and the river lies a railed-in plot of grass called **Croppies Acre**, with a monument on the spot where the executed rebels of 1798 were buried. During the Great Famine, Ireland's largest soup-kitchen was set up on the esplanade, where policemen supervised mass feedings from a 300-gallon pot. The quay is now named Wolfe Tone Quay, after the Rebellion's leader (see pp.82–83). The prostitution racket centred on Heuston Station, just across the river, leaves a tidemark of condoms on the sheltered side of Croppies Acre.

PHOENIX PARK

Map 3, A3; Bus #25, #25A, #66, #66A, #66B or #67A from Middle Abbey Street.

Phoenix Park, a rolling landscape over twice the size of London's Hampstead Heath or New York's Central Park, is a pleasure to visit at any time of year – but be sure to leave before dusk, as it's unsafe after dark. Since the attractions are scattered over seven hundred hectares, it's also wise to con-

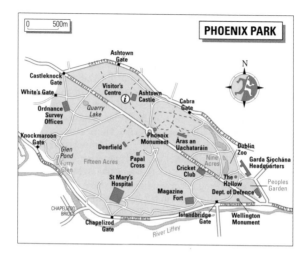

serve your energy by getting there by bus – though if you've already walked as far as the Collins Barracks, it's only another ten minutes to the main entrance off Parkgate Street.

Ryan's pub at no. 28 Parkgate Street is the ideal place to take a break for refreshments; see p.223.

Landscaped in the English fashion, the park harbours three hundred **deer** which bask on the Fifteen Acres or roam the woods nearby. Frequented by joggers and dog-walkers on a daily basis, and families at the weekends, it's also a venue for **cricket**, **football** and **hurling** matches in season, and occasional pop **concerts** over summer.

The name "Phoenix" is a corruption of the Irish *fionn uisce* ("clear water"), from the days when this land belonged to St John's Priory in Kilmainham, before the Reformation.

After the Restoration of Charles II, the duke of Ormond supervised the construction of a viceregal lodge which remained a private preserve until 1747, when it was opened to the public by Lord Chesterfield.

For decades, Head Ranger Nathanial Clements ensured that "every impropriety was vigorously expelled", but after his death in 1777 the "gates were opened wide to Tag, Rag and Bobtail" and the Sabbath was profaned by hurling matches "productive of blasphemous speaking, riot, drunkenness, broken heads and bones". Eventually, up to three hundred tents were pitched on the Fifteen Acres for gambling and drinking on Sundays – a fitting spot for a Temperance rally in 1875. A tradition of political meetings going back to 1792 reached its zenith with the Land League demonstration of 1880, whose 30,000-strong crowd set a record only surpassed by religious events, with 500,000 at the Eucharistic Congress of 1932, and over twice that number attending Papal Mass in 1979.

On entering the park you'll find the 1980s' **Peoples Garden**, the only part with formal flowerbeds and hedges, which merges into the hillocks and ponds landscaped in the 1830s by Decius Bruton, who also laid out **Chesterfield Avenue.** Near the Parkgate St entrance to the park stands the **Wellington Monument**, a 61-metre-high granite obelisk which bears reliefs cast from cannons captured at Waterloo, depicting the triumphs of the "Iron Duke".

Off the avenue to the right, **Dublin Zoo** (Mon–Sat 9.30am–6pm, Sun 10.30am–6pm; £5.50, children £3, family £15) dates back to 1830 – the second oldest in Europe. In recent years the zoo's decline led to a public campaign for its closure, but the zoo has been granted £15 million to modernize and extend its premises into something fit for the next millennium. Where the zoo once boasted of having bred the *MGM* lion, it now lays stress on breeding endangered species for subsequent release into the wild.

PHOENIX PARK

The Phoenix Park Murders

The Phoenix Park Murders of 1882 shocked society on both sides of the Irish Sea. One Saturday evening in May, the viceregal Chief Secretary and Under-Secretary were strolling home along Chesterfield Avenue when four men jumped out of a hansom cab, stabbed them to death and escaped towards Chapelizod. The killings struck fear into every official in Ireland, where cold-blooded assassination had never been encountered before. *The Illustrated London News* blamed a "foul conspiracy of the enemies of civilized society – Nihilists or Anarchists, or Fenians, or by whatever name they may be called", aiming "to subvert all regular Government, for the purpose of Communistic plunder". Most Irish nationalists were equally appalled, as Parnell had just been released from jail after making a pact with Gladstone, and the murdered Chief Secretary was Gladstone's nephew. Parnell offered to resign, to forestall any imputation of support for the murders, but was dissuaded by Gladstone. It was soon discovered that the assassins belonged to a Fenian splinter group, the **Invincibles**, as one of their comrades turned state's evidence that got them hanged at Kilmainham Jail. (He was later killed by Fenians aboard a boat bound for South Africa, where he hoped to start a new life.) A plaque on the roadside of the Polo Grounds marks the spot where the murders took place; the five Invincibles are remembered by a monument in Glasnevin cemetery.

Heading up the avenue past the Army and Garda athletic grounds and Nine Acres polo fields, you'll see the Palladian **Áras an Uachataráin** (Presidential Residence), which was built in 1751 as the viceregal lodge. Queen Victoria stayed here during her first visit to Ireland in 1849, and appeared not to notice the Famine at all, while the young Winston Churchill spent three years at the nearby "Little Lodge" when his father was secretary to his own father, the duke of Marlborough. The lodge became the home of the Irish president in 1937, and proudly flies the Harp from its flag-post. Since Mary Robinson announced that she wouldn't be seeking a second term, a new Irish president will be moving in by 1998.

A spur road across the way leads to a 27-metre-high stainless steel **Papal Cross**, on the spot where John Paul II celebrated Mass on September 29, 1979. Further along, at a crossroads, Lord Chesterfield's **Phoenix Monument** resembles an eagle more than a mythical bird and obfuscates the origin of the park's name. One road leads towards **Deerfield**, the US Ambassador's residence; the other to a **Visitors Centre** (daily 9am–5pm; £2, children/students £1, family £5) featuring a reconstruction of the Knockmaree cist grave found on the Fifteen Acres in 1838, which is older (c. 3500–3000 BC) than the famous Neolithic passage tomb at Newgrange (see p.163).

The ticket for the centre includes a tour of **Ashtown Castle**, a slender seventeenth-century tower house built to safeguard the family and assets of a distant ancestor of Daniel O'Connell. The tower has such defensive features as a "murder hole" by the door and a spiral staircase with a "trip step" on the threshold of the living quarters.

For more seclusion, head off past the Ordnance Survey Offices to the **Glen Pond** and **Furry Glen** on the edge of the **Fifteen Acres**, a huge meadow once used for military manoeuvres.

Beyond St Mary's Hospital (formerly the Hibernian Military School a path continues to the derelict **Magazine Fort**, dug into a hilltop in 1734. "Lo, here's proof of Irish sense/ here Irish wit is seen/ where nothing's left worth defence. They build a magazine", quipped Swift. After the British left, the fort became the main arms depot of the

Irish Army until a daring raid by the IRA in 1939 got away
with over one million rounds of ammunition, since when
its bunkers have been impregnably secured against interlop-
ers and abandoned to the elements.

THE GRAND CANAL
AND AROUND

Although it hasn't been used commercially for over twenty years, parts of the **Grand Canal** are still very pleasant for a stroll – the stretch between Lower Mount Street and Lower Leeson Street is especially attractive, with some good places to stop for a drink around the Richmond Bridge. There are a few low-key tourist attractions further out along the water, notably **Shaw's birthplace** and the **Irish Jewish Museum** off Portobello Road, with the **National Print Museum** at Beggars Bush as a possible detour between the two.

To the south of the Grand Canal lies leafy middle-class Ballsbridge and its adjacent suburbs. The Royal Dublin Society (see p.261) and Lansdowne Road (see p.264) are in this part of town, but unless you're going to a sporting event at one of these venues, or are staying in accommodation hereabouts, it's not a district you're likely to explore. To the south of Ballsbridge, however, you'll find a trio of minor sights that merit a brief excursion: the **Pearse Museum**, **Rathfarnham Castle** and the miniature medieval tower house of **Drimnagh Castle**.

The Grand and Royal canals

True Dubliners, it's said, are born within the confines of the city's two canals: the Grand Canal, which makes a six-kilometre loop around south Dublin, and the Royal Canal, which performs a similar loop through north Dublin.

The **Grand Canal**, which was intended to link Dublin to a vast area of central Ireland, had two branches: one joined the River Barrow to extend navigation as far south as Waterford, the other met up with the great natural waterway of the River Shannon. Work began in 1756 but proceeded so slowly that only 20km had been dug by 1763, when the Dublin Corporation took over the project to speed things up, handing it back to private investors in 1772. Nine years later the first cargo barges began operating between Dublin and Sallins, and passenger services started the following year. Boats terminated at the St James's Street Harbour near the Guinness brewery until the opening of the Circular Line, encircling the southside to meet the Liffey at Ringsend. The inauguration of the Grand Canal Basin locks in 1796 marked the completion of the longest canal system in Ireland and Britain, extending for 550km (of which the Shannon and Barrow account for about 250km).

While much of its revenue came from shipping turf (Dublin's fireplaces burnt 40,000 tonnes a year), the Grand Canal Company ran five hotels along the route for passengers on horse-drawn barges that carried up to eighty people. By 1852 services had been killed off by the railways, but cargo was still transported by barge for another century, with diesels replacing horsepower after 1911. The last barge haulage company went bust in 1950, and a decade later Guinness stopped transporting its stout by barge from St James's Street Harbour, which was filled in in 1974.

The **Royal Canal** to the north of Dublin was a later rival venture by John Binns, a director of the Grand Canal who quit after taking offence to a jest and vowed to wreck its business. The Grand Canal Company claimed breach of charter but failed to stop it, though they did win a stipulation that once the Royal Canal had advanced 22km from Dublin, it had to run at least 6km away from their own canal. The duke of Leinster was a major backer, but insisted it be routed past his mansion near Maynooth. As a result, construction of it proved longer and costlier than anticipated, and never made a profit; in 1840 it was bought by a railway company as a route for their line (which still runs alongside the canal through the northside), and in 1961 it was closed for navigation as so much of it had dried up. Since realizing its tourist potential, the stretch between Dublin and Mullingar has been restored, and work on the next section is well advanced.

WATERWAYS VISITORS CENTRE

Map 3, J5. June–Sept daily 9.30am–6.30pm; Oct–May Wed–Sun 12.30–5pm; £2, students/children £1, family £5.

Raised on stilts above the water of the canal, in the manner of an ancient bogland settlement, the **Waterways Visitors Centre** is a purpose-built tourist attraction that strives to convey the beauty of Ireland's waterways from a Dublin backwater. It's no substitute for a holiday on the Shannon, but if you're considering such a trip it's worth a visit, as it provides a good overview – and it sells maps and guidebooks. The pavilion's open-plan interior relies on pictorial displays to cover the history and ecology (a video monitor upstairs runs through the scenic highlights), and there are models to explain how to design a canal or build a coracle. While the exhibits are informative, virtually the only genuine artefact is a deep-sea diving suit worn by canal repairmen until the 1930s. Having fallen into disuse in the 1950s, the canal system has revived since the 1970s thanks to tourism, so it's unfortunate that the romantic image of the waterways conjured up by the centre is weakened by the grimy vista of the Grand Canal Basin and its downstream locks from the rooftop viewing platform.

NATIONAL PRINT MUSEUM

Map 3, J7. May–Sept Mon–Fri 10am–12.30pm & 2.30–5pm, Sat, Sun and bank holidays noon–5pm; Oct–April Tues & Thurs 2–5pm; £2.50, students/children £1.50, family £5.

It's possible to walk from the Waterways Centre to the leafier stretches of the Grand Canal in about ten minutes, or to take a detour to the **National Print Museum** in the former chapel of the **Beggars Bush Barracks** on Haddington Road. It contains all kinds of printing equipment, from an eighteenth-century "handcaster" to the earliest Apple word-processors, most of which are still in working order. Built by the British in 1830, the barracks were constructed in an effort to control a lawless area on the edge of Dublin – Beggars Bush – and were the first barracks to be handed over to the Free State in 1922. It was here that Erskine Childers was executed for possessing a revolver during the Civil War – an ironic end for someone who became a Nationalist hero for smuggling 900 rifles into Ireland in 1914. The barracks now house the Irish Labour Court.

FROM MOUNT STREET TO RICHMOND BRIDGE

There's a verdant stretch of canal between Mount Street and Richmond Bridge that isn't far from the centre of town and has a choice of approaches. One is from Merrion Square along **Mount Street Upper** past **St Stephen's Church** (named "Pepper Canister" after its fluted cupola); another is by Lower

Baggot Street, which has lots of lively pubs along its initial Georgian stretch and beyond the Bank of Ireland building.

The stretch of **canal** by Lower Baggot Street is 3–6m wide at this point, with swans on the cleaner parts, shaded by trees that once provided cover for prostitutes and their clients (it was here that Joyce lost his virginity). In the 1950s and 1960s, *Parson's Bookshop* by Baggot Street Bridge (now a café) was a meeting place for writers like Brendan Behan and the poet Patrick Kavanagh, who lived nearby and produced a short-lived "journal of literature and politics" called *Kavanagh's Weekly*, written largely by himself (with contributions from Behan and Flann O'Brien). After Kavanagh's death in 1967, his home on Pembroke Road was found to contain little more than a bed, and his friends erected a plain memorial **seat** on the Mespil Road side of Baggot Street Bridge in accordance with his wish: "O commemorate me with no hero-courageous/Tomb – just a canal-bank seat for the passer-by". A lifesize **statue of Kavanagh** muses on a bronze bench on the other side of the canal.

A mile or so past Kavanagh's statue you'll reach a trio of **pubs** as the canal dwindles to a ditch near the Portobello Bridge: *The Barge*, right on the corner, *The Portobello*, before the Richmond Bridge, and *The Lower Deck* just around the block from **Portobello House**. Originally a hotel for passengers at the terminus of the Grand Canal, this was Jack B. Yeats's last residence, and now serves as a college.

THE SHAW BIRTHPLACE

Map 3, F7. May–Oct Mon–Sat 10am–6pm, Sun & holidays 11.30am–6pm; £2.40, students £2, children £1.15.

There are two places of interest in the sidestreets beyond Richmond Bridge, whose houses are dwarf versions of the Georgian houses of Dublin's centre. No. 33 Synge Street

George Bernard Shaw

Born in Dublin in 1856, **George Bernard Shaw** was technically a member of the privileged Ascendancy, but his father's failed attempt, after leaving the civil service, to make money meant that Shaw grew up in an atmosphere of genteel poverty and, by the age of sixteen, was earning his living in a land agency. When his mother left his father for a singing teacher and took her two daughters with her to London, Shaw soon joined them and set about educating himself. Subsidized by his mother's meagre income, he spent his afternoons in the British Museum's reading room and his evenings writing novels.

Shaw's novels were unsuccessful, but his plays were a different matter entirely and he was acclaimed the most important British playwright since the eighteenth century. However, Shaw recognized his foreignness as being a big part of his success: "the position of foreigner with complete command of the same language has great advantages. I can take an objective view of England, which no Englishman can." In the 1890s, influenced by the drama of Ibsen, he began to write plays hinged on moral and social questions rather than romantic or personal interests – *Man and Superman*, *Caesar and Cleopatra*, *Major Barbara*, *St Joan*, and, of course, *Pygmalion,* from which the musical *My Fair Lady* was adapted. As well as a dramatist he was an active pamphleteer, critic, journalist and essayist, on subjects ranging from politics and economics to music. Shaw was rewarded the Nobel Prize for literature – which he refused. He died in Hertfordshire, England, in 1950.

was the **birthplace of George Bernard Shaw**, and is now a museum with Victorian period-furnishings. Shaw lived here until he was ten and recalled that "neither our hearts nor our imaginations were in it". This "loveless" atmosphere arose from his parents' failing marriage and the strain of keeping up appearances when the family was sinking into debt – a mood conveyed by the claustrophobic rooms and a terse inscription acknowledging that "Bernard Shaw, author of many plays", lived here.

THE IRISH JEWISH MUSEUM

Map 3, F8. May–Sept Sun, Tues & Thurs 11am–3.30pm; Oct–April Sun only 10.30am–2.30pm; closed on Jewish holy days; free.

Further along the widening canal, you can turn into Kingsland Parade and take the second turning on the left to find the **Irish Jewish Museum** at 3 Walworth Road. Opened in 1985 by President Chaim Herzog of Israel, who was born in Belfast and educated in Dublin, the museum relates the history of the Jewish community in Ireland (the first were Portuguese and Spanish Jews, fleeing the Inquisition), who established a synagogue off Dame Street in the 1720s. The house itself functioned as a synagogue from 1915 until the mid-1970s, when its congregation moved to the suburbs. Upstairs you can see a wedding canopy, circumciser's instruments and other artefacts of Judaic culture.

RATHFARNHAM CASTLE

Map 2, F6. June–Sept daily 10am–6pm; May 10am–5pm; April Sun only; Oct daily 10am–5pm; £1.50, students/children 60p. Bus #16 or #16A from O'Connell Street.

Rathfarnham Castle has been undergoing restoration since 1987, and work is far from finished, but if you're interested in historic monuments and their conservation, the guided tour is worthwhile. Though evidence suggests that a fortified dwelling existed here in Norman times, the castle you'll see today was built in the closing years of the sixteenth century by Sir Adam Loftus, a Yorkshireman who came to Ireland as the Lord Deputy's chaplain and went on to become Archbishop of Dublin and the first Provost of Trinity College.

A solid block with four square corner towers, the castle lost its battlements in the 1720s, when it passed from the Loftus family into the hands of "Speaker" Connolly, who rented it out to tenants. In 1767, it returned to the family in the person of Nicholas Hume-Loftus, earl of Ely, an eccentric who erected a triumphal arch at the north entry to the grounds. At one point he was nearly judged insane, but escaped committal thanks to his uncle, Henry Loftus, who defended him in court and inherited Rathfarnham after his death. It was Henry who made Rathfarnham a byword for luxury and refinement, hiring Sir William Chambers and James "Athenian" Stewart to remodel the rooms, and installing aviaries and menageries in the grounds. However, his heir had little interest in the area and by the end of the century the castle had been abandoned and its art collection dispersed to other estates. In 1913 part of the land was sold off for a golf course, while the castle was bought by the Jesuits. The kitchen wing has been fully restored, but the principal rooms have yet to be furnished.

PEARSE MUSEUM

Map 2, G6. Daily: Nov–April & Sept–Oct 10am–1pm & 2–5pm; May–Aug 10am–1pm & 2–5.30pm; free. Bus #16 from O'Connell Street or Rathfarnham Castle.

If you're interested in the background to the 1916 Easter Rising, it's worth visiting the **Pearse Museum** in former St Enda's School in Rathfarnham village. The school was run by Pádraig Pearse from 1910 and set about promoting Gaelic culture by teaching its curriculum in Gaelic and encouraging students to take part in sports such as hurling, Gaelic football, camogie and handball. Sadly, the school attracted fewer pupils than Pearse had hoped for and in 1916, facing bankruptcy, it closed down. It was from here that Pearse and his brother Willie went out to fight on Easter Monday of that year. As a signatory to the Proclamation of the Irish Republic, Pearse was one of the first leaders to be executed at Kilmainham Jail (see p.88). His idealism and heroism are the leitmotif of a twenty-minute audiovisual show, entitled "This Man Kept a School".

The museum also has a nature study centre with a self-guiding trail around **St Enda's Park** (open until slightly later than the museum), which features riverside walks, a waterfall and a walled garden where outdoor concerts are held during the summer.

DRIMNAGH CASTLE

Map 2, E5. April–Oct Wed, Sat & Sun 10am–5pm; Nov–March Sun 2–5pm; £1.50, students £1, children 50p. Bus #56A from Eden Quay, via Christ Church, Saint Patrick's and the Coombe.

Drimnagh Castle is well worth the bus journey through the pebble-dashed suburb of Drimnagh, three miles south-west of the centre. Visible from Long Mile Road, behind a Christian Brothers School, the castle's rugged profile attests to eight hundred years of inhabitation and alterations.

The **tower house** was built in the thirteenth century by the Anglo-Norman Barnewall family, who occupied it for nearly four hundred years, but its defensive role declined as the lawless clans of the Wicklow Mountains were subdued. Sir Adam Loftus of Rathfarnham Castle leased Drimnagh in the seventeenth century, replacing some of the arrow-slit windows with mullioned ones, adding a rooftop fumerelle

DRIMNAGH CASTLE

for smoke to escape, and a front staircase to supersede the low ground-floor entrance beneath a "murder hole", designed to force attackers to stoop as lime or boiling water was poured on their heads.

Inside, the **spiral staircase** unusually turns anti-clock wise, as stairways were built to favour the defender's sword-hand and Sir Hugh Barnewall was left-handed. At the top is a garderobe (toilet) sited conveniently near the **Great Hall**, which was an all-purpose living room and sleeping quarters. Its floor would originally have been strewn with rushes, but restorers have surfaced it with tiles bearing the coats of arms of the Barnewall, Loftus and Lansdowne families. Over the centuries there have been sightings of the **ghost of Eleanora**, Hugh de Barnewall's niece, who is said to have killed herself on hearing that she was destined to marry her cousin. The Jacobean-Tudor minstrels' gallery and the hammer-beamed roof of Roscommon oak are modern replicas. Some of the crafts people involved in their creation were honoured by statues in medieval guise, carved on the beams. The chandeliers come from the film *Excalibur*, which was shot in Ireland at the Powerscourt Estate (see p.156).

Behind the house are a small seventeenth-century French-style **garden** with bay hedges and a **poultry-run** for diverse breeds of fowl. The aim is to restore the grounds to something of the self-sufficiency that prevailed in medieval times and persisted as late as 1954, when Drimnagh was vacated by the Hatch family, who lived and ran a dairy business here.

THE OUTSKIRTS

A huge arc of coastline has effectively become part of the greater Dublin metropolitan area, but even so, you'll feel like you're leaving the city behind as you head down the coast. You'll pass **Dún Laoghaire** with its great harbour overlooked by the Martello Tower, immortalized in *Ulysses,* and the charming seaside towns of **Dalkey** and **Killiney**, with the Wicklow Mountains on the outskirts of **Bray**, further south.

All of these places are accessible from Dublin by frequent DART trains, making it easy to visit several in a day's outing. The DART isn't quite as useful for northerly outskirts. The Botanical Gardens and Prospect Cemetery are in suburban **Glasnevin**, east of which you'll find the exquisite Casino in **Marino** and the dunes and seabirds on **Dollymount Strand**, just offshore from Clontarf.

The headland of **Howth** is the scenic highlight of this part of Dublin, with a cliffside walk as fine as any on the south coast. Beyond Howth **Malahide** deserves a visit for its delightful castle, while **Donabate** is home to the quirky Newbridge House and a traditional farm. Both are accessible by suburban trains or buses from Dublin.

SOUTH ALONG THE COAST

The DART line south follows the course of Ireland's first railway, opened in 1834, which ran from Dublin to Kingstown (as Dún Laoghaire was then called) where, at the townsfolk's insistence, it terminated on the outskirts. After their intolerance had abated, the railway was extended to Dalkey along the route of a quarry-railroad called "The Metals", and finally right down to Arklow – though the DART itself terminates at Bray.

Boarding a train in the centre, you'll catch a first glimpse of the sea on the horizon at **Sandymount**. Two stops later, the track starts to trail along beside Dublin Bay, past the UNESCO-designated bird sanctuary of **Booterstown Marsh**, whose wading birds are visible from the station platform. Glimpses of the sea alternate with views of the railway as you pass through Blackrock and Monkstown, till Dún Laoghaire harbour comes into view.

Dún Laoghaire

By DART, or bus #7, #7A or #45A from Trinity College. Night buses (Thurs–Sat) from College Street.

The seaside town of **Dún Laoghaire** (pronounced "Dunleary") is virtually a suburb of Dublin but there's still a residue of a resort atmosphere here. The harbour, now a port for ferries from Britain and the base for lightships and yacht clubs, was built to hold a great fleet within its two mile-long granite piers and was the largest artificial harbour in the world at the time of its construction (1817–42).

The **East Pier** has all the requisites for an edifying stroll: a bandstand, a lifeboat memorial, a compass pointer, and an anemometer for measuring windspeed (one of the first in the world when installed in 1852). Along the landward side are the crusty members-only Royal Irish Yacht Club (dating from 1850), Royal St George Yacht Club (1863) and National Yacht Club (1876) – with the non-élitist National Sailing School over on the **West Pier**.

Just inland from the Carlisle Pier, which is within the harbour, stands an odd **monument to George IV** (commemorating his state visit of 1821), which was described by Thackeray as "a hideous obelisk, stuck upon four fat balls, and surmounted by a crown on a cushion". The king had been expected to disembark here, but landed, visibly drunk, at Howth instead, though he tried to make amends by departing from Dún Laoghaire. One of George's balls is newer than the others; the original was blown away by the IRA, who also put paid to a statue of Queen Victoria that stood nearby. A little way uphill is Andrew O'Connor's sculpture **Christ the King**, which the civic fathers purchased in 1949 but kept in storage till 1979 because Church authorities objected to it.

Further inland, the former Mariners' Church on Haigh Terrace is a fitting home for the **National Maritime Museum** (April & Oct Sun 1–5pm; May–Sept Tues–Sun 1–5pm; £1.50, children 80p, family £4). Its star exhibit is a giant clock-work driven **Baily Optic** which was used in Howth lighthouse from 1902 to 1972. Vying for second place is a French ship's longboat captured at Bantry Bay in 1796 from Wolfe Tone's failed invasion, and sea charts and other items from the German U-boat that landed Sir Roger Casement in 1916. Ask to see the brass nail from *HMS Bounty* – one of the few that the mutineers didn't use to barter sexual favours from the Tahitians. Among the scale models is one of Brunel's early steamships, *The Great Eastern* (1858), which proved a commercial failure as a passenger ship but laid the first transatlantic cable between Ireland and North America.

To blow any cobwebs away, try the **Dublin Bay Sea Thrill** (£12 per person). You'll be togged up to withstand a deluge of spray on this forty-minute zoom about in a high-speed inflatable. Trips depart every hour from 9.30am in summer, but less regularly during other seasons; the ticket office (✆260 0949) is just outside the Arts Centre by the entrance to Carlisle Pier.

Sedate **boat trips** down to Sandycove, Dalkey Island and Killiney Bay can be arranged at short notice for £40 (the boat can carry twelve passengers) at *Dún Laoghaire Boat Charter* (✆282 3426) on the East Pier.

Sandycove

By DART, or bus #8 from Dún Laoghaire.

Not far down the coast from the East Pier, Dún Laoghaire merges into **Sandycove**, a quieter suburb whose most famous son was Roger Casement, the British diplomat turned Irish rebel. Casement made his name as a consul championing the rights of indigenous tribes in the Belgian Congo and the Peruvian Amazon, and retired with a knighthood convinced that Irish freedom was his next cause. In 1914 he travelled to Berlin to enlist German support; he returned by U-boat shortly before the Easter Rising, but was soon captured. Charged with high treason, Casement was stripped of his honours and hanged at Pentonville prison in London.

Today, Sandycove is more widely associated with James Joyce, who for a brief period lived in the Martello Tower – now a Joyce museum and the starting point of the Bloomsday pilgrimage. Originally it was just one of 21 such towers built against the threat of French invasion in 1804–06. Their walls are 2.4m and an armoured door 3.6m off the ground was the sole means of entry, making them almost impregnable – but they never fired a shot in anger. You'll see other Martello towers at Dalkey, Bray, Howth and Sandymount.

The Sandycove tower is called the **James Joyce Tower** (April–Oct Mon–Fri 10am–1pm & 2–5pm, Sun & holidays 2–6pm; £2.40, concessions £2, children £1.15), not so much for its association with his life – Joyce spent barely a week here in August 1904, four months before eloping with Nora Barnacle – but more because it features so prominently in the opening chapter of *Ulysses*. The characterization of "stately, plump Buck Mulligan" was Joyce's revenge on his host, Oliver St John Gogarty. On the sixth night of Joyce's stay, a fellow guest, Samuel Chenevix Trench, had a nightmare about a panther and fired some shots into the fireplace; Gogarty seized the gun and shot down a row of saucepans above Joyce's head, shouting, "Leave him to me!". Joyce took the hint and left promptly.

All of the items on show are donations to the museum, which was opened in 1962 by Sylvia Beach, who first published *Ulysses*. An edition illustrated by Matisse vies for attention with a plaintive letter from Joyce to Nora, accusing her of "treating me as if I were simply a casual comrade in lust", and such odd exhibits as a pandybat of the kind with which Joyce was beaten for "vulgar language" at school. In the first-floor guardroom, Gogarty's abode has been recreated complete with a lifesize ceramic panther representing Trench's *bête noire*. The spiral staircase emerges on the rooftop gun platform where Buck Mulligan did his ablutions at the start of the novel.

From there you can see right over the backyard of **Geragh**, a Constructivist seaside villa which the architect Michael Scott built for his family in the 1930s. Beyond it lies a knobbly brown headland with a famous bathing place known as the **Forty Foot Pool** (so called not for its size

SANDYCOVE

but because the 40th Regiment of Foot used to be stationed in a battery nearby). The pool was long reserved for
male nude bathing: nowadays both sexes can use it but
"Togs must be worn" – though nude bathers still get away
with it before 9am. If you're tempted to join them, bear in
mind the water temperature only varies by about 5°C
throughout the year, so you'll find it pretty chilly.

Dalkey and Killiney

By DART or bus #8 from Dún Laoghaire or Sandycove.

Just down the coast from Sandycove is the charming seaside
town of **Dalkey** (pronounced "Dawky"), immortalized in
Flann O'Brien's satirical novel *The Dalkey Archive*. On
sunny days its narrow streets and cliffside villas have an
almost Mediterranean lushness that makes Dublin itself
seem a little cold and grey. Historically, Dalkey has thrived
on comparisons with the capital: for two hundred years, it
was the only natural harbour on the east coast of Ireland.
Goods unloaded here filled Dalkey's warehouses and swelled
its coffers, until the dredging of the Liffey in the sixteenth
century wiped out its business and Dalkey dwindled to a
village. In time, though, Dalkey's beauty ensured that fresh
comparisons were made, as well-to-do Dubliners built seaside homes and the advent of the railway brought day-trip-
pers with it. Today, its nostalgic old quarter merges into a
commuter-belt hinterland under the cover of forested
slopes and azaleas.

From the DART station it's a short walk down Railway
Road to Castle Street, distinguished by two fortified warehouses from the fifteenth century, when Dalkey was dubbed
the "Port of the Seven Castles". **Goat Castle**, across the
way from **Archibold Castle**, serves as Dalkey's town hall,
with a **Visitor Centre** alongside. Further north stands

Bulloch Castle, built by the Cistercians in 1180 to protect the fishing harbour not far from Sandycove.

Dalkey's main attraction is the lovely walk down Coliemore Road past Georgian houses and Victorian villas, to the harbour facing Dalkey Island, and out along the cliffside **Vico Road** to view the fabulous coastline.

From mid-April till the end of summer there are daily boat trips, weather permitting, from Coliemore Harbour (✆283 4298; £5 return) to **Dalkey Island**, 300m offshore. First inhabited 8500 years ago (the dwelling sites are marked by thickets of nettles), the island was known in Gaelic as *Deiliginish* (from which Dalkey derives), a name which recalls a spiked wooden fort (*Deilig* means "thorn" or "spike") that once existed there. Here you'll find another Martello tower and the ruins of an early Irish Church, St Begnet's, on the other side of the saddle-shaped island. A curious ritual involving the "King of Dalkey", complete with crown and sword, is still occasionally enacted here: it started out as a student prank, but became increasingly political until it was stamped out by Lord Clare in 1797. **Fishing** trips can be arranged through the *Dalkey Island Hotel* (by the harbour); you can charter a boat for the day or hire a rowing boat for a few hours.

Dalkey Hill is definitely worth climbing; steps and a path ascend steeply from Vico Road, or there's an easier route from the park on Ardbrugh Road. Shavians can track down **Torca Cottage**, where George Bernard Shaw spent much of his boyhood. En route to the summit there's a fine view of Dalkey **quarry**, where the granite blocks that form the walls of Coliemore Harbour and the great piers of Dún Laoghaire were hewn. To give your lungs a workout, follow the ridge up to **Killiney Hill**, where a park has been laid out for visitors to enjoy the glorious **view** of Dublin Bay and the Wicklow Mountains.

DALKEY AND KILLINEY

Killiney, in the next bay, is the Irish equivalent of Beverly Hills, where stars like Mel Gibson, Tom Cruise, George Michael and Lisa Stansfield own property alongside such indigenous luminaries as Chris De Burgh, Bono and The Edge, writers Maeve Binchy and Hugh Leonard, and film director Neil Jordan. Celebrity-spotting aside, the real attraction is the wide grey **beach** running the length of the bay.

Bray

Beyond Killiney the coast relapses into humdrum suburbia, but things pick up as you approach **Bray**, whose rugged headland contrasts with the softer flanks of the Wicklow Mountains. Its fine surroundings make amends for the resort, which is a poor relation to Dalkey and Dún Laoghaire. Though the amusement arcade and places to eat and drink are open year round, Bray only really comes alive in the summer, especially during the **International Festival of Music and Dance** (see p.257) in August. The **Oscar Wilde Autumn School** (see p.259) in October marks the end of the festive calendar. Details of both events are available from the **tourist office** (daily 10am–5pm; ✆286 6796) in the Old Court House on Main Road, which doubles as a **heritage centre** devoted to local history and the achievements of Sir William Dargan, the builder of the Dublin–Kingstown railway and founder of the National Gallery.

Bray Head is worth climbing for the view of town and the hills enclosing the bay. The leeward side partakes of the softness of Wicklow, the "Garden of Ireland", where trees and plants from five continents flourish in gardens that throw open their gates during the **Wicklow Gardens Festival** (mid-May to mid-June). A full list of the gardens and viewing days is available from the tourist office. The easiest to reach is the seventeenth-century French-style garden of

Killruddery House (May, June & Sept daily 10am–5pm; £1.50), off the Southern Cross Route on the edge of Bray (bus #84 from Main Street or a 20-minute walk from Strand Road). By paying £2.50 extra you can tour Killruddery House, the Tudor-Revival seat of the earls of Meath, which was a famous hunting lodge for generations.

NORTH TO HOWTH AND BEYOND

Heading northwards from the centre of Dublin, you don't catch sight of the sea from the DART until you're nearly at Sutton, and don't have long to enjoy the view before the line terminates at Howth, the rugged northern headland of Dublin Bay. Aside from Howth, the bay's only real seaside spot is Dollymount Strand, a few miles from the centre. The other main attractions are in the suburbs of Glasnevin and Marino, and out beyond Howth in Malahide and Donabate. While buses are the only way to get to Glasnevin, Marino and Dollymount, Malahide and Donabate can also be reached by train from Connolly Station. You'll need to catch a **suburban train** bound for Drogheda, which can also be boarded at Howth Junction – an interchange between the DART and suburban lines (not to be confused with Howth, the DART terminus). Until 1959, Dubliners enjoyed riding the famous Hill of Howth trams, which crested the summit of the peninsula; bus #31B does the same today, *sans* romance – though the view is still pretty spectacular.

Glasnevin: the Botanic Gardens and Prospect Cemetery

Bus #13, #19 or #19A from Upper O'Connell St.

Glasnevin was a village on the cattle-road from Meath and it remained quite bucolic until the establishment of two civic amenities catalyzed its evolution into a genteel suburb of pebble-dashed maisonettes and B&Bs. Glasnevin now coexists uneasily alongside Finglas, a sprawl of new estates built to rehouse inner-city slum-tenants, which is rough enough for the Alsatian dogs to walk around in pairs (so locals joke).

As buses swing off Botanic Road on to Glasnevin Hill you'll see the gates of the **National Botanic Gardens** (March–Oct Mon–Sat 9am–6pm, Sun 11am–6pm; Nov–Feb 10am–4.30pm, Sun 11am–4.30pm; free), founded by an act of the Irish Parliament in 1795. Ireland's mild climate makes it an excellent place for growing exotic species, and its Botanic Gardens were the first in the world to raise orchids from seed and the first in Europe to grow pampas grass and the giant waterlily. Some 20,000 species and varieties flourish over nineteen hectares of rockeries and arboretums, and in cast-iron glasshouses that are early masterpieces of the genre. The **Curvilinear Range** was fabricated by Richard Turner, a Dublin ironmaster who built the Palm House at Kew Gardens in London; its newly restored ironwork is sublime. The **Palm House** is showing its age, but the new **Alpine House** is a worthy addition to Turner's legacy.

Alongside the Botanic Gardens lies the Glasnevin or **Prospect Cemetery** (daily 8.30am–4pm; free), a place ennobled by the remains of national heroes. Established as a burial place for Catholics by Daniel O'Connell in 1832, its jungle of Celtic crosses, shamrocks, harps and other patriotic iconography is elucidated by **guided tours** (Sun 11.30am). The 51-metre-high Round Tower is a monument to O'Connell, whose body was interred in its crypt in 1869, having been brought home from Genoa in 1847. Similar pomp attended the burial of Parnell, whose tomb is topped by a huge granite boulder; his beloved Kitty was buried with far less ceremony in Sussex. Other historical figures among the 11.5 million dead at Glasnevin include Roger Casement, Michael Collins, Arthur Griffith, Jim Larkin, Countess Markievicz and Éamon de Valera; from the arts, Gerard Manley Hopkins, Maud Gonne Macbride and Brendan Behan. The main entrance is on a small square at the end of Prospect Avenue, where *Kavanagh's* **pub** has consoled mourners since 1833.

The Casino at Marino

Map 2, F4. May daily noon–4pm; June–Sept 9.30am–6.30pm; Oct daily 10am–5pm; Nov Sun & Wed only noon–4pm; £2, students/children £1, family £5. Bus #123 from O'Connell Street, or #20A, #20B, #27, #27A, #27B, #42, #42B or #42C from Beresford Place.

Marino, off Malahide Road 5km northeast of O'Connell Street, originally enjoyed a sweeping view of Dublin Bay that made it an ideal location for a stately home. It was here that the Earl of Charlemont endeavoured to bring the civilization of ancient Rome and Renaissance Italy to Ireland by creating a splendid park and a mansion to display the antiquities he had collected during his nine-year Grand Tour of Europe. While nothing remains of Marino House you can still admire the elegant folly that was the *pièce de résistance* of his estate. Regarded as one of the finest Neoclassical buildings in Ireland, its construction preoccupied Charlemont from 1758 to the 1770s.

The **Casino** cost £20,000 (equivalent to about £3 million today) and was designed by Sir William Chambers – the architect of Charlemont's town house on Parnell Square (now the Hugh Lane Gallery).

Its most remarkable feature is the way Chambers plays with your perception of its scale, so what outwardly appears

THE CASINO AT MARINO

147

to be a one-roomed pavilion contains two floors of rooms designed to appear larger than they are. To maintain the illusion, the "doorway" is a dummy with only one panel that opens, and the large windows are masked to hide the fact that they illuminate two levels, with curved panes of glass to reflect the outside world. With equal ingenuity, the downpipes that carry rainwater into underground cisterns are hidden in the columns, and the chimney pots are disguised as urns.

Among the curiosities on the top floor are a child's bed that could be extended as the infant grew, and the earl's own bedroom, with a huge "boat" bed modelled on one at Versailles. Charlemont married in late middle age after he fell out with his brother and decided to sire an heir so that his sibling would be disinherited. In public life, he was regarded as one of the most enlightened and cultivated men of his day; his belief in Irish self-government led him to become the first commander-in-chief of the Irish Volunteers and to leave his deathbed to vote against the Act of Union in the last session of the Grattan Parliament.

If you're catching a bus back into town, try to sit upstairs on the left for a view of **Marino Crescent**. This elegant row of Georgian houses was once nicknamed "Ffolliot's revenge" after the man who built the crescent out of spite, to block Charlemont's view of the sea. To further upset him, Ffolliot ensured that the side facing Marino House was an unsightly jumble of chimneys and sheds. No. 15 was the **birthplace of Bram Stoker**, the author of *Dracula*, and now hosts an annual summer school devoted to the author and his creation.

As bus #42 runs on to Malahide, it's easy to visit the Casino en route to (or back from) Malahide Castle (see p.151).

Dollymount Strand

Bus #32X from St Stephen's Green, or the Fairview/Clontarf Road near Marino.

In fine weather it's pleasant to stroll along **Dollymount Strand**, the popular name for **North Bull Island**, which was built in 1821 to prevent Dublin Harbour from silting up, at the suggestion of Captain Bligh of *HMS Bounty* fame. Besides holidaying Dubliners, the island accommodates over 40,000 **birds**, many of them Arctic migrants. Shelducks, curlews and oystercatchers wade upon the mudflats and larks nest in the dunes (now designated a UNESCO Biosphere Reserve), which also sustain foxes, shrews, badgers, rabbits and many plant species. You can find out more at an **interpretive centre** at the end of the causeway road from the mainland, one mile's walk from the bus stop on James Larkin Road.

Howth

By DART or bus #31B from Lower Abbey Street or Howth Road (near Marino).

A rugged peninsula at the northernmost point of Dublin Bay, **Howth** derives its name from the Danish *hoved*, or "cape", and is pronounced to rhyme with "both". While the DART gives you a glimpse of the northern coast of the peninsula, the bus crosses the summit, with views right across Dublin Bay to the Wicklow Mountains, and even the Mountains of Mourne on fine days.

For the best places to stay in Howth see p.176 and p.182; for the nicest places to eat see pp.214–215.

Howth **village** is a sleepy place of steep streets and dramatic views. Poised above Harbour Road but accessible by

HOWTH

Church Street, the Gothic shell of **St Mary's Abbey** dates from the fourteenth to the seventeenth centuries and traces its origin to the first church founded by the Norse King Sitric, in 1042. You can see a fair bit of the interior without going to the trouble of obtaining the keys from Mrs O'Rourke at no. 3 Church Street, but will need them to view the fifteenth-century double tomb of Lord and Lady Howth. St Mary's offers a fine view of Howth harbour and Ireland's Eye, and there's food and music to be enjoyed at *Ye Olde Abbey Tavern*, on the road below.

Howth Castle, built in 1564, is the oldest inhabited house in Ireland and is a weather-beaten and battlemented veteran of numerous restorations down to the present century. For many years the St Lawrence family kept open house at mealtimes, a custom said to have arisen from an incident in 1575, when Grace O'Malley, the "Uncrowned Queen of the West", was turned away because the family was at dinner, and reacted by kidnapping their eldest son and holding him until Lord Howth promised to keep his gates open at mealtimes in the future. Although the castle isn't open to the public, you can wander along to a barn that enthusiasts have turned into a **National Transport Museum** (June–Aug daily 10am–5pm; Sept–May Sat, Sun & bank holidays noon–5pm; £1.50, children 50p, family £3), with vehicles from buses to fire engines and armoured cars, including a Hill of Howth tram. In spring, don't miss the **rhododendron glades** behind the *Deer Park* golf club, where 400 species flourish in the peaty soil below Mud Rock. Just downhill is a prehistoric **dolmen**, its gigantic 91,000-kilo capstone balanced on a dozen smaller rocks.

On a fine day you can enjoy Howth's famous **Cliff Walk**, with imposing rockscapes and superb views south past the mouth of the Liffey to the Wicklow Mountains, and north to the flatlands of the Boyne. The footpath runs right around the peninsula, but the four-kilometre arc from the Nose of Howth to the lighthouse is the most scenic. You can get there by walking out along Balscadden Road – which commits you to the whole distance – or conserve your energy by taking a #31B bus to the summit, and cutting down to the **Baily Lighthouse** on the southeast point. Built in 1814 on the site of a Celtic fort (*baile*), it was, until March 1997, the last manned lighthouse on Ireland's coastline. From the so-called summit, you can climb to the 171-metre **Ben of Howth.**

Malahide

Map 1, E3. **Castle** April–Oct Mon–Fri 10am–5pm, Sat 11am–6pm, Sun & holidays 11.30am–6pm; Nov–March Mon–Fri 10am–5pm, Sat, Sun & holidays 2–5pm; £2.95, students/children £2.45, family £7.95. Combined ticket for **Castle** and **Newbridge House** £4.75, unwaged £3.70, children £2.35, family £11.75, can be obtained at either site. Bus #42 from Beresford Place (or Marino), or suburban train from Connolly Station or Howth to Malahide Junction (no services on Sun).

A few miles up the coast from Howth, the old feudal estate of **Malahide** lends its name to a commuter village of pretty houses and quiet streets sloping gently down to a yachting marina. Its chief attraction is **Malahide Castle**, a medieval tower house that was modified and expanded over the 800 years that it was owned by the Talbot family. The Talbots were of Anglo-Norman origin but remained Catholic until the eighteenth century; dispossessed while Cromwell was in power, they regained Malahide after the Restoration, and it stayed in the family until the death of Lord Milo in 1975, when the estate was acquired by Dublin County Council. Its charm lies in its disparate styles, as the twelfth-century

MALAHIDE

tower house evolved from a defensive to a domestic building while retaining the look of a romantic castle. The first room, whose stone walls are hidden behind dark Jacobean panelling, was the principal one in the **tower house**. The Virgin carved over the fireplace was the family totem and is said to have disappeared during the years that Malahide was given to Cromwell's general, Myles Corbet, as a reward for his signature on the death warrant of Charles I.

You then pass into the **west wing**, then on to the family **bedrooms**, featuring a four-poster bed which is said to have belonged to the actor David Garrick. From there you descend to the **Great Hall**, whose oak hammer-beam ceiling and minstrels' gallery date from 1475. The low door in the corner is known as Puck's Door, after the **ghost** of a servant who fell asleep on the night when invaders attacked, and hanged himself in shame. It's said to appear whenever there are changes Puck dislikes and made its last appearance in 1975, when the contents of the castle were auctioned. A picture of the Battle of the Boyne is flanked by portraits of "Fighting Dick" Talbot and thirteen other family males who breakfasted here on the morning of the battle, never to return. The tour ends in a small **library** with Flemish wall-hangings and an exquisite inlaid table. In 1928, many of the papers of James Boswell (the great-grandfather of Emily Boswell, who married the fifth Lord Talbot) were found here, including an unexpurgated draft of his *Life of Johnson*.

Having seen the castle, most visitors make a beeline for the **Fry Model Railway** (April–Sept Mon–Thurs 10am–6pm, Sat 11am–6pm, Sun & holidays 2–6pm; June–Aug also Fri 10am–6pm; Oct–March Sat, Sun & holidays 2–5pm) installed in the old Corn Store. The nation's largest model railway layout (covering 240 square metres), it represents Ireland's transport system in all its diversity, from canal barges to the DART and ferry services.

Another sight in the vicinity is the fifteenth-century **Church of St Sylvester**, wherein lies Maud Plunkett, the heroine of Gerald Griffin's ballad *The Bride of Malahide*, who was "maid, wife and widow" in one day, after her husband was killed in battle on their wedding day (she later married a Talbot). On the west gable is a *sheela-na-gig*, a relic of pagan times featured on many medieval Irish churches. Finally, there is the twenty-acre **Botanic Gardens** laid out by Lord Milo early this century, which contain 5000 species from Australia, New Zealand and Chile.

Newbridge House

Map2, H1. April–Sept Tues–Fri 10am–5pm, Sat 11am–6pm, Sun & bank holidays 2–6pm (weekdays closed 1–2pm); Oct–March Sat, Sun & bank holidays 2–5pm; £2.75, students £2.45, children £1.50, family £7.50. Bus #33B from Eden Quay, or suburban train from Connolly Station or Malahide (no services Sun).

Next stop along the Malahide line is **Donabate**, a trim commuter village that is graced by **Newbridge House**, a solid brownstone edifice built in 1737 for Charles Cobbe, archbishop of Dublin from 1742 to 1765. It remained in the Cobbe family until 1985, when the estate was sold to Dublin County Council.

The **Dining Room** has a lovely Rococo ceiling commissioned by Lady Betty Beresford, who married the archbishop's son. Off the adjacent library lies the family's **Museum of Curiosities**, containing all sorts of shells and artefacts from around the world, including an African chief's umbrella and the mummified ear of a sacred Egyptian bull. The **inner hall**, beyond, leads to the upper floor via a stairway featuring a portrait of one of Swift's beloveds – either Stella or another woman called Vanessa (it

NEWBRIDGE HOUSE

is not known which) – and the magnificent **Red Drawing Room**, added to the house around 1760. Finally, you descend to the basement, where the **laundry** features a manually operated washing machine and an early vacuum cleaner, while the **kitchen** is crammed with fascinating devices such as a duck-press for squeezing juice from poultry, and a mousetrap that drowned its victims. The house remained unelectrified until the 1960s, when it was wired up for the filming of *The Spy Who Came in from the Cold*.

Attached to the house is a **traditional farm** (£1, students/children 80p, family £2), home to various breeds of sheep, fowl, pigs and cattle. In the coach house you can see the gilded ceremonial coach made for "Black Jack" Fitzgibbon, who was such an unpopular Lord Chancellor that someone once threw a rat through the window during a procession.

DAY-TRIPS FROM DUBLIN

It's feasible to travel to most parts of the country in less than a day from Dublin, making the list of possible excursions endless. In this chapter we've concentrated on six places within a short range of the capital which represent a geographical and historical cross-section of what's on offer, covering an arc from the Wicklow Mountains to the neolithic sites of the Boyne Valley.

To the south, the **Wicklow Mountains** are modest in height (the highest peak is under 1000m), but have remained very sparsely populated – for many centuries they were bandit country. From a tourist's point of view, three attractions stand out from the rest: the **Powerscourt Estate**, famous for its splendid gardens; the early monastic site of **Glendalough**; and **Russborough House**, renowned for its decoration and art collection.

The landscape is less inspiring to the west, with small towns and villages fast becoming suburbs of Dublin. But if you're interested in stately homes and the lifestyle of the old Anglo-Irish Ascendancy, it's worth taking a suburban bus out to Celbridge to explore **Castletown House**, which was founded by William Connolly, one of the most influential figures of Dublin's golden age.

The **Valley of the River Boyne** in County Meath, north of Dublin, has the distinction of being Ireland's richest pasture land. The area known as the *Brú na Bóinne* (Palace of the Boyne) is the site of three prehistoric passage graves – **Newgrange**, **Knowth** and **Dowth** – that are among the most remarkable prehistoric structures in Europe. We haven't covered Dowth in this chapter as it's currently closed to the pubic.

While all of these places can be reached by public **transport**, Newgrange and Powerscourt necessitate changing bus or walking some distance, so you might prefer to go on an **organized tour** from Dublin. There are two main companies involved, *Gray Line* and *Bus Éireann*. Bookings for both can be made in the Dublin Tourism Centre on Suffolk Street (see pp.9–10); *Gray Line* coaches depart from there, while *Bus Éireann* trips leave from Busáras (where you can also make bookings, see pp.9–10 for details). To be sure of getting a place during the summer reserve a day or two ahead – especially for Newgrange. The price of the tour includes admission charges for the site.

POWERSCOURT ESTATE

Map 1, E7. Gardens March–Oct daily 9.30am–5.30pm; £3, students £2, children £1. **Waterfall** Daily summer 9.30am–7pm; winter 10.30am–dusk; £1.50, students £1, children 80p. Bus #44 from Hawkins Street (off Burgh Quay) or #85 from Bray DART station to Enniskerry.

Nestled in the foothills of the Wicklow Mountains, the picture-postcard village of **Enniskerry** originally belonged to the **Powerscourt Estate**, which was owned by a dynasty founded by one of James I's generals, Richard Wingfield. The great house, 1km from Enniskerry, is one of the largest Palladian mansions in Ireland, but its real attraction are the magnificent gardens which are blended into the backdrop of the Great Sugar Loaf and other Wicklow peaks.

The greystone **house** with its twin copper domes was designed by Richard Cassels for the first Viscount Powerscourt and took a decade to build (1731–41). Gutted by fire in 1974 – on the eve of a party to celebrate the completion of extensive restoration – it's now owned by the Slazengers (makers of tennis racquets and sportswear), who financed its restoration by selling off some of the land for housing. A section of the ground floor was due to reopen as this book went to press.

The twenty-hectare **Garden** is entered through the gilded **Bamberg Gate**, which originally belonged to Bamberg Cathedral in Bavaria. The great stone terrace, with its angels of Fame and Victory, was designed in 1840 by Daniel Robertson, who used to be wheeled about in a barrow, clutching a bottle of sherry while working on the job. When his creative powers were exhausted and the bottle was empty, he'd call it a day. Fourteen years later, the seventh viscount began the **Italian Gardens**. Overlooked by a grand staircase, they lead down to the circular **Triton Lake** whose eponymous statue (based on Bernini's fountain in Rome) spurts jets of water nearly 30m into the air.

At the far end of the terrace the land falls away sharply, enhancing the beauty of the North American conifers planted by Robertson. Behind the **Pepper Pot Tower** is the Killing Hollow, where the last of the O'Toole bandit clan was beheaded, and a little further down are the **Japanese Gardens**. Skirting the Triton Lake, you can carry on to the **Pet Cemetery**, where the graves of family dogs and horses are accompanied by that of a cow which

POWERSCOURT ESTATE

produced seventeen calves and over 100,000 gallons of milk during her lifetime.

From the gardens, it's about a six-kilometre walk through rhododendron woods to the famous **Powerscourt Waterfall**. At 119m it's the highest in Ireland, leaping diagonally down the rockface into a valley where it joins the River Dargle. From the car park you can follow a two-kilometre **nature trail** past giant redwoods, through a mulchy undergrowth of ferns and bluebells. You may also spot sika **deer**, introduced from Japan in 1858.

GLENDALOUGH

Map 1, D8. Daily summer 9am–6.30pm; winter 9.30am–5pm; free. **Visitors Centre** same hours; £2, students/children £1, family £5. Accessible by St Kevin's bus service from St Stephen's Green, daily 11.30am, £5 one-way, £8 return.

Deeper into the Wicklow Mountains lies **Glendalough** (the "valley of the two lakes"), a magical setting for one of the best-preserved monastic sites in Ireland. Despite the car parks and the coach parties, there is a sense of peace and spirituality around here that makes it easy to imagine how hermits and monks once lived. The **Visitors Centre** features a film that sets Glendalough in the context of ancient monasteries elsewhere in Ireland and has a model of how it probably looked in those days.

The monastery's foundation is attributed to St Kevin, a scion of the royal house of Leinster who studied under three holy men before retreating to Glendalough to fast and pray in solitude. His piety attracted followers, and in 570 he became abbot of a monastic community. As a centre of the Celtic Church, the monastery became famous throughout Europe for its learning, and despite being sacked by the Vikings, Normans and English, it was restored each time, until being dissolved during the Reformation. However, as the pope decreed that seven visits to Glendalough would procure the same indulgence as one pilgrimage to Rome, pilgrimages continued until the mid-nineteenth century, when a local priest banned gatherings due to the licentious behaviour of the pilgrims following their devotions on St Kevin's day (June 3).

You enter the grounds through a double stone archway that was once surmounted by a tower. The nearest ruin is the **Cathedral**, dating from the early ninth century, whose roofless nave and chancel contain numerous grave slabs. Among the tombs outside stands **Saint Kevin's Cross**, a granite monolith that was left unfinished. Nearby is a small **Priest's House** from the twelfth century, above the door of which are carved three barely discernible figures, thought to represent Kevin and two abbots. Further downhill is a two-storied edifice with a steeply pitched roof and a bell-turret, known as **Saint Kevin's Kitchen**, though it was probably an oratory. The most impressive structure is the thirty-metre-high *Cloigtheach* or **Round Tower**, which served as a belfry, watchtower and place of refuge – the doorway high above the ground would have been reached by a ladder that could be pulled up in times of danger. (Such towers were a distinctive feature of Irish monasteries.) Further west, outside the enclosure, you'll see the remains of **Saint Mary's Church**, which is believed to have been the first building in the lower valley, and may mark the site of Kevin's grave.

Downhill from the Kitchen is a footbridge, on the far side of which is the hollowed-out **Deerstone**, so-called after a legend claiming that tame deer squirted their milk into it to feed the motherless twins of one of Kevin's followers. By following the signposted "Green Road" skirting the Lower Lake, you'll come to the ruined **Reefert Church** and the start of a path to **Saint Kevin's Cell**, or rather the spot where he slept on a promontory overlooking the Upper

Lake. He later moved into a cave halfway up the cliff – dubbed **Saint Kevin's Bed** – to avoid the advances of a maiden called Kathleen. She eventually found his hiding place and, awaking one morning to find her beside him, he reacted with the misogyny characteristic of the early church fathers by throwing her into the lake, where she drowned. (Kevin himself is said to have died in 617 or 618, at the age of 120.) The cave is only accessible by boat from the far shore of the lake in summer.

RUSSBOROUGH HOUSE

Map 1, B7. April, May, Sept & Oct Sun 10.30am–5.30pm; June–Aug daily 10.30am–5.30pm; 45min tour of main rooms and paintings £2.50; outside official opening hours, ✆045/65239. Bus #65 from Eden Quay.

Five kilometres south of Blessington stands the classic Palladian structure of **Russborough House**, designed, like Powerscourt, by the German architect Richard Cassels (with the assistance of Francis Bindon). The house was constructed for Joseph Leeson, son of a rich Dublin brewer who became MP for Rathcormack then **Lord Russborough** in 1756. Russborough epitomizes the great flowering of Anglo-Irish confidence before the Act of Union deprived Ireland of its parliament, much of its trade and its high society.

The **lake** in front of Russborough provides the house with an idiomatically eighteenth-century prospect – it is actually a thoroughly twentieth-century reservoir, created by damming the Liffey, which provides Dublin with twenty million gallons of water a day.

The chief reason why Russborough is so firmly on the tourist trail is its collection of **paintings**. The German entrepreneur Alfred Beit (1853–1906), co-founder with

Cecil Rhodes of the De Beer Diamond Mining Company, poured the fortune he derived from that enterprise into amassing works of art. His nephew, Sir Alfred Beit, acquired Russborough in 1952, which explains why such an extraordinary collection – featuring Goya, Murillo, Velazquez, Gainsborough, Rubens and Frans Hals – are kept in this obscure corner of County Wicklow.

Russborough has been burgled twice: first in 1974, when Bridget Rose Dugdale stole sixteen paintings to raise money for the IRA (her booty, worth £18 million, was recovered undamaged from a farmhouse in County Cork a week later); and again in May 1986. Some of the paintings taken in this second heist have since been retrieved in The Netherlands. Nowadays security is tight, and visitors are herded around the house in groups, with little chance to study the paintings – or anything else – in detail. You can, however, take a second tour for no extra charge.

CASTLETOWN HOUSE

Map 1, B5. March Sun & bank holidays 2–5pm; April–Sept Mon–Fri 10am–6pm, Sat 11am–6pm, Sun & bank holidays 2–6pm; £2.50, students/children £1, family £6. Bus #67, #67A, #66X or #67X from Middle Abbey Street to Celbridge.

Some 20km west of Dublin, on the upper reaches of the River Liffey, the village of **Celbridge** is the site of one of Ireland's great Palladian mansions, **Castletown House**. Castletown is remarkable for its size and ostentation, but ongoing restoration work means that it will be closed until some time in 1998, so be sure to phone first to avoid disappointment (☏628 8252).

Castletown was built for William Connolly, a publican's son from Donegal who made his fortune by dealing in forfeited estates after the Battle of the Boyne, as legal adviser to William III. Unanimously elected Speaker of the Irish House of Commons in 1715, he was acknowledged as the richest man in Ireland by the 1720s. Later he joined the Hellfire Club, holding sessions of debauchery at his hunting lodge outside Dublin. Castletown was begun in 1722, in a somewhat haphazard fashion, and the interior was still unfinished when he died seven years later. Work on the house didn't resume until his nephew, Tom Connolly, inherited it in 1758. The driving force was his wife, Lady Louisa, who was only fifteen years old when she assumed responsibility for the job, which carried on into the 1770s. Castletown was sold by the Connolly family in 1965, and would have been demolished to build houses if the property developers hadn't gone bust. Desmond Guinness stepped in to buy the house on behalf of the Irish Georgian Society, which used Castletown as its headquarters until 1994.

When the restoration is completed you'll pass through the pine-panelled Brown Study into the **Red Drawing Room**, which is covered in torn French damask. Its ceiling was designed by Sir William Chambers for Lady Louisa, as was the adjacent **Green Room**. The **Print Room**, next door, is the only surviving example in Ireland of the eighteenth-century fad for gluing prints onto walls. A splendid yellow and blue silk canopied bed dominates the **State Bedroom**, beyond.

The upper floor is reached by a grand cantilevered **staircase** with bronze banisters, whose walls are decorated with wonderful plasterwork by the Franchini brothers, and a painting of bears being savaged by hunting dogs. The **Blue Bedroom** is more Victorian than Georgian, with another amazing bed, surmounted by the three feathers of the Prince of Wales. Best of all is the **Long Gallery**, with its Pompeiian murals and gilded sconces bearing busts of poets and philosophers.

From the gallery's windows you can see the "**Connolly Folly**" two miles away. This bizarre structure appears to be a monument to chimney-sweeping, but was actually a memorial to William Connolly. His widow also commissioned the **Wonderful Barn**, a weird conical tower with an external stairway, which can be seen from the M4 motorway. Both projects were set up to provide relief work for estate workers hit by the famine-ridden winter of 1739. Unfortunately, the land on which they stand no longer belongs to the estate, and both are too far from the house to reach on foot.

NEWGRANGE

Map 1, B1. Daily March & April & Oct 9.30am–5.30pm; May & late Sept 9am–6.30pm; June to mid-Sept 9am–7pm; Nov–Feb 9.30am–5pm; £3, students/children £1.25, family £7.50. **Visitor Centre**: £2, students/children £1, family £5. Suburban train from Connolly Station to Drogheda, then a bus to the Visitor Centre. *Gray Line* tours Mon & Tues 10am, Thurs & Sat 2.30pm (£14.50); *Bus Éireann* tours April Sat & Sun 10am, May–Sept Sat–Thurs 10am, Oct Thurs & Sat 10am (£16).

Newgrange, a Neolithic tumulus situated about 13km west of Drogheda, is an artificial mound built between 3500 and 2700 BC, when stone was the only material available for use as tools. The mind boggles at the effort required to transport the building materials, which amounted to 450 giant boulders and over one million sackfuls of small stones – a task believed to have taken forty years. Though evidently important, its purpose remains unclear: a burial place, a cenotaph, a solar temple or a kind of astronomical chart have all been suggested as functions.

To confuse matters, the mound is surrounded by later additions, such as the **Great Circle** of massive standing stones, of which a dozen of the estimated 35 originals remain upright. There are also series of concrete **slabs** and wooden **stakes**, the former representing the remains of a satellite passage grave which has largely been destroyed over the centuries, the latter marking the centre point of deep pits whose purpose remains unknown.

The mound itself covers about an acre. It has been so completely restored that at first sight it reminds you of a grounded flying saucer, but once you accept the incongruity, its sparklingly new appearance heightens the wonder. The white quartz **retaining wall** gives some hint of the power this stone must have had for the builders, since the nearest source is the Wicklow Mountains. The base is girdled by a ring of 97 granite **kerbstones** weighing between four and eight tonnes apiece. The stones were quarried in the Mourne Mountains of County Down – it's estimated that it would have taken eighty men four days to drag one from the quarry to the river, whence it was transported by boat to Newgrange.

The most important feature, and one which distinguishes Newgrange from Dowth and Knowth, is the **roof-box** above the entrance, containing a slit through which the light of the rising sun penetrates the tomb on the **winter solstice** (December 23). At 8.58am, the rays start edging their way slowly up the passage, to illuminate the chamber at the far end with an orange glow, which fades away fifteen minutes later. Guided tours feature a speeded-up "recreation" of this phenomenon, using electric light; there's a nine-year waiting list to witness the real event, though the effect is almost as good a couple of days before or after the solstice.

The **passage** extends for 19m into the tumulus (about a quarter of its depth), sloping gently upwards so that the floor of the chamber at the end is the same height off the ground as the roof-box. The **chamber** is roughly cross-shaped with a corbelled roof of huge slabs that stands exactly as it did some 5000 years ago, without renovation or repair. When the chamber was excavated in 1967 the charred bones of four or five people were found, which some take as proof that only priests and rulers were buried here – others argue that is where bodies were merely laid out before being interred elsewhere (a theory given credence by the discovery of hundreds of cremated remains in other tumuli).

Newgrange can only be entered on guided tours of no more than thirty people at once, so you may have to hang around for a while. To spread the numbers out a bit, you'll be taken first to a newly opened **Visitor Centre** on the other side of the River Boyne, whence shuttle-buses run to the site.

KNOWTH

Map 1, B1. Daily May to mid-June 10am–5pm; mid-June to mid-Sept 9.30am–6.30pm; mid-Sept to Oct 10am–5pm; £2.

To reach **Knowth**, carry on up the road from Newgrange and take a left, whereupon you'll see a makeshift wooden watchtower overlooking the site. Major excavations have been going on here since 1962, but recently about a third of the complex has been opened to the public. Though there's less to see for visitors, the discoveries at Knowth have already surpassed what was excavated at Newgrange. At Knowth alone, about 250 decorated stones have been found: over half of all known Irish passage grave art.

Several periods of occupation by different cultures have been identified, from the **Neolithic**, when the original passage tombs were built (3000–2000 BC), through occupation by the Beaker people (2000–1800 BC) (so called

KNOWTH

because of a distinctive beaker left with each of their dead), and a late **Celtic** settlement in the early centuries AD. Early **Christian** occupation has been identified from the eighth to twelfth centuries, and finally **Norman** usage (twelfth and thirteenth centuries) brought an extensive settlement and a glut of *souterrains* (underground passages and chambers).

The main passage tomb is about twice the size of that at Newgrange – with a tunnel over 30m long leading to the central chamber – and even more richly decorated. At Knowth there is also a smaller second passage tomb within the main tumulus, and up to seventeen **satellite tumuli.** Structurally the main mound is similar to the one at Newgrange, with a cruciform chamber, high corbelled roof and richly decorated stones, but here there is also evidence of settlement around the mound.

LISTINGS

ACCOMMODATION

D espite the many new places that have sprung up around the city centre recently, the ever-rising demand for **accommodation** means that there's hardly a slack season any more. Unless you're willing to risk a frustrating search for a bed, it's necessary to make **reservations** if you're arriving at the weekend (Fri–Sun) any time of year; on week-days over summer; or around Easter or major sporting events. How far in advance depends: one or two weeks should be okay in February or October, but one or two months is more appropriate for peak times. If you arrive without a reserva-tion, it's possible to book on the spot at any of the Dublin Tourism offices (see p.6). With a credit card, this can also be done by phone (☎605 7777) or fax (☎605 7787), or by using the touch-interactive videos outside the offices. In each case, there's a fee of £3 per booking. Alternatively, you can run through the listings here and phone around yourself.

Hotels in Dublin are mostly quite expensive and some-times no more comfortable than good guesthouses. **Guesthouses** and **bed-and-breakfasts** (B&Bs) are plenti-ful but variable – we've selected what we think are the best. For those on a tight budget, **hostels** are the cheapest option. Our listings under these headings are divided into **central** (meaning within the Grand and Royal canals) and various **suburban** areas. Thanks to the DART it's quite feasible to stay in a seaside town like Dún Laoghaire or Howth and commute into Dublin.

Accommodation prices

Accommodation prices vary throughout the year, with the highest rates from June to September, during events like international rugby championships, and over Christmas, Easter and St Patrick's Day. Our listings for **hotels**, **guesthouses** and **B&Bs** feature a code (eg ③) signifying the high-season rate for *one* person sharing a double room (reckon on 15–20 percent more for single occupancy), as follows:

① £10–£15	③ £20–£30	⑤ £40–£60	⑦ £80–£100
② £15–£20	④ £30–£40	⑥ £60–£80	⑧ over £100

For **hostels** and **campsites**, the low- and high-season prices appear in £, again referring to what one person will pay.

HOTELS

The majority of the best hotels are on the southside, either in or around Temple Bar or St Stephen's Green. If you don't have any luck in here, the next best location is Ballsbridge, which is within walking distance of the city centre. Further out the seaside ports of Dún Laoghaire and Dalkey offer an attractive alternative to staying in the centre. At less than half an hour's journey on the DART from the city centre, it's also worth considering picturesque Howth village, at the northern end of Dublin Bay.

The telephone code for the Dublin area is ⓒ01.
Calling Dublin from abroad (or Northern Ireland),
dial ⓒ00-353-1, followed by the subscriber's number.

Adams Trinity Hotel

Map 6, D5. 28 Dame Lane ℂ670 7100; fax 670 7101.
Small, new, old-fashioned-looking hotel overlooking Dame Street, near Temple Bar and Dublin Castle. Ask about special weekend rates. **⑥**

Bewley's Hotel

Map 6, F4. 19–20 Fleet St ℂ670 8122; fax 670 8103.
Cosy, friendly three-star hotel in Temple Bar. Non-smoking rooms. Restaurant and bar. Secure parking nearby. **⑤**

Buswell's Hotel

Map 4, F7. 23–27 Molesworth St ℂ676 4013; fax 676 2090.
Small, comfy three-star hotel in a Georgian house near the National Museum. Non-smoking rooms. Bar and restaurant. **⑥**

Central Hotel

Map 6, E6. 1–5 Exchequer St ℂ679 7302; fax 679 7303.
Refurbished nineteenth-century establishment on the corner of South Great George's Street, not far from Dublin Castle and Temple Bar. Bright pink walls hung with modern Irish art. Non-smoking rooms. Breakfast not included. **④**

The Clarence Hotel

Map 6, C4. 6–8 Wellington Quay ℂ670 9000; fax 670 7800.
Ultra-stylish five-star Temple Bar hotel owned by U2, containing *The Kitchen* nightclub (see p.232) and the award-winning *Tea Rooms* restaurant (see *Restaurants*). All rooms with video, candles and Egyptian linen, plus penthouse suites (£400–£1450) used by the likes of Tina Turner and Simon Le Bon. **⑦**

Conrad International Dublin

Map 4, E10. Earlsfort Terrace ✆676 5555; fax 676 5424.
Formerly the *Hilton*, this five-star pile stands opposite the
National Concert Hall, just off St Stephen's Green. All
facilities. Disabled access. Breakfast not included. ⑧

Georgian House Hotel

Map 4, G9. 18 Lower Baggot St ✆661 8832; fax 661 8834.
A three-star, family-friendly hotel in a Georgian house, 5min
from St Stephen's Green. Bar and seafood restaurant. ⑤

The Gresham Hotel

Map 5, H4. 20–22 Upper O'Connell St ✆874 6881; fax 878 7175.
Dublin's oldest hotel, and the best on the northside. Classy, yet
family-friendly. Safe parking. Breakfast not included. ⑦

Harcourt Hotel

Map 4, C10. 60 Harcourt St ✆478 3677; fax 475 2013.
Pleasant two-star hotel not far from St Stephen's Green. George
Bernard Shaw once had a flat in one of the houses, now knocked
together. Some rooms en suite, others not. Bar and restaurant. ⑤

Harding Hotel

Map 6, B5. Copper Alley ✆679 6500; fax 679 6504.
Attractive new two-star *USIT* hotel facing Christ Church
Cathedral. The twin/triple rooms are good value for three
people. Restaurant and Viking-theme bar with pool table. ④

Jury's Christchurch Inn

Map 6, B5. Christchurch Place ✆454 0000; fax 454 0012.
A three-star eyesore opposite Christ Church. Their flat room-

HOTELS: CENTRAL

rate makes it a good option for anyone with children. Bar and restaurant. Disabled access. ④

Longfields

Map 4, H9. 9–10 Lower Fitzwilliam St ℂ676 1367; fax 676 1542.
Small, award-winning three-star hotel near Merrion Square, with an excellent restaurant. ⑤

Mont Clare Hotel

Map 4, G7. Merrion Sq ℂ661 9555; fax 661 5663.
Charming renovated townhouse in the heart of Georgian Dublin. Bar and restaurant. Breakfast not included. ⑥

Ormond Hotel

Map 5, F6. Upper Ormond Quay ℂ872 1811; fax 872 1909.
Historic (it features in *Ulysses*), luridly decorated and shabby hotel on the north bank of the Liffey, used by lawyers and witnesses attending the nearby Four Courts, and right next to the *Temple of Sound* nightclub. ④

The Shelbourne Hotel

Map 4, F8. St Stephen's Green North ℂ676 6471; fax 661 6006.
Dublin's most prestigious hotel, and a society watering hole. Elegantly furnished period interiors and a buzzing social life, plus an excellent restaurant and bar (see p.224). Breakfast not included. Open all year. ⑧

Wellington Hotel

Map 6, D4. 21–22 Wellington Quay ℂ677 9315; fax 677 9387.
A small, new, inexpensive hotel in Temple Bar, whose flat room-rate makes it a good option for those with kids. ④

HOTELS: CENTRAL

The Westbury Hotel

Map 4, D7. Henry St ©679 1122; fax 679 7078.
Large and glittering five-star pile just off Grafton Street,
attached to a mall. Open all year. **⑧**

BALLSBRIDGE

Berkeley Court

Map 3, I7. Lansdowne Rd ©660 1711; fax 661 7238.
Hideous outside but plush within, as befits the flagship of the
Doyle group, which also runs *Jury's* (below). Non-smoking
rooms; five-star facilities. Open all year. Breakfast not
included. **⑧**

Burlington Hotel

Map 3, H8. Upper Leeson St ©660 5222; fax 660 3172.
Four-star complex within walking distance of the centre. Non-
smoking rooms. Disabled access. Open all year. **⑥**

Jury's Hotel & The Towers

Map 3, J7. Pembroke Rd ©660 5000; fax 660 5540.
Huge five-star place with a lively atmosphere, 3km from the
centre. Pool and a 24hr coffee dock. Disabled access. Open all
year. **⑧**

Lansdowne Hotel

Map 3, I7. 27 Pembroke Rd ©668 2522; fax 668 5585.
Popular with rugby fans because of its proximity to Lansdowne
Road stadium, this small, comfy hotel is within walking
distance of the centre, in pleasant, leafy surroundings. **⑤**

DALKEY AND KILLINEY

The Court Hotel

Map 1, F6. Killiney ℗285 1622; fax 285 2085.
An enormous Victorian pile near the DART station. All
rooms en suite and non-smoking. Seafood and French
restaurants; bar. ④

Dalkey Island Hotel

Map 7, H2. Coliemore Rd, Dalkey ℗285 0377; fax 285 0141.
A refurbished Georgian hotel overlooking Dalkey Island. All
rooms en suite. Conservatory-like bar; seafood restaurant.
Honeymooners can be driven around in a vintage Rolls
Royce. Open all year. ⑤

Fitzpatrick Castle Hotel

Map 7, H2. Killiney ℗284 0700; fax 285 0207.
A ex-stately home with fine views and four-star facilities.
Indoor pool, tennis, golf course and riding. Breakfast not
included. ⑥

DÚN LAOGHAIRE

Kingston Hotel

Map 7, C3. Adelaide St ℗280 1810; fax 280 1237.
All rooms en suite; the ones sleeping five are a good deal at
£85–£95. Bar, restaurant and disco. ④

Port View Hotel

Map 7, B3. Royal Marine Rd ℗280 1663; fax 280 0447.
A little way inland of the DART station. Twenty rooms, some
of them en suite. Bar and lounge. ③

Deer Park Hotel

Map 8, B3. Howth ✆832 2624; fax 839 2405.

In the grounds of Howth Castle, about 15min walk from the DART. Popular with golfers (the links are right outside) and famous for its rhododendrons. ⑤

St Lawrence Hotel

Map 8, D2. Harbour Rd ✆832 2643; fax 839 0346.

Nice, old-fashioned place overlooking the harbour, within easy reach of everything. Open all year. ②

Sutton Castle Hotel

Map 8, A4. Sutton ✆832 2688; fax 832 4476.

Off Shielmartin Road on the southwest side of the peninsula; bus #31B runs fairly close by. Three-star facilities and great views of Dublin Bay. ⑤

GUESTHOUSES AND B&BS

Guesthouses and **bed-and-breakfasts** (B&Bs) come in all shapes and sizes throughout the city. Though guesthouses are supposedly superior to B&Bs, this is contradicted so often in practice that it's wisest to focus on the specifics of a place rather than its category. Places in the centre (mostly north of the Liffey) tend to be more expensive and less attractive than in suburbs beyond the Grand and Royal canals, so you'll need to decide which factors are most important. You can count on hot water, central heating and a TV lounge if nothing else; breakfast is usually included. Unless stated otherwise, the vast majority are closed over

Christmas; some operate for a shorter period of the year (as indicated).

Anchor Guest House

Map 5, J4. 49 Lower Gardiner St ✆878 6913; fax 878 8038.
A tastefully refurbished Georgian house. All rooms are en-suite with TV and phone. Infants free; child discount. ③

Clifden House

Map 5, H2. 32 Gardiner Place ✆874 6364; fax 874 6122.
Nine pleasant en-suite rooms with TV. Child discount; babysitting. Breakfast not included. Open all year. ③

Fitzwilliam

Map 4, G9. 41 Upper Fitzwilliam St ✆660 0448; fax 676 7488.
A posh southside guesthouse near Merrion Square, with a restaurant, bar and en-suite rooms with TV and phone. Parking. Child discount; babysitting. Breakfast not included. ④

The Grey Door

Map 4, F10. 23 Upper Pembroke St ✆676 3286; fax 676 3287.
Another superior southside establishment, with two award-winning restaurants, and very classy non-smoking rooms. Open all year. ⑤

Maple Hotel

Map 5, J4. 75 Lower Gardiner St ✆ & fax 874 5239.
Cosy, friendly guesthouse run by the Sharkey family for thirty years. All rooms en-suite with TV. Convenient for the Busáras and airport buses, and not far from O'Connell Street and the Liffey. ④

Marian Guesthouse

Map 5, H2. 21 Upper Gardiner St ℰ874 4129.
Six rooms with shared bathrooms, and a garden. Same rates year round, with no extra charge for single occupancy. Open all year. ②

Othello Guesthouse

Map 5, J4. 74 Lower Gardiner St ℰ855 4271; fax 855 7460.
A dozen en-suite rooms with TV. Child discount; cot available. Parking. Breakfast not included. Open all year. ③

Staunton's on the Green

Map 4, E8. 83 St Stephen's Green ℰ478 2300; fax 478 2263.
Swankiest option on the southside: an, elegant Georgian house overlooking the Green, with a private garden. All rooms en-suite with phone and TV. Bar. Family friendly. Open all year. ⑤

Stella Maris Guesthouse

Map 5, H1. 13 Upper Gardiner St ℰ874 0835; fax 668 0483.
Nine rooms, five of them en-suite. Parking. Child discount. Breakfast not included. ③

Talbot Guesthouse

Map 5, I5. 95–97 Talbot St ℰ & fax 874 9672.
The newest, most centrally located northside guesthouse, close to O'Connell Street and the Liffey. All rooms en-suite and non-smoking, with TV and phones. Child discount; cot available. Disabled access. ④

The Townhouse

Map 5, J4. 47–48 Lower Gardiner St ℰ878 8808; fax 878 8787.
A snazzily refurbished Georgian house that once belonged

to the playwrights Dion Boucicault and Lafcadio Hearn.
All rooms en-suite with TV, fridge and tea maker. Fine
healthy breakfast. Secure parking. Higher rates at weekends.
The classiest guesthouse on the northside, with a hostel
attached. ⑤

BALLSBRIDGE AND SANDYMOUNT

Mrs Maureen Bermingham

Map 2, G5. 8 Dromard Terrace ℂ668 3861.
Ivy-covered period house near the beach; bus #3 or
Sandymount DART station. Old-fashioned comfort but no en-
suite facilities. Non-smoking rooms. Child discount;
babysitting. Open May–Sept. ①

Mrs Bridget Brady

Map 3, J7. Northumberland Lodge, 68 Northumberland Rd ℂ660
5270; fax 668 8679.
A spacious Victorian house with its own garden. Six rooms
with phones and TV, all en-suite. Child discount; cot available.
③

Mrs Cathy Cotter

Map 2, G5. Lansa House, 68 Merrion Rd ℂ668 0416; fax 660 0803.
A mock-Tudor house opposite the RDS. Four en-suite rooms
with TV and phone. Child discount and baby sitting. Totally
non-smoking. ④

Mr & Mrs Kane

Map 2, G5. 49 Beach Rd ℂ660 2969.
Right on the seashore in Sandymount. Five rooms, three of
them en-suite. Open all year. ②

Mrs M. Smyth

Map 2, G5. 21 Sandymount Rd ☎668 3602.
Quiet location close to the seafront. Four rooms with shared facilities. Open all year. ②

CLONTARF AND DRUMCONDRA

Mrs Nuala Betson

Map 2, G4. The Villa, 150 Howth Rd, Clontarf ☎ & fax 833 2377.
Comfortable detached house near the DART and a bus stop (#32, #32A, #31, #31B). Most rooms en-suite with TV. Child discount. ②

Mary Dunwoody

Map 2, G4. Eldar, 19 Copeland Ave, Clontarf ☎833 9091.
Semi-detached house in the vicinity of the Casino. Four rooms, two en-suite, the others with showers. Totally non-smoking. Open April–Oct. ②

Kathleen Hurney

Map 2, G4. 69 Hollybank Rd, Drumcondra ☎837 7907.
Four comfy rooms with TV, two of them en-suite. Near the bus stop for easy access to the centre. Child discount. Totally non-smoking. ②

Eugene & Ou Maguire

Map 2, G4. Griffith House, 125 Griffith Ave, Drumcondra ☎837 5030.
Detached house with a garden. Four bedrooms with TV, one en-suite. Child discount and babysitting. Non-smoking. ②

DALKEY AND KILLINEY

Mrs N. Carey

Map 7, G3. Ballincea Heights ©284 4750.
Located at one of the highest points in Killiney, yet bus #59 stops conveniently close. Three rooms, one of them en-suite. Open all year. ③

Mrs Margaret Jackson

Map 7, G3. Desmar, 15 Railway Rd ©285 8203.
Small B&B close to Dalkey DART station. Four rooms with shared bathrooms. Closed Nov–Feb. ④

DÚN LAOGHAIRE AND SANDYCOVE

Mrs Helen Callanan

Map 7, C3. 1 Rosmeen Gdns ©280 6083.
The first and one of the best of the many B&Bs off Summerill Road, midway between Dún Laoghaire and Sandycove and Glasthule DART stations. Four non-smoking rooms with TV, two of them en-suite. ②

Mrs Anne Dalton

Map 7, C3. Annesgrove, 28 Rosmeen Gdns ©280 9801.
Another recommended option, further down Dún Laoghaire's B&B street. Four rooms, two en-suite; no smoking. ②

Mrs Marie Dunne

Map 7, C3. 30 Rosmeen Gdns ©280 3972.
Three cosy rooms with shared facilities, also recommended. Open May–Sept. ②

Margaret Campbell

Map 8, H5. Highfield, Thormanby Rd ℘832 3936.
As its name suggests, up towards The Summit. Three rooms
with TV, two of them en-suite. Child discount; cot available.
②

Kitty Rickard

Map 8, H4. Gleann Na-Smol, Killrock Road, off Nashville Rd
℘832 2936.
Half a dozen rooms, mostly en-suite, at the bottom end of
Thormanby Road, within walking distance of the harbour. ②

HOSTELS

Hostels are busy all year – all the best ones are sure to be
full at weekends, so always book ahead. While there are
some fine hostels in great locations on the southside – near
Trinity or Christ Church for example – it pays to be
choosier on the northside. The majority are affiliated to
Independent Holiday Hostels (IHH), so Hostelling
International cards aren't required. Hot showers, luggage
rooms, payphones and TV lounges are standard; other facilities vary. The prices below refer to what one person will
pay (with seasonal fluctuations), and include bed linen and a
light breakfast unless stated otherwise.

CENTRAL

Abraham House

Map 5, J4. 82–83 Lower Gardiner St ℘855 0600; fax 855 0598.
A large, well-run hostel near the Busáras and Connolly Station;

bus #41 from the airport stops outside. Dorms sleeping 10 (£7–£10), 6–8 (£7.50–£10.50) or 4 (£9–£11.50) persons; double (£11–£13.50) and single (£13–£18) rooms. En-suite four-bed dorms (£11–£13) and doubles (£13–£15), too. Kitchen; laundry; bureau de change; secure parking. Open 24hrs all year.

Ashfield House

Map 4, E5. 19–20 D'Olier St ℗679 7734; fax 679 0852.

A good option near College Green and Temple Bar, just across the river from the Busáras. Spacious, clean and friendly. En-suite facilities throughout. Dorms sleeping 12 (£7.50–£10), 6 (£9–£11.50) or 4 (£11–£13) persons; double (£15–£18) and single (£17–£20) rooms. Kitchen; laundry. Open 24hrs all year.

Avalon House

Map 4, B8. 55 Aungier St ℗475 0001; fax 475 0303.

Housed in a red-brick Victorian medical school, 5min walk from St Stephen's Green, or 10min from Temple Bar. Friendly, but the rooms are cramped and noisy, and the shared bathrooms co-ed with showers that cut off every 30 seconds. Six-person dorms (£7.50–£10.50); double (£12–£14) and four-bed (£10–£12) rooms. No kitchen, but a good café. Open 24hrs.

Backpackers Citi Hostel

Map 5, J5. 61–62 Lower Gardiner St ℗855 0035.

A new, rather spartan hostel in a Georgian house near the Busáras and the river. The rooms are light and the kitchen is well-designed. Dorm beds (£6–£7) and doubles (£12.50) only. Breakfast not included. Open 24hrs all year.

Backpackers Euro Hostel

Map 5, J4. 80–81 Lower Gardiner St ⓒ836 4900.

The grungy prototype of the *Citi Hostel*, it has rooms (£15) with broken locks in the so-called *City Manor Guesthouse*, and horrible basement dorms (£7.50). However, the staff are nice, the kitchen is okay and the place may get a refit in the future. Breakfast not included. Open 24hrs all year.

Cardijn House (or Goin' My Way)

Map 5, I4. 15 Talbot St ⓒ878 8484.

Small, family run *IHH* hostel above a newsagents, close to O'Connell Street and the river. Twin rooms (£12–£13) and dorms sleeping 6 (£9–£10) or 8 (£7–£8). The ones at the back of the garden are vulnerable to thieves entering through the skylights. Kitchen. No lock out, but a midnight curfew. Closed over Christmas and New Year.

Dublin International Youth Hostel

Map 5, G2. 61 Mountjoy St ⓒ830 1766.

Way up near the Black Church and Upper Dorset Street (bus #41 from the airport), the northside headquarters of *An Óige* is a well-equipped 460-bed hostel in an ex-convent that's barricaded against the 'hood. *An Óige* or Hostelling International members pay £9.50 for a dorm bed; non-members £10, plus a £1.25 surcharge. To stay here, you must have or hire a sleeping sheet. Open all year.

Globetrotters Tourist Hotel

Map 5, J4. 46 Lower Gardiner St ⓒ873 5893; fax 878 8787.

Convenient for the Busáras and the airport bus, and within walking distance of the southside. The cosy, tasteful dorms sleep 6–12 people (£10–£14), with security-coded doors and individual bed lights for a peaceful night's sleep. Their breakfast is the best you'll get in any hostel in Dublin, and the decor and standards are a lot higher, too.

Kinlay House

Map 6, B5. 2–12 Lord Edward St ℃679 6644; fax 679 7437.
Cheerful *USIT* hostel near Christ Church Cathedral (bus #50, #54, #65 & #77). Generally fine, though some rooms suffer from traffic noise. Dorms sleeping 4–6 (£12–£13), some en suite (£12–£13); double rooms (£12.50–£13.50), en suite (£13–£14); and singles (£17.50–£18.50) without. Free towel and soap. Café; kitchen; bike hire; laundry (£5). Open 24hrs, all year.

Oliver St John Gogarty's

Map 6, F4. 18–21 Anglesea St ℃671 1822; fax 671 7637.
Comfy, stylish hostel next to the eponymous pub in the heart of Temple Bar. En-suite 6–10-bed dorms (£10–£14), quadruple (£11–£14), triple (£12–£15) and double (£14–£18) rooms, plus snazzy four-person rooftop apartments (£100) with kitchen, TV and washing machine. No communal facilities, alas.

Strollers Tourist Accommodation

Map 6, E5. 29 Eustace St ℃677 5614.
Another new place in Temple Bar, slightly less chic and without en-suite facilities, but with a café and a small rooftop garden. Their eight-bed dorms (£11), quadruple (£13) and double (£15) rooms cost the same all year.

DONNYBROOK

Morehampton House

Map 3, I8. 78 Morehampton Rd ℃668 8866; fax 668 8794.
A converted Victorian house in the embassy belt beyond the

HOSTELS: CENTRAL

Grand Canal, readily accessible by bus (#10, #46A or #46B from Trinity College; #46A from Dún Laoghaire). Dorms sleeping 12 (£6.95–£7.95), 8 (£8.95–£11.95) or 4–6 (£9.95–£12.95) persons; twin rooms (£11.50–£15); and larger family rooms for two (£16.50–£22.50) or three (£11–£15) adults, with the option of en-suite (£2 extra). Prices include towel and soap, but not breakfast. Open 24hrs. Garden; kitchen; laundry; bike hire.

DÚN LAOGHAIRE

The Old School House

Map 7, B3. Eblana Ave ©280 8777; fax 284 2266.

A converted Christian Brothers school in a backstreet off the seafront, 10min walk from the ferry terminal, and 20min ride from Dublin by DART. Friendly, clean and cosy. Dorms with 6 (£8–£9) or 4 (£8.50–£9.50) beds (with en-suite for £1.50 more), and double rooms (£11–£12). Kitchen; meals served; bike hire. Open 24hrs.

STUDENT ACCOMMODATION

As an alternative to staying in a hostel or B&B, you can rent **student accommodation** during the summer holiday (mid-June to mid Sept). The rooms are better set up for self-catering than hostels, with a camaraderie arising from the fact that so many of the guests are foreign students attending courses – which makes it imperative to book months ahead.

Trinity College

Map 4, E5. College Green ©608 1177; fax 671 1267.

Not cheap, but the setting is unique and utterly central. Singles (£28) with a shared kitchen and bathroom, or superior en-suite singles (£36) or four-bed rooms (£30) with a shared kitchen/lounge, in one of the many halls of residence on campus.

Trinity Hall

Map 2, F6. Dartry Rd, Rathmines ℗497 1772.

A pleasant hall of residence in grounds near the Botanical Gardens (bus #14 or #14A from Pearse Street near Trinity College). Single (£16) and double (£15) rooms with shared facilities, or en-suite (£25 per person). Sports facilities. Breakfast included.

UCD Village

Map 2, F5. Belfield ℗269 7111; fax 269 7704.

A complex of modern self-catering apartments on the UCD campus, about 5km south of the centre (bus #46), with single bedrooms at comparable rates to Trinity Hall's, plus a kitchen.

CAMPING

There are two **campsites** on the outskirts of Dublin, one in Clondalkin, the other between Killiney and Bray. Both are mainly aimed at caravaners, and relatively few backpackers use them for the simple reason that by the time you've taken fares into account it's unlikely to be any cheaper than staying in a hostel in Dublin – and involves far more effort.

Camac Valley Caravan and Camping Park

Map 2, A7. Corkagh Demesne, Clondalkin ℗462 0000; fax 462 0111.

On the southwest edge of Dublin, in a national park off the Naas road (bus #68 or #68A from town; 40min). An attractive setting and decent facilities. Campers pay £5 per tent plus £1 per person. Open all year.

CAMPING

Shankill Caravan and Camping Park

Map 1, E6. Off Dublin Rd, Shankill ℗282 0011.
South of Killiney, 16km from the centre; access by DART
(20min) and direct buses (#45, #45A, #46 or #84; 45min).
Campers pay £6 per tent plus £1 per person. Pitches can't be
booked in advance. Open all year.

EATING

Dublin may not be the gastronomic capital of the world, but the phenomenal expansion in the range of **places to eat** since the 1980s means that almost any taste is nowadays catered for. Dubliners are now far more sophisticated in their eating habits than a decade ago, creating a virtuous circle of rising expectations and standards that shows every sign of continuing.

Most restaurants, bistros and upmarket cafés offer a **lunchtime** set menu of two to four courses for about half the cost of their evening fare. Alternatively, you could see what pubs have to offer; carvery lunches, seafood, steaks, hearty Irish stew or nourishing soups (usually made from vegetables) are typical, but you can find more exotic dishes at trendier pubs around Temple Bar and Grafton Street.

While **dinner** offers the widest scope, you'd be wise to book a table if you're going to eat after 7.30pm, as the best places fill up fast. Prices in the evening are invariably higher than at lunchtime, whether you go for a set menu or *a la carte* – though quite a few establishments have an "early-bird menu" before 7pm, for less than you'd pay later on.

If all else fails, **fast-food** outlets are rarely far away. O'Connell Street has the highest concentration, with *McDonald's*, *Wimpy*, *Burger King* and *Pizzaland* as well as a branch of *Beshoff's*, Dublin's traditional fish-and-chips emporium. Another homegrown fast-food chain is *Abrakebabra*, a kebab eatery with outlets on the corner of Aston Quay and Westmoreland Street, by Merchant's Arch in Temple Bar, and at other locations around the city.

**If you'd prefer to make your own meals, see p.250
for details of the best places to buy food.**

In the listings below, **prices** are indicated by the terms "cheap" (under £5); "inexpensive" (£5–£10); "moderate" (£10–£20); "expensive" (£20–£30); and "very expensive" (over £30). For restaurants, these refer to the cost of a starter, main course and dessert for *one* person; it's harder to specify what this might cover in cafés, but basically a meal, however you define it. The cost of **drinks** is *not* included in these estimates. Beer rarely costs much more than you'd pay in a pub, but wine is a lot dearer than anywhere else in Europe, owing to the high tax levied by the government. On the plus side, few restaurants impose a **service charge** unless you're dining in a group of ten or more, so tipping is discretionary (but certainly expected). Places where there *is* a service charge for individuals are indicated in our listings, as are the few places that *won't* accept payment by **credit card**.

CAFÉS AND QUICK MEALS

The distinction between **cafés** and restaurants is often arbitrary, as many of the newer places that call themselves cafés are restaurants (or at least bistros) in all but name. This section is essentially a run-through of the best places to eat if what you want is a quick, unpretentious bite to eat – and includes a few fine pubs. All the places listed are in the centre of Dublin – the vast majority of them on the southside.

Beshoff's

Map 4, E4. 14 Westmoreland St. Daily 11am–3am.
Map 4, P3. 7 Upper O'Connell St. Daily 11am–3am. Cheap.

A Dublin institution, albeit not as grand as *Bewley's* (see below). Ivan Beshoff was a survivor from the mutiny on the battleship *Potemkin*, who settled in Ireland and opened a fish shop in Howth and then a café in Dublin, which his heirs turned into a chain of outlets with counter service and old-fashioned decor. The menu varies with the catch, but you can be sure of getting a plate of fresh fish and chips for £3. The O'Connell Street *Beshoff's* has a fine view from its upstairs windows.

Bewley's Oriental Cafés

Map 4, D7. 78 Grafton St: Sun–Thurs 8am–1am, Fri & Sat 7.30am–4am.
Map 4, D3. 11–12 Westmoreland St: Mon–Wed 7.30am–9pm, Thurs–Sat 7.30am–11pm, Sun 8.30am–9pm.
Map 4, C6. South Great George's St: Mon–Sat 7.30am–6pm (Thurs till 8pm). Cheap.

As integral to Dublin life as Guinness, *Bewley's* cafés have been a meeting place for Dubliners for generations. Founded by a Quaker family in 1840, they embody the ethos of the ordinary made sublime: hearty hot breakfasts and lunches, sticky buns and cakes, consumed on marble-topped tables in panelled rooms. The Grafton Street branch is embellished by Harry Clarke's *Birds of Paradise* window, a small theatre and a museum, and the Westmoreland Street *Bewley's* retains its original wooden pews. Owing to its late opening hours, the one on Grafton Street attracts clubbers and nightbirds; it's also a meeting place for chess players. Try the waitress-service section on the first floor for elegance and potted palms at much the same prices as downstairs.

CAFÉS AND QUICK MEALS

Billboard Café

Map 3, F7. 43 Lower Camden St.
Sun–Wed 7am–10.30pm, Thurs–Sat 24hrs. Inexpensive.

A friendly café whose all-night weekend opening hours attract clubbers from the *POD* and Gardaí from the Harcourt Street headquarters. They do Irish breakfasts all day, and have a jukebox for those who feel bereft of music once they've left the *POD*. A Dublin classic.

Blazing Salads II

Map 4, D7. Powerscourt Townhouse Centre, off Grafton St.
Mon–Sat 9am–6pm. Inexpensive.

Despite the excruciating pun, the food and setting are great. Its marvellous vegetarian menu includes dairy-, gluten- and sugar-free dishes, while the tables overlook the shopping centre's atrium, adapted from the courtyard of a Georgian mansion, where live music at lunchtime soothes shoppers and diners (see *Live music*) .

Leo Burdock's

Map 6, B6. Werburgh St.
Mon–Fri 12.30–11pm, Sat 2–11pm. Cheap.

Dublin's best loved fish-and-chippie, near Christ Church Cathedral. Though the coal-powered fryer has gone, everything else remains the same. Great nosh and cheerful service. Queues at lunchtime, after work and during pub hours. Carry-out only; no credit cards.

Café Auriga

Map 6, E4. Temple Bar Sq.
Mon–Sat noon–11pm. Moderate.

Chic café on two levels, with glass walls overlooking whatever's happening on the square outside. Light, modern food such as smoked salmon with mozzarella and roasted tomato, or curried cod with mash. A place for power lunches and romantic assignations.

Café-en-Seine

Map 4, E7. 40 Dawson St.
Daily 11am–11pm. Inexpensive.

The pub that revolutionized Dublin's pub scene, inspiring a host of imitators. A long elegant bar of *fin de siecle* design, with tables on the pavement outside. Serves coffee and pastries all day, carvery lunches, and a snack menu till 8pm. Their Sunday brunch (noon–5pm) features *oeufs Benedict* and other light French food, accompanied by live jazz (see p.218).

Café Java

Map 3, G5. 5 South Anne St Mon–Fri 7.45am–7pm (till 8pm Thurs), Sat 9am–6pm, Sun 10am–6pm.
Map 3, H8. 145 Leeson St Mon–Fri 8am–6pm, Sat 9am–5pm, Sun 11am–5pm. Cheap.

Popular breakfast, lunchtime and coffee stop, offering such light meals as poached eggs with bacon or chicken with yogurt. The coffees are as good as you'd expect from the food, and they serve wine, too.

Café Kylemore

Map 4, D3. O'Connell St/North Earl St.
Mon–Sat 8am–9pm, Sun noon–8pm. Cheap.

Kylemore is a chain of bakeries whose flagship café on the corner of O'Connell Street resembles a fusion of *Bewley's* and a motorway cafeteria, serving hot breakfasts all day and hearty lunches featuring chips with almost everything. To buttress the bistro-image purveyed by all the brass and bentwood chairs, they have a drinks licence.

Coffee Bean

Map 4, E6. 4 Nassau St.
Daily noon–11pm. Inexpensive.
Not a coffee shop, but a café popular with office workers and college students. The cooking is subtle and tasty, making use of produce from the shop downstairs, with a selection of vegetarian dishes as well as plenty of choice for carnivores. Customers have a good view over the wall into Trinity College, across the street.

Cornucopia

Map 6, G6. 19–21 Wicklow St.
Mon–Wed 9am–8pm, Thurs 9am–9pm, Fri & Sat 9am–10pm. Inexpensive.
A wholefood shop and café of long standing, somewhat eclipsed by newer places like *Juice*, but still well regarded by veggies. Their hot breakfast (till 11am) includes vegetarian sausages. You can enjoy a good lunch here for £5, but dinner costs more.

Fitzer's

Map 6, F4. Temple Bar Square: Mon–Sun noon–11.30pm.
Map 4, E7. 51 Dawson Street: Mon–Sat noon–4pm & 5.30 –11.30pm.
Map 4, H7. National Gallery: Mon–Sat 11am–5.30pm (Thurs till 8.30pm).
Map 2, F5. RDS: Mon–Sun noon–3pm & 6–11.30pm. Moderate.
A chain of cafés, each with an individual identity. The newest, in Temple Bar, has a cool high-tech design; Dawson Street's attracts a trendy crowd and has tables outside in the summer; while *Fitzer's* in Ballsbridge revels in the grandeur of the Royal Dublin Society dining rooms. The National Gallery branch is lacking in ambience, but the food is just as good. Menus change daily, so expect anything from calamari with pickled chillies to Cajun bean casserole. Lots of choice for vegetarians; sells alcohol.

CAFÉS AND QUICK MEALS

The Gotham Café

Map 4, D7. 5 South Anne St.

Tues–Sat 11am–midnight. Moderate.

Buzzy, child-friendly café specializing in Cal-Ital food. Does great pizzas, chargrilled chicken with peanut sauce, spicy prawn salad, and other yummy concoctions. You can enjoy lunch for under £10, and dinner for less than £15. Go for it.

The Irish Film Centre

Map 6, E4. 6 Eustace St.

Daily 11am–11pm. Inexpensive.

One of the coolest hangouts in Temple Bar. Its minimalist bar-restaurant is great for a lunchtime snack, or a full meal before the show. Serves bar food – including cakes and pastries – all day, and meals in the evening (Mon–Sat from 6pm). Plenty of vegetarian choice on an eclectic menu; vegetable pâtés, burgers, chicken, jambalaya with bananas all recommended (see *Drinking* and *Theatre & Cinema*) .

Juice

Map 4, C6. South Great George's St.

Daily 8am–2.30pm & 6.30–10.30pm. Inexpensive.

Juice is a chic vegetarian eating place with not a sweaty sandal in sight. Its imaginative macrobiotic food could be described as Californian or Pacific Rim; the drinks list features juices, lassis and organic wines.

Kilkenny Design Centre

Map 4, E6. First floor, 6 Nassau St.

Mon–Sat 9am–9pm (Thurs till 8pm). Inexpensive.

A popular eatery and coffee spot above one of Dublin's slickest shops (see p.249). Does carvery lunches, tangy salads, freshly

CAFÉS AND QUICK MEALS

baked pies and a different stew each day. Packed at lunchtime, so be prepared to queue (see *Shopping*).

Odessa

Map 6, F5. 13–14 Dame Ct.
Daily noon–midnight. Moderate.
Exotic snacks and outré decor make this one of the city's trendiest new cafés; downstairs is good for gossiping in big squashy sofas. Breakfast served noon–4pm. The lunch and dinner menus feature ceviche, tandoori chicken, marinated tofu and other dishes "for cosmopolitan palates". You can have lunch for less than £10. If you can't afford that, the nearby *Stag's Head* is recommended (see opposite).

Oliver St John Gogarty

Map 6, F4. 58–59 Fleet St.
Mon–Sat noon–10pm. Moderate.
The best-known tourist pub in Temple Bar, *Gogarty's* does pub lunches and an all-day bar menu, with a wider range of dishes on their second-floor restaurant (£8 minimum charge per person). Specializes in Irish cooking: prawns, oysters, salmon, spiced beef, steaks and rack of Wicklow lamb. Traditional music on the floor below from 9pm nightly.

Pasta Fresca

Map 4, D7. 3–4 Chatham St.
Mon–Sat 8am–11.30pm, Sun 12.30–8.30pm. Inexpensive.
Ireland's first fresh pasta shop when it opened a decade ago, *Pasta Fresca* still delights the ciabatta-loving classes. Its "restaurant" consists of a few tables and chairs in the window, serving fresh pasta and other Italian dishes, that's always busy at lunchtime.

CAFÉS AND QUICK MEALS

The Stag's Head

Map 6, F5. Dame Ct, off Dame St.
Mon–Fri 12.30–3.30pm & 5.30–7.30pm, Sat 12.30–2.30pm.
Cheap.

A mosaic of a stag's head on the pavement alerts you to the presence of this delightful Victorian pub, in an alley across the road from the Central Bank. Simple pub grub, cooked to perfection: Irish stew, ham and cabbage, roast spuds and chips. The hours above refer to when food is available; drinking hours are longer, naturally (see p.224).

Well Fed Café

Map 6, E4. Crow St.
Mon–Sat noon–9pm. Cheap.

A relic of the days when Temple Bar was "alternative" rather than mainstream, the *Well Fed Café* is a workers co-op run in tandem with a small shop selling cards, candles etc. Along the corridor between the two is a noticeboard for courses and events. The café is self-service and vegetarian, with shared tables. It does healthy, filling salads, soups and casseroles, plus a sinful chocolate cake with dollops of cream.

Winding Stair Café

Map 6, C3. 40 Lower Ormond Quay.
Mon–Sat 10.30am–6pm. Cheap.

A secondhand book emporium on three floors, linked by a staircase that inspired the bookshop's name (taken from a poem by Yeats). Their café has large windows overlooking the Ha'penny Bridge, with soups, salads, sandwiches and cakes that are good enough to stand on their own merits. A popular spot for lunch.

CAFÉS AND QUICK MEALS

RESTAURANTS

The majority of Dublin's restaurants are in the centre of the city (defined here as anywhere between the Grand and Royal canals, though almost all of them are on the southside), but the suburbs and seaside resorts also feature a selection of places (listed separately, by location). Wherever they're situated, it's always advisable to book in the evenings.

CENTRAL

Ayumi-Ya Japanese Steakhouse

Map 3, I7. 132 Lower Baggot St, ⌀622 0233.
Mon–Thurs 12.30–2.30pm & 6–11.30pm, Fri till 12.30am, Sat 6pm–12.30am. Moderate.

Authentic Japanese food at affordable prices, for homesick salarymen in Dublin's business quarter. The service is calm despite the rapid turnover. You can slurp down noodles (the best in town) at the counter, or take a table to savour the steaks (they do all kinds, including a vegetarian one). There's also a full sushi menu, and a wonderful take-away service in Bento boxes. Highly recommended.

Bad Ass Café

Map 6, F4. 9–11 Crown Alley ⌀679 5981.
Daily 11am–midnight (last orders 11pm). Inexpensive/Moderate.

Once deeply hip (Sinéad O'Connor was a waitress here), the *Bad Ass* is still popular with tourists and Dubliners on an evening out in Temple Bar. Snort at the puns on the menu while you work out what kind of pizza or pasta you fancy and see your order whizzed across the room by an overhead pulley. Sells alcohol.

Captain America's

Map 4, D7. 44 Grafton St ✆671 5266.

Mon–Sun noon–1am. Moderate.

Youthful, rock-themed burger joint with a full bar. Not *Planet Hollywood*, but they do boast a few items of rock memorabilia, and Chris de Burgh used to busk here before he became a star. Fun if you like that sort of thing, and fairly child-friendly.

Chameleon

Map 6, E4. 1 Lower Fownes St, ✆671 0362.

Wed–Sat 5.30–11pm, Sun 3–11pm. Moderate.

Temple Bar's only Indonesian restaurant, *Chameleon* is friendly and relaxed, with a family atmosphere. They do lots of vegetarian dishes, but carnivores can enjoy themselves, too. Their speciality is the *Rijsttaffel*, or Rice Table, a banquet of assorted dishes and dips (£10–£14).

Chez Jules

Map 4, E5. D'Olier Chambers, 16A D'Olier St ✆677 0499.

Mon–Fri noon–3pm & 5–11pm, Sat 1–11pm, Sun 1–10pm. Moderate.

Friendly, unpretentious French-style bistro with lots of seating for groups, close to *Ashfield House* hostel and Trinity College. They specialize in seafood and chargrilled steaks, but vegetarians can always find something decent on the menu. Good-value set lunches and early-evening meals (before 7pm).

The Cedar Tree

Map 4, D6. 11 St Andrew's St ✆677 2121.

Mon–Sat noon–5pm & 5.30–midnight, Sun noon–5pm & 5.30–11.30pm. Moderate.

Located in a cavernous basement off Suffolk Street, *The Cedar Tree* is equally good for a quiet lunch or a lively evening out. Its

RESTAURANTS: CENTRAL

dazzling array of meze dishes are best appreciated by a group of friends, with lots of wine to wash it down. Vegetarians love the diversity of dishes based on pulses and grains, that belies the notion that Middle Eastern cooking is all about kebabs.

Chicago Pizza Pie Factory

Map 4, D8. St Stephen's Green West ✆478 1233.
Mon–Sat noon–11.30pm. Moderate.
Another American-style place with rock associations: it stands on the site of the Dandelion Market, where U2 used to play before they made it big. Does tasty deep-pan fried pizzas. Youthful clientele. Full bar. Located next to the St Stephen's Green shopping centre.

Cooke's Café

Map 4, D6. 14 South William St ✆679 0536.
Mon–Sat 12.30–3.30pm & 6–11.30pm. Expensive.
Accomplished cooking in cool, terracotta surroundings. Very fashionable, very new wave. Expect to find anything from veal kidney sautéed in brandy to scallops in Noilly Prat. *Upstairs at Cooke's* now offers a cheaper way of sampling this delicious food, plus a range of salads and breads.

Da Pino

Map 6, C5. 38–40 Parliament St ✆671 9308.
Daily: noon–midnight (last orders 11.30pm). Inexpensive.
One of the best of the many Italian restaurants in Temple Bar. Italians come here to enjoy spaghetti carbonara, *zuppa di cipolla* and other classic dishes. The welcome is warm and the decor sympathetic. The restaurant possibly stands on the site of the *Eagle Tavern*, where the notorious Hellfire Club was founded.

Eastern Tandoori

Map 4, D6. 34–35 South William St ℡671 0506.
Mon–Sat 12.30–2.30pm & 6pm–midnight, Sun 6pm–midnight.
Moderate.

A comfortable, relaxed North Indian restaurant, with excellent food and service. The combination has proved such a winner that the Khan family has opened other *Eastern Tandooris* in Malahide and Cork city.

Elephant & Castle

Map 6, F3. 18 Temple Bar ℡679 3121.
Mon–Fri 8am–11.30pm, Sat 10.30am–midnight, Sun
12.30pm–midnight. Moderate.

A hit with Dubliners from the outset, its panache and informality has had a huge influence on the culinary scene in Temple Bar, and Dublin generally. Imagine a neighbourhood diner that just happens to be in the coolest part of town, and does gourmet burgers, breakfasts or late-night meals with a Cajun-Creole or Pacific Rim spin. Clubbers celebrate their hangovers with Sunday brunch at the *E&C*; on weekdays, you needn't feel ashamed of ordering the spicy chicken wings as a snack for two.

Gallagher's Boxty House

Map 6, F3. 20 Temple Bar ℡667 2762.
Mon–Sat noon–11.30pm. Moderate.

Though Dubliners slightly call it "GBH", many tourists love the jolly atmosphere and traditional Irish food. A *boxty* is a potato pancake cooked on a griddle, offered with a variety of meat and vegetable stuffings. *Coddle* is a thick stew of sausages, bacon, onions and potatoes. For a uniquely Irish dessert, try the brown bread ice-cream. *Gallagher's* is right next to the *Elephant & Castle*, an ironic juxtaposition of *ancien* and *nouvelle* Irish cooking.

Good World Restaurant

Map 4, C6. 18 South Great George's St ☏677 5373.
Daily: noon–3am. Moderate.

Sited near several pubs off Dame Street, its late hours ensure a boisterous clientele after closing time, and the reputation of its dim sum packs patrons by day. Dublin's Chinese community is divided on whether the *Good World* or the *Imperial* (see below) does better dim sum, but relishes putting both to the test. Come here early on a Sunday to get a place upstairs. Their standard menu is also admirable, with prices well below the *Imperial's*.

Imperial Chinese Restaurant

Map 6, G6. 12A Wicklow St ☏677 2580.
Daily noon–midnight. Expensive.

A large room buzzing with Chinese customers, who generally rate it the best restaurant in Dublin. Others, too, have discovered the joys of its superb dim sum (served 12.30–5pm), and a Sunday brunch at the *Imperial* rivals brunch at the *E&C* as a sociable experience. You can feed a whole family for £10. *A la carte* in the evening is dearer, but the ingredients and cooking are so fine that you won't complain.

Khan's Tandoori

Map 4, D7. 51 South King St ☏677 8408.
Mon–Thurs 12.30–3pm & 6pm–midnight, Fri & Sat till 1am, Sun 6pm–midnight. Moderate.

Beside the *Gaiety Theatre* off the top of Grafton Street, it attracts shoppers at lunchtime and pubbers in the evening. The Punjabi cuisine is authentic, and the staff are friendly and helpful.

Lord Edward Seafood Restaurant

Map 6, B5. 23 Christchurch Place ①454 2420.
Mon–Fri 12.30–2.30pm, Tues–Sat 6–10.45pm. Expensive.

Around the corner from *Leo Burdock's*, the legendary chippie, the *Lord Edward* represents the other end of the pescatorial scale. Dublin's oldest seafood restaurant, above a pub opposite Christ Church Cathedral, it is a venerable club-like institution dedicated to simple cooking with the very freshest fish, savoured by barristers. Lunches are half the price of dinners.

Marks Bros

Map 4, C6. 7 South Great George's St ①677 1085.
Tues–Sun 6–11pm. Moderate.

Long known as a daytime sandwich bar, *Marks Bros* has now become a vibrant vegetarian restaurant offering such dishes as wild mushroom risotto and ginger-coated tofu and vegetarian tempura, accompanied by a reasonably priced wine list. Recommended.

La Mezza Luna

Map 6, E4. 1 Temple Lane ①671 2840.
Mon–Fri 10am–11pm, Sat 10am–11.30pm, Sun 10am–10.30pm. Moderate.

Overlooking Dame Street, but entered from the lane around the corner, this popular and lively Italian restaurant does a variety of pizzas and pasta dishes, especially good value at lunchtime.

Milano

Map 4, E7. 61 Dawson St.
Daily noon–midnight. Moderate.

The first venture of the British *Pizza Express* chain in Ireland, *Milano* offers a familiar and affordable range of tasty pizzas and pastas in a ritzier setting than one associates with *Pizza Express*. Currently an "in" place to eat and be seen for the bright young things of Grafton Street. You can lunch here for under £10.

Mongolian Barbecue

Map 6, F4. 7 Anglesea St ℘670 4154.
Mon–Fri noon–3pm & 6.30–11pm, Sat noon–11pm, Sun 1–10pm.
Inexpensive.

On the strength of this cheery theme-restaurant, you can't help feeling that if the Mongols had eaten this well at home, they wouldn't have bothered to carve out an empire. All you can eat of noodle stir-fries, composed from a wide range of exotic ingredients and fried on the spot. Great value at lunchtime (£5.95; Sun £7.95) or in the evenings (£9.95), when you'll never get a table without booking.

Morel's Bistro

Map 4, F10. 14–17 Lower Leeson St ℘662 2480.
Mon–Fri 12.30–2.30pm & 6–10pm, Sat 6–10pm. Moderate.

Snazzy, eclectic bistro beneath the *Stephen's Hall Hotel*. The bright decor complements such zestful dishes as monkfish tempura with lime and coriander, or wood pigeon with roast shallots and crispy bacon. The service and wines are fine too. Children are also welcome; they even provide high chairs and colouring sets. There is another *Morel's* in Sandycove (see p.213).

Nico's

Map 6, E5. 53 Dame St ℘677 3062.
Mon–Fri 12.30–2.30pm & 6pm–12.30am, Sat 6pm–12.30am. Expensive.

A highly successful Italian restaurant popular with theatre-goers and courting couples. The food is good solid stuff like carbonara and risotto, but the real secret of its success is the atmosphere, enlivened by the dramatic flounces of the waiters, and piano music as the night wears on.

The Old Dublin

Map 3, E6. 90–91 Francis St ✆454 2028.
Mon–Fri 12.30–2.15pm & 7–11pm, Sat 7–11pm. Expensive.
Long established amid the antiques shops of the Liberties, *The Old Dublin* offers a hybrid of Irish, Scandinavian and Russian cuisine, with zestfully prepared dishes like coddle, gravadlax, borscht and blinis, that work well together. Early-bird menu before 8pm.

101 Talbot

Map 5, I5. 100–101 Talbot St ✆874 5011.
Mon 10am–3pm; Tues–Sat 10am–11pm. Moderate.
One of the very few good restaurants on the inner northside, conveniently close to the *Abbey Theatre*. Seedy Talbot Street is left behind as you climb the stairs to a lovely spacious dining room, as open to shoppers wanting a quick sandwich as families indulging in a leisurely brunch. Flavoursome dishes like mung bean and aubergine stew keep vegetarians coming back, and the service never falters. Lunch noon–3pm, dinner 6–11pm.

La Paloma

Map 6, F3. 17B Asdills Row ✆677 7392.
Daily noon–1am (last orders at midnight). Moderate.
A cosy, friendly Spanish restaurant just off the main drag in Temple Bar. Taped flamenco music, hot pink walls and a yellow ceiling contribute to the Iberian ambience, a stone's throw from the Liffey. Does good, cheap tapas noon–7pm, with pricier paellas and tortillas later on. Recommended.

RESTAURANTS: CENTRAL

Il Pasticcio

Map 6, E4. 12 Fownes St ©677 6111.
Mon–Thurs 12.30–11pm, Fri 12.30–11.30pm, Sun 2–10pm.
Moderate.
Small, lively Italian restaurant with contemporary art on the
walls. Their wood-baked pizzas are among the best in town,
their pasta rich and filling, and the salads and desserts delicious.
Like most places in Temple Bar, their lunchtime and early-bird
menus cost less than eating after 7pm.

Patrick Guilbaud

Map 3, I6. James Place East, off Lower Baggot St ©676 4192.
Tues–Sat 12.30–2.30pm & 7.30–10.15pm. Very expensive.
An elegant French restaurant that once stunned foodies with its
flair and prices, this modestly eponymous establishment still has
bags of cachet. Many critics hold Guilbaud's nouvelle cuisine to
be the best in Dublin. Overall a serious contender among the
culinary heavyweights – if not number one, for the *coup de gráce*
it delivers to your wallet.

Peacock Alley

Map 4, C6. 47 South William St ©662 0760.
Mon 6.30–11pm, Tues–Fri 12.30–2pm & 6.30–11pm, Sat
6.30–11pm. Very expensive.
Ultra-fashionable restaurant dedicated to "Mediterranean
Provincial" cuisine, on the same street as the Powerscourt
Townshouse (which has several good places to eat should you
decide that you can't afford the *Peacock*). Ravioli with lobster
and goat's cheese appears at lunch, while the evening menu
features rack of lamb with rosemary mashed potatoes, chicken
stuffed with organic greens, and other treats. Worth a serious
splurge.

Poco Loco

Map 6, C5. 32 Parliament St ℰ679 1950.
Mon–Sat 5pm–midnight. Moderate.
Small, lively Temple Bar bistro with hand-painted tables and other colourful touches, offering straightforward Tex-Mex interpretations of Mexican dishes that can be sampled in combination plates for £10 or less. Sometimes there's a guitarist as the night wears on.

The Rajdoot Tandoori

Map 4, D7. 26–28 Clarendon St ℰ679 4274.
Daily 1–2.30pm & 7.30–10pm. Moderate.
Despite being in the Westbury Mall off Grafton Street, and far plusher than other Indian restaurants, the *Rajdoot* keeps a keen eye on its rivals, so you'll be pleasantly surprised by the prices – especially at lunchtime. Lots of choice for vegetarians, and excellent service. The only drawback is the limited opening hours.

The Shalimar

Map 4, C6. 17 South Great George's St ℰ671 0738.
Mon–Thurs noon–2.30pm & 6pm–midnight, Fri & Sat till 1am, Sun 6pm–midnight. Moderate.
A long-established rival of the *Rajdoot*'s that's recently opened a Balti House in its basement. You can choose between tandooris, biryanis and other classic Punjabi dishes, or a simpler keema or kofta downstairs – both with lots of options for vegetarians. Always busy, but especially as the pubs close.

South Street Pizzeria

Map 4, C6. South Great George's St.
Daily 11am–1am. Moderate.
Sited across the road from Exchequer Street, the *South Street Pizzeria* is one of the most popular hangouts on a street noted

RESTAURANTS: CENTRAL

for its pubs and restaurants. Relaxed and friendly atmosphere, smashing pizzas, a wine bar and cheap lunchtime specials. What more could you ask for?

Tante Zoe's

Map 6, E4. 1 Crow St ⚹679 4407.
Mon–Sat noon–3pm & 6pm–midnight, Sun 6pm–midnight. Moderate.
The first Cajun/Creole restaurant to open in Temple Bar, it remains popular for continuing to serve decent food at affordable prices and managing to be fun. Go for the inexpensive lunchtime or early-bird menu and you won't regret it; not all of the main dishes are winners.

The Tea Rooms

Map 6, D4. The Clarence Hotel, 6–8 Wellington Quay ⚹670 7766.
Mon–Fri 12.30–2.30pm & 6.30–10.30pm, Sat 6.30–11.30pm, Sun 6.30–10pm. Expensive.
Dublin's most stylish hotel, *The Clarence* (see p.171), has a fabulous restaurant that's one of the coolest places to be seen in town. Its stunning design provides a perfect foil to the eclectic menu, offering ten different starters and a dozen main courses, from Thai soup to steamed cod with aubergine blinis. Though the atmosphere isn't hidebound, you'll feel a prat if you don't dress up a bit, and it's considered deeply uncool to gawk at U2 (who own the hotel) or any star guests that breeze in. Worth a splurge.

Thunder Road Café

Map 6, F4. Temple Bar ⚹679 4057.
Daily noon–midnight (Thurs–Sat till 12.30am). Moderate.
Temple Bar's version of the *Hard Rock Café*: burgers, nachos and other American grub, served amid a cacophony of loud music, video screens, dancing customers and singing waiters. As an

indication of the image they aspire to, the no-parking sign outside makes an exception for Harley Davidsons. In reality, more weenyboppers than bikers, but what the hell. Teenagers love it.

Tosca

Map 6, G5. 20 Suffolk St ✆679 6744.
Daily 12.30–3.30pm & 6.30–11pm. Moderate.
Located between Grafton Street and the Dublin Tourism Centre, this modernist temple to southern European food and wine has won over those who expected to see its owner, Norman Hewson (brother of U2's Bono), fall flat on his face. Aside from its cool halogen spot-lit interior, *Tosca* is known for its zestful salads and pastas, with lots of choices for vegetarians. The menu changes daily, and the wine list is imposing. Though quite laidback at lunchtime, it gets very busy at night.

Trocadero

Map 6, F5. 3 St Andrew St ✆677 5545.
Mon–Sat 6pm–midnight, Sun 6–11.30pm. Expensive.
Looks like an obnoxiously rich trattoria, but in fact is pleasant, friendly and has excellent food. One of Dublin's oldest Italian restaurants, its walls are hung with plaudits in the form of signed photographs of visiting showbiz luminaries. The place comes into its own late at night when it fills up with theatre folk. There's an early-bird menu for those who'd rather save money than socialize.

Unicorn

Map 4, F8. Merrion Court, off Merrion Row ✆676 2182.
Mon–Thurs 12.30–3pm & 6–11pm, Fri & Sat till midnight. Expensive.
This Italian haunt of *bien pensant* media folk and politicos was run for decades by the Sidoli family. Following the trauma of a change of ownership, its regulars are happy to find that the

RESTAURANTS: CENTRAL

trattoria fare and plain, no-nonsense interior haven't altered, and their interactions still make the *Unicorn* what it is – a Dublin institution. The other hangout that counts in this world is *Doheny and Nesbitt's* pub, across Lower Baggot Street (see p.219).

Le Vigneron

Map 6, F4. 6 Cope St ℂ671 5740.
Mon–Sun 12.30–11pm. Moderate.

Archetypal French restaurant and bistro in Temple Bar. Its food – from several regional traditions – is rather unpredictable, and the real attraction is its wine list – one of the best in Dublin – with over 100 French wines, many of which are available by the glass. The bistro downstairs is livelier and cheaper than the restaurant.

Yamamori Noodles

Map 4, C6. 71–72 South Great Georges St ℂ475 5001.
Mon–Wed 12.30–2.30pm & 5.30–11pm, Thurs & Fri till 11.30pm, Sat 12.30am–11.30pm, Sun 5–11pm. Moderate.

Trendy, fun Japanese restaurant in the heart of publand, more conveniently located than the *Ayumi-Ya* on Baggot Street. Delicious noodles, teriyaki, tempura, sushi and sashimi. You can eat well at lunch for under £10; in the evenings you must get there early (or book) to stand any chance of getting a table.

BALLSBRIDGE

Chandni

Map 3, J7. 174 Pembroke Rd ℂ668 1458.
Mon–Sat 12.30–2.30pm & 6–11.30pm, Fri & Sat till midnight. Moderate.

A comfortable and sophisticated Indian restaurant that caters to a similar clientele. The cooking isn't so adventurous, but it rarely disappoints. To spice things up, from time to time the *Chandni* features an Indian dancer.

RESTAURANTS: BALLSBRIDGE

Lobster Pot Restaurant

Map 3, J8. 9 Ballsbridge Terrace ✆668 0025.
Mon–Fri 12.30–3pm & 6–10.30pm, Sat 6–10.30pm. Expensive.
A cosy haven for seafood lovers, serving sumptuous bisques and the catch of the day with lashings of wine and cream. For something less rich, the *Marrakesh* and *Roly's Bistro* are next door. (Bus #5, #7, #7A, #8 or #45 from College Green or Merrion Square North.)

Marrakesh

Map 3, J8. 11 Ballsbridge Terrace ✆660 5539.
Daily noon–2.30pm & 6–11pm (Fri & Sat till 11.30pm). Moderate.
Dublin's only Moroccan restaurant, the *Marrakesh* is a quiet upstairs venue for savouring real *harira* soup, pigeon and almond pie, couscous, and other specialities. For a serious feast, go for the *mechoui* or saddle of lamb (which must be ordered in advance) and a spread of mezes. Don't miss the desserts, either; try the *beghrir* with a sauce of honey, orange and butter.

Roly's Bistro

Map 3, J8. 7 Ballsbridge Terrace ✆668 2611.
Daily noon–3pm & 6–10pm, Fri & Sat till 10.30pm. Moderate.
Roly's appeals to power-lunchers and residents of Ballsbridge alike, by providing adventurous bistro cooking at a reasonable price, in a stylish yet relaxed setting. Try the fricassee of prawns with vanilla sauce, or salmon trout with saffron and fennel sauce.

BRAY

Orchard Court

Map 1, F6. 36 Main St ✆286 3347.
Daily 12.30–3pm & 6–11pm. Moderate.
A decent high-street Chinese restaurant, offering Cantonese, Sichuan and Pekinese cuisine. You can find Main Street by

RESTAURANTS: BRAY

bearing inland from the DART station along Quinsborough Road.

Tree of Idleness

Map 1, F6. The Strand ✆286 3498.

Tues–Sat 7.30–11pm, Sun 7.30–10pm. Moderate/Expensive.

An award-winning Greek-Cypriot restaurant on the seafront, serving the freshest seafood, wonderful moussaka and suckling pig, accompanied by a great wine list and excellent service. You can enjoy a four-course *table d'hote* menu for £20 or less, but the 10-percent service charge could well push the final bill closer to £25 or £30. What the hell. People travel right out from Dublin to dine here.

DALKEY

Guinea Pig Fish Restaurant

Map 7, G3. Railway Rd ✆285 9055.

Daily 6pm–midnight. Expensive.

Just downhill from the DART station, en route to Dalkey's high street, this little award-winning seafood restaurant offers a five-course meal of asparagus, salmon, crab, seafood chowder and dessert for £25. You'll pay well over £30 going *a la carte*, so it's certainly a tempting deal.

P.D.'s Woodhouse

Map 7, G2. 1 Coliemore Rd ✆284 9399.

Mon–Sat 6–11pm, Sun 1–9.30pm. Expensive.

A pub-like restaurant that's currently cool in Dalkey, with garden tables for those balmy summer days. Char-grilled steaks are a speciality; the kebabs, seafood, baked potatoes and crunchy salads are also fine. £10 minimum charge after 7pm.

BLACKROCK, DÚN LAOGHAIRE & SANDYCOVE

Ayumi-Ya

Map 2, G6. Newpark Centre, Newtownpark Ave, Blackrock
©283 1767.
Mon–Sat 6–11.30pm, Sun 5.30–9.45pm. Moderate.

It's worth a trip to neighbouring Blackrock to sample the
delights of this more formal version of the *Ayumi-Ya Japanese
Steakhouse* in the city centre. Excellent sashimi, tempura, noodles
and grilled or ginger-cured salmon. The teppan-yaki tables are
for serving a special menu that's cooked before your eyes. You
can get there from Dún Laoghaire by DART (to Blackrock
station, then bus #114 to the Newpark Centre) or bus #45 (to
the corner of Stradbrook Road and Newtownpark Avenue).

Brasserie na Mara

Map 7, B3. The Harbour, Dún Laoghaire ©280 0509.
Mon–Sat 1–2.30pm & 7–10.15pm. Expensive.

A successful venture into restauranting by Irish Railways, in the
former station buffet uphill from the ferry terminal. Giant
drapes and mirrors create a stylish setting to enjoy Adrian
Spellman's cooking. Try the deep-fried hake in a tortilla crust,
or the rilette of duck and foie gras. The set dinner costs less
than £20, but you can easily surpass that dining *a la carte*.

Morel's Bistro

Map 7, D3. 18 Glasthule Rd, Sandycove ©230 0210.
Mon–Sat 6–10pm, Sun 12.30–2.30pm & 6–10pm. Moderate.

Morel's in Sandycove proved so popular that it soon spawned an
offshoot in the city centre. The cooking is modern, but not
eclectic: blue shark on a bed of spinach, roast lamb with basil mash,
and marinated salmon with mustard sauce are typical offerings. Try
finishing off with a chocolate terrine in espresso sauce.

Odell's

Map 7, D3. 49 Sandycove Rd ℂ284 2188.

Mon–Sat 6–10.30pm, Sun 6–9.30pm. Moderate.

Sadly only open in the evenings, this friendly bistro is noted for its generous helpings of Cajun dishes given a Mediterranean workover or a pinch of Chinese spicing. Check out the early-bird menu.

HOWTH

Adrian's

Map 8, G3. 8 Abbey St ℂ839 1696.

Mon–Sat 12.30–3.30pm & 6–9.30pm, Sun 6–8pm. Moderate.

Just uphill from Harbour Road in a converted house painted to resemble a giant aquarium. The food is as playful as the exterior, ranging from a chowder snappy spliced with whiskey to a curried chicken garnished with fried banana. There are some nice dishes for vegetarians, too.

Casa Pasta

Map 8, G3. 12 Harbour Rd ℂ839 3828.

Mon–Sat 6pm–midnight, Sun 1–11pm. Moderate.

A big success since it opened in 1993; the views of the harbour are only partly to credit, as the Italian cooking is great. Pasta with shrimps, fetuccine with pesto, spicy chicken wings and deep-fried brie are only some of the treats on offer.

El Paso

Map 8, G3. 10 Harbour Rd ℂ832 3334.

Mon–Fri 6–11pm, Sat 1–11pm, Sun 2–11pm. Moderate.

Though it seems a bit incongruous to find a Tex-Mex Steakhouse on the seafront of a fishing town, the *El Paso* is the Real McCoy for delicious steaks, nachos, tortillas and all the rest (including vegetarian dishes), with a special afternoon menu on Sat (1–6pm) & Sun (2–6pm).

King Sitric's Fish Restaurant

Map 8, H3. East Pier, ✆832 5235.
Mon–Sat 6.30–11pm. Expensive.
Howth's equivalent of the *Lord Edward* in Dublin, the *King Sitric* is a fine, old-fashioned seafood restaurant whose ingredients are landed at the pier nearby. Don't expect exotic sauces or vegetables, just the fruits of the sea, perfectly cooked and presented.

DRINKING

"Good puzzle would be cross Dublin without passing a pub"
— James Joyce, *Ulysses*

Dubliners boast, with ample justification, that the best **pubs** in the world are to be found in their city. The public house stands at the very centre of Irish social life, and any visitor seeking the "craic" for which Dublin nightlife is so famous should have little trouble tracking it down in one of the city's hundreds of pubs and bars.

In general, pubs are open from 11.00am to 11.00pm during the winter months, and until 11.30pm in the summer, but in recent years some flexibility has been introduced into Ireland's arcane licensing laws and it is increasingly common for city-centre pubs to keep serving until well after midnight.

All pubs serve draught beers in units of pint and half-pint (the latter is invariably referred to as "a glass"), with pride of place being reserved for the city's most famous tipple, Guinness, which really does taste infinitely superior in its hometown, where it's always granted the requisite seven minutes settling time, however busy the barman or thirsty the customer. You'll also find Irish whiskey like Paddy's,

Powers and Jameson's, as well as a variety of other spirits and, depending on the premises, a wide range of the imported bottled beers, "alcopops" and wines.

The economic boom which Dublin has enjoyed of late has had some negative consequences for the city's pub culture. A trend towards "quaintification" has seen many modest old pubs gutted and refitted with bulk-purchased turf baskets, moth-eaten books and blackened fire-irons, and practically every fortnight another soulless pastiche opens in Temple Bar or the Grafton Street area, quickly to be colonized by tourists, stag parties and pickpockets. Nevertheless, there are many genuinely historic licensed premises still trading in more or less the same condition that Joyce's hero Leopold Bloom would have found them in 1904.

In recent years these traditional pubs have been joined by a huge array of more youth-orientated and cosmopolitan bars. The new and old co-exist quite happily and the compact nature of the city centre means that you can find yourself careening between a succession of nicotine-stained Victorian snugs and ultra-hip designer watering-holes in the course of a single riotous evening.

The Brazen Head

Map 3, E5. 20 Lower Bridge St.
Below Christ Church and just across the river from the Four Courts stands the pub which is a leading contender for the impressive title "oldest pub in Europe". There has been a tavern on the site of the *Brazen Head* since Viking times, and it is said to be haunted by the ghost of one of Ireland's greatest martyred patriots, Robert Emmet. Impromptu Irish traditional "sessions" are encouraged here, attracting fiddlers, whistlers, *sean-nós* singers and Irish music fans from far and wide.

Café-en-Seine

Map 4, E7. 40 Dawson St.

This swanky, high-ceilinged enormo-pub is where thrusting young professionals come to ogle haughty teenage models. The raised benches that line its walls make it an ideal location for people-watching, talent-spotting and gossip-causing. Good coffee and sandwiches at lunchtime (see p.193).

The Chocolate Bar

Map 4, D10. Harcourt St.

Nestling in the armpit of Dublin's hippest nightclub, this Gaudi-inspired watering hole is where Dublin's truly trendy young things congregate to swig alcopops and imported bottle beers before swaggering around to the club. Mean cocktails and wonderful sink-into sofas.

The Clarence Hotel

Map 6, D4. Wellington Quay.

The Clarence was bought some years ago by U2 and modernized at vast expense – its wood-panelled octagon-shaped public bar is the very epitome of studied cool, eerily illuminated by artificial daylight however late the hour. If you're lucky, you may spot a star guest who's wandered down from the £1450-a-night penthouse suite for a nightcap and a bit of company.

Davy Byrne's

Map 4, D6. 21 Duke St.

Davy Byrne's "moral pub" receives a particularly honourable mention in Joyce's epic novel as the place where Leopold Bloom takes a break from his famous perambulation across Dublin for a Gorgonzola sandwich and a glass of burgundy. It's been extensively redecorated over the years, so little of its 1904 ambience remains, but it's still a popular place of resort for both natives and visitors. Food's still OK, too.

The Dockers

Map 3, J4. 5 Sir John Rogerson's Quay.

Rock fans from around the world make pilgrimage to this cosy establishment, located on the somewhat dilapidated quays east of the centre, just around the corner from the original site of Windmill Studios, where U2 recorded their early albums. Although the studio itself has now moved, Bono and the boys are still known to drop by for the occasional pint between tours.

Doheny and Nesbitt

Map 4, G9. 5 Lower Baggot St.

This tiny, atmospheric, smoke-filled room looks as if it's hardly changed since the beginning of the century. Its cosy snugs are frequently packed with *Irish Times* hacks, but if you can't stand the pace here, there's a slightly less hectic lounge upstairs.

The Front Lounge

Map 6, C4. Parliament St.

One of Temple Bar's runaway success stories, this enormous and airy bar has been thronged since the day its doors first opened a couple of years ago. The designer watering hole of choice for arty Dubliners, gay and straight alike. Comfortable sofas, highly ironic decor and good coffee. As New York as Dublin pubs get.

The Globe

Map 4, C6. 11 South Great George's St.

Outrageously popular with the sassy and fashion-conscious youth of Dublin, this loud and lively bar is invariably packed at weekends, and busy every night. It is pleasantly dark-wooded and discreetly lit, wih an upbeat, sociable atmosphere that makes it a perfect prequel to a night's clubbing.

Grogan's

Map 4, D6. 15 South William St.
Young literary and artistic types are to be found slouching on the comfortable benches of this eccentric establishment. Works by well-known local artists hang on the walls and from the ceiling, and a new generation of impoverished painters, sculptors and poets nurse slowly sipped pints while awaiting discovery, dreaming perhaps of one day being added to the fantastic stained glass celebration of famous *Grogan's* regulars from the past.

Hartigan's

Map 4, F10. 100 Lower Leeson St.
As featured by Ireland's comic genius Flann O'Brien in *At-Swim-Two-Birds*, and latterly the stomping ground of students from the nearby medical schools of UCD and College of Surgeons, this spartan bar has made few concessions to the passage of time or modern notions of comfort. But what it lacks in decor and seating is more than made up for in history and attitude. And, given the good-natured riotousness that frequently erupts (especially after college rugby matches), the lack of breakable furniture is perhaps understandable.

Hogan's

Map 4, C6. 35 South Great George's St.
Another favoured haunt of the city's bright young things, this large and extremely busy bar is not for those seeking a quiet contemplative drink. The volume of the eclectic music mix often renders meaningful conversation well-nigh impossible, but the excitable crowd that throng this lively joint seem to manage more than adequately with sign language and knowing looks.

Hughes's

Map 5, E6. 19 Chancery St.

The local for habitués of the neighbouring Four Courts, this venerable establishment quenches the thirst of barristers, litigants, and Guards (as the police force, officially the Gardaí, are generally known) without fear or favour. In the evening it hosts excellent traditional music sessions.

The International Bar

Map 6, G6. 23 Wicklow St.

On three compact floors, this charming and civilized old pub is an unspoilt gem within a stone's throw of Grafton Street. The magnificent carved shelving behind the ground floor bar are worth a visit alone, and the gently reclining red velour seats support the bottoms of both ordinary Dubliners and the comedians, songwriters and musicians who perform in the tiny and informal venue upstairs.

The Irish Film Centre

Map 6, E4. 6 Eustace St.

Another oasis of calm in the commercial storm: the narrow passageway entrance opens up into a hidden architectural marvel, an ancient courtyard now covered and converted into a room three storeys high. Spacious and cultured, this is a pleasant spot for a pint and a cappuccino at any hour of the night or day, and film buffs can browse the specialist bookshop or view cult movies in the adjoining cinema (see p.239).

Keogh's

Map 4, D7. South Anne St.

Until just last year the family whose name adorns this wonderful old establishment lived upstairs, reputedly the last resident publicans in the city centre. To the collective relief of Dublin's more discerning drinkers, the new owners have scarcely touched the wonderful mahogany interiors, and there are few happier places to be than in the innermost seat of the tiny snug, a pint settling on the table in front of you, discussing life with new-found best friends.

McDaid's

Map 4, D7. Harry St.
One of Dublin's best known literary pubs, this small, high-ceilinged bar boasts the dubious distinction of having been the preferred watering-hole of Ireland's most famously dipsomaniac writer, Brendan Behan. It remains more-or-less intact, and is highly popular with locals and visitors alike.

Mulligan's

Map 4, E4. 8 Poolbeg St.
This establishment is generally accepted to be the home of "the best pint in Dublin", an accolade which alone justifies a visit to its low-ceilinged premises. A favoured haunt of print workers and journalists, this no-nonsense two-room bar is the genuine article, unaffected by either fashion or prosperity.

O'Donoghues

Map 4, F8. 15 Merrion Row.
One of Dublin's most famous musical pubs where many of Ireland's foremost traditional and folk groups (the Chieftains and the Dubliners, to name but two) began their musical careers squashed in together at the window seat. The sessions are as energetic as ever, and as popular – if you want a good seat get there early.

DRINKING

O'Neill's

Map 6, G5. 2 Suffolk St.

A series of interconnecting rooms knocked together, this large pub has been a home from home for generations of students and lecturers from nearby Trinity College. Also much favoured by office workers as a lunching spot, who come for the healthy portions of buffet food and sandwiches served.

The Palace Bar

Map 6, G3. 21 Fleet St.

An elegant and sociable outpost of Old Dublin on the eastern boundary of Temple Bar, this handsome bar attracts a mixed crowd of drinkers drawn in by the quality of the pint and the relative tranquillity of its ambience in comparison to the surrounding piped-music tourist-traps.

The Porter House

Map 6, C4. 16 Parliament St.

Opened just last year, Dublin's first microbrewery serves a wide selection of its excellent and playfully monikered own-brand beers on three busy floors, attracting both curious locals and visitors enticed by the bright, bustling interior and enormous vats visible from the street.

Ryan's

Map 5, A6. 28 Parkgate St.

Situated near the entrance to the Phoenix Park, this stately establishment can fairly claim to be the president of Ireland's local. The quality of its Guinness is legendary, and its regulars hotly dispute the claim of *Mulligan's* of Poolbeg Street to the city's finest pint. The sensitive and notoriously travel-sickness-prone liquid, they triumphantly point out, has by far the shorter distance to travel to reach *Ryan's*, the St James Street Brewery being a mere river-breadth away.

The Shelbourne Hotel

Map 4, F8. St Stephen's Green.
The Horseshoe Bar in the magnificent *Shelbourne Hotel* is the place where politicians, gossip columnists, solicitors and advertising executives repair every Friday evening to flirt, swagger and carve up the world. The back bar attracts a somewhat younger crowd of suit-wearers and mobile-phone-owners, while the more civilized drawing room provides a welcome respite from the vicious gossip and the crowds.

Slattery's

Map 5, F6. 129 Capel St.
This cheery and unpretentious pub has been hosting excellent traditional music sessions for many years, and is well worth the short walk across Capel Street Bridge away from the more self-conscious establishments that proliferate in the Parliament Street area. This is where real Dubs come to hear their ballads.

The Stag's Head

Map 6, E5. 1 Dame Court.
One of Dublin's prettiest old bars, favoured by students and workers alike. Its dark woods and stuffed fauna evoke the ambience of a slightly scruffy hunting lodge. Extremely lively at weekends when the crowds overflow out onto the pavements, eventually turning the narrow street into a traffic-impassable beer garden. Great pub grub too (see p.197).

DRINKING

Thomas Read's

Map 6, D5. 1 Parliament St.

Actually two bars knocked into one, this lively establishment serves a globe-spanning selection of bottled and draught beers to its young-ish regulars. By day, its large windows and strategic location on the corner of Parliament and Dame streets, just opposite Dublin Castle, make it the perfect place to while away a few hours watching the city flow by outside, keeping your strength up by sampling its excellent array of food, coffee and cakes.

Toners

Map 4, G9. 139 Lower Baggot St.

This Victorian bar, just across the road from *Dohney and Nesbitt,* is one of Dublin's finest. Dark and cosy with a refreshingly plain exterior, its snugs and glazed partitions are perfect for making and breaking confidences.

LIVE MUSIC AND CLUBS

The international success of artists like Sinéad O'Connor, Hothouse Flowers and, particularly, U2 has created a huge boom in the Irish **music** industry, and Dublin can fairly claim to be Europe's Second City of Rock after London. The capital's proximity to London, and its reputation as a music-friendly town, means that most international rock, pop and country acts include a Dublin date on their tours, and the vibrant local music scene throws up a seemingly inexhaustible supply of young guns. Any night of the week you'll find a wide variety of music listed in the pages of magazines like the iconoclastic *Hot Press*, the lively *In Dublin* and the excellent and widely available freesheet *Dublin Event Guide*. For larger shows, you may need to book in advance – the ticket shop at HMV on Grafton Street is your best bet. At smaller venues you can generally pay at the door; prices vary from about £5 to £15 depending on the act.

Some of the best Irish traditional music can be heard for nothing at the informal sessions that take place in various pubs (see *Drinking*).

For many years Dublin's **club** scene comprised a cluster of cramped, expensive and mostly unlicensed basements on Leeson Street. "The Strip", as the Leeson Street clubs are collectively known, still exists to snare the unwary. These days, however, there are many better options for those looking to keep the night alive. After a somewhat late start, club culture has now arrived in Dublin with a vengeance. Venues crop up or disappear so rapidly that the only way to find the hottest draws is to pick up one of the listings mags. The places we've listed are the pick of the durable clubs. Expect to pay anything from £5 to £12 for entrance, depending on the coolness of the club and the reputation of the DJ.

Many of Dublin's pubs and live music venues morph into clubs on selected nights, notably the *Mean Fiddler*, *Whelans*, the *Music Centre*, the *Irish Film Centre* and the *DA Club*.

The **classical music** scene in Dublin isn't too hot, but the RTE Symphony Orchestra gives regular performances at the National Concert Hall in Earlsfort Terrace (℗671 1533), the main venue for classical concerts. In addition, concerts are often held in Powerscourt Townhouse, the Bank of Ireland in Foster Place, the RDS in Ballsbridge and at the Municipal Gallery of Modern Art on Parnell Square. Operas are performed at *The Gaiety Theatre* on South King Street twice yearly and both St Patrick's and Christ Church cathedrals host organ recitals, while lunchtime performances can be heard at St Ann's on Dawson Street and the St Stephen's on Mount Street. Choral and organ recitals are given occasionally at Trinity and UCD, and you can hear the best of the city's students at the schools of music in Chatham Street and Westland Row.

LIVE MUSIC VENUES

Bad Bob's

Map 6, D4. 35-37 East Essex St ℂ677 5482.

This well-run and popular establishment models itself on an American honky-tonk, with a small stage and a large central bar. It specializes in bringing country music to its thirty-something clientele, and you can see both local and international artists perform here seven nights a week.

The DA Club

Map 3, I2. 3-5 Clarendon Market, off North William St ℂ671 1130.

The small but perfectly formed *DA Club* hosts a variety of musical styles on its two floors. Its adventurous booking policy means that some of Dublin's hottest young talent can be found strutting their stuff on the extremely tiny stage, and serenading you through the surprisingly sophisticated sound system.

Eamon Doran's

Map 6, E4. 3A Crown Alley ℂ679 9114.

A large, rather soulless joint, but young bands can be heard here most nights, often two or three per evening. You're unlikely to have heard of any of them before, and with an occasional honourable exception, you're unlikely to hear of them again. Still, if you can deal with the wildly varying standards of the performers, the venue itself is clean and the crowd are out for a good time.

The Furnace

Map 6, G3. 2 Aston Place ℂ671 0088.

As you might expect of a venue run by the Union of Students in Ireland, the beer in this mid-sized venue is cheap and the often quite well-known bands booked tend to be at the noisier and more youth-orientated end of the spectrum. Good spirits and plastic glasses abound.

The International Bar

Map 6, G6. 23 Wicklow St ⟨⟩677 9250.

For those who want to spot the next great Dublin songwriter taking his or her first faltering steps towards superstardom, every Tuesday young hopefuls come out to play a song or two at the unamplified Songwriter's Night in the minuscule room upstairs at *The International Bar* - don't even whisper during songs, no matter how woeful – with up to twenty performers per night, there'll be somebody better along in a minute.

The Mean Fiddler

Map 4, C9. 26 Wexford St ⟨⟩475 8555.

This trendy, 800-capacity venue with a seriously cool interior is part of the London's *Mean Fiddler* chain, and many burgeoning international acts touring their UK halls are routinely booked for a date here. Excellent sightlines and sound system.

The Music Centre

Map 6, E4. Curved St, Temple Bar ⟨⟩679 0533/4.

This is one of the jewels in Temple Bar's crown – a custom-built facility whose amenities include an impeccable, if slightly antiseptic venue for audiences of up to 650. The bar area outside also features frequent free shows by burgeoning songwriters.

The National Stadium

Map 3, 8E. South Circular Rd ⟨⟩453 3371.

Frequently used medium-sized venue holding between 1000 and 2000 people, depending on whether or not the seats are taken out. As you'd expect of an ageing hall designed primarily to host boxing matches, the facilities for audiences are fairly spartan, but the excellent sightlines and acoustics compensate.

LIVE MUSIC VENUES

Olympia Theatre

Map 6, D5. 72 Dame St ☎677 7744.

This wonderful old Victorian theatre is frequently used for live music - quieter and more established international and Irish acts tend to play early-evening sets, with late-night gigs reserved for more good-time performers to entertain the audience drawn in by the promise of the theatre's late alcohol licence (see p.237).

Point Theatre

Map 3, J4. East Link Bridge, North Wall Quay ☎836 3633.

The venue of choice for most visiting superstar acts, the cavernous *Point Theatre* is a huge and charmless converted warehouse on the north bank of the Liffey, about one mile east of O'Connell Street, with a capacity of between 4000 and 7000, depending on whether the show is seated or standing. The acoustics and sightlines are good, but considering its size and status, the venue is surprisingly bereft of facilities for the humble punter.

Red Box

Map 4, D10. 35 Harcourt St ☎478 0225.

Far more plush than other similar-sized venues in the city, the recently opened Red Box is a tailor-made and lovingly designed 1000-capacity hall located upstairs from *The POD* nightclub (see p.233), and owned by the same organization.

The SFX

Map 5, H1. 28 Upper Sherrard St ☎874 5227.

This 1500-capacity hall is one of Dublin's oldest and most popular rock venues, and has hosted some of the city's most exciting rock and pop gigs over the last two decades. The advent of new venues and *The SFX*'s unfashionable location has diminished its popularity somewhat, but it's still a great place to see your heroes play.

Whelans

Map 4, C9. 25 Wexford St ⊘478 0766.

With its welcoming 350-capacity, two-level room, this is perhaps the city's best place to see live music up close. Its intimate atmosphere makes it a particularly ideal venue for acoustic and roots music, and the list of international stars who've graced its compact stage is a mile long.

CLUBS

The Andrew's Lane Theatre

Map 6, F6. 9 St Andrew's Lane.

Thurs–Sun 11pm till late.

On weekend nights, after the last playgoer has gone, this small modern theatre throws its doors open to a very different public. Expect user-friendly trip-hop and jazzy beats.

Break for the Border

Map 4, C7. Lower Stephen's St.

Wed–Sat 11pm–2am.

This enormous Western-themed restaurant attracts hundreds of good-natured punters in pursuit of dance, drink and the opposite sex. The mainstream music policy is more than compensated for by the clientele's impressive dedication to the pursuit of good times.

La Cave

Map 4, C7. 28 South Anne St.

Mon–Sun 11pm till late.

A veritable institution, this tiny basement wine bar is famous for its improbable tendency to transform itself into an impromptu carnival if the crowd and the mood are right:

CLUBS

the staff distribute battered percussion instruments from behind the bar so that energetic revellers can play along to the intoxicating Brazilian and African rhythms as they dance.

The Gaiety Theatre

Map 4, D7. South King St.
Fri & Sat 11.30pm–2.30am.

On Friday and Saturday nights Dubliners out for a good night throng the beautiful old *Gaiety Theatre* for the highly popular *Velure*, a multi-event club night which offers live bands (predominantly jazz and samba), DJs and even film screenings in the array of backstage bars and green rooms.

The Kitchen

Map 6, D4. East Essex St.
Mon–Wed 11.30pm–2am, Thurs–Sun 11pm–2am.

Housed beneath the *Clarence Hotel* (see p.171), *The Kitchen* is equally trendy in design, and perhaps even more adventurous in its booking of cutting-edge turntable wizards. Its location and the fame of its owners mean that this is another place where gaining entry can be tricky, and you'll almost certainly have to queue.

Lillie's Bordello

Map 4, G6. Adam Court, Grafton St.
Mon–Sun 11pm till late.

Rock stars – would-be, has-been and actual – quaff and bitch with supermodels in the velour-bedecked *Lillie's Bordello*. Don't worry unduly if you're asked whether or not you're a member – practically nobody is. Regulars get priority and rarely pay the reasonably hefty (£8) entrance fee, but if you beat the after-pub crowd, act relaxed and don't look too dishevelled you should get in easily enough. If you do gain admittance you'll have the dance floor more or less to yourself: the regulars are far too cool to boogie. Bonus points if you manage to sneak into the genuinely exclusive Library.

The POD

Map 4, D10. 35 Harcourt St.
Wed–Sat 11pm–2.30am.

The phenomenally popular *POD* (short for Place Of Dance) on Harcourt Street is a match for anything that New York, Berlin or Tokyo has to offer, boasting ultra-modern décor and a tooth-loosening sound system. *The POD* is home to the hottest local DJs, the most popular venue for international dance acts, and the hangout of choice for many a visiting celebrity. The clientele are intimidatingly chic, and the door policy, especially at weekends, can be tough. Dress to impress and get there early.

Renard's

Map 4, F6. South Frederick St.
Mon–Sun 11.30pm–3am.

Popular with Dublin's small but self-important music and media pack. Claustrophobes may find the ground-floor bar preferable to the sweaty basement dance floor.

Rí-Rá

Map 4, C6. South Great George's St ℅677 4835.
Thurs–Sun 11.30pm–2.30am.

The records spun at *Rí-Rá* (pronounced Ree-Raw) can range from trip-hop to world music to hard funk, depending on night and mood: this club manages to be both informal and fashionable and draws an eclectic and friendly crowd.

CLUBS

System

Map 4, D7. 21 South Anne St.

Fri & Sat 11pm–3am.

Younger and less élitist than many of the city's new breed of nightclub, *System* specializes in hard, fast techno, served up at a deafening volume. Dress light, or you'll expire.

Temple Theatre

Map 5, H2. North George's St, off Temple St.

Fri & Sat 9pm–2am.

A recent addition to the Dublin dance scene, clearly inspired by UK mega-clubs like *Cream* and *Ministry of Sound*, this enormous restored church is drawing youthful club fans by the hundreds, who come for the excellent sound and lights, the regular top international DJs and the sheer scale of the place.

THEATRE AND CINEMA

As befits a city with a rich literary past, **theatre** flourishes in Dublin. The traditional diet of Irish classics at the "establishment" theatres is now spiced by experimental or fringe programmes at newer, smaller venues. Theatres operate from Monday to Saturday; evening performances usually begin at 8pm, and there may be matinees, too. Credit-card booking is widely available – tickets are cheap (£4–£12), and it's also worth enquiring about cheaper stand-by tickets on weekdays, or cut-price Monday-night shows. A highlight of the year is the **Dublin Theatre Festival** (see p.259), which runs for two or three weeks in late September/early October.

Dublin has numerous **cinemas** showing mainstream films (mostly in and around O'Connell Street), which are often released earlier in Ireland than in Britain, plus two art-house cinemas. The *Irish Film Centre*, the *Screen* and the *Savoy* are the venues for the **Dublin Film Festival** (see p.255) in March. All cinemas operate a policy of cheap seats before 5pm (6.30pm in some cases), seven days a week.

Check *In Dublin, The Event Guide* or the *Irish Times* for details of what's on.

THEATRES

The Abbey Theatre

Map 4, E3. Lower Abbey St ℂ878 7222.

This is the National Theatre of Ireland, founded by W.B. Yeats and Lady Gregory in 1902. The original building was destroyed by fire in the 1950s and replaced by the current, ugly building in 1966. It tends to show Irish classics (by Synge, Sheridan, O'Casey, Wilde etc), plus new offerings by contemporary playwrights such as Brian Friel (see also *Peacock Theatre*).

Andrew's Lane Theatre

Map 6, F5. Between St Andrew St and Exchequer St ℂ679 5720.

Situated just off Dame Street, in what appears to be the middle of a car park, this theatre specializes in contemporary Irish drama, and generally has two shows on the go at once. Under the same management as the *Gate*.

City Arts Centre

Map 4, G4. 23 Moss St, off St George's Quay ℂ677 0643.

The centre includes a full-time theatre with a focus on community-based drama, and also does projects with youth groups and the disabled. Well worth investigating.

Crypt Arts Centre

Map 6, D6. Dublin Castle ℂ761 3387.

A new venue in the crypt of the Chapel Royal, staging everything from heavyweight drama to rock concerts by little-known bands. Used by *Amharclann na Híde*, the only Dublin theatre group to perform in Gaelic.

THEATRE

Focus Theatre

Map 3, H8. Pembroke Place, off Sussex Rd ℭ676 3071.
An occasional venue for fringe theatre.

Gaiety Theatre

Map 4, D7. South King St, off Grafton St ℭ677 1717.
An old-style playhouse with velvet curtains and gilded boxes, that usually hosts musicals, pantomimes and other family entertainments. On Fridays and Saturdays it becomes an after-midnight club (see p.232).

Gate Theatre

Map 5, H4. Beside the Rotunda Hospital on Parnell Sq ℭ874 4045.
Founded in 1928, it has a longstanding rivalry with the *Abbey* and a reputation for staging adventurous, experimental drama as well as established classics, in a stark auditorium. Student stand-by tickets Monday to Thursday, subject to availability.

Olympia Theatre

Map 6, D5. Dame St ℭ677 7744.
Somewhat similar to the *Gaiety*, this old-style music hall has been through many incarnations since it opened in 1749, with a roll-call of luminaries from Charlie Chaplin and Noel Coward to Mary Black and Jack Dee. Nowadays it hosts musicals, stand-up comedy shows and medium-sized gigs, with late-night Friday and Saturday concerts under the title of "Midnight at the Olympia"(see *Live music*).

Passion Machine Theatre Company

Map 5, H2. 30 Gardiner Place, off Mountjoy Sq ℭ878 8857.
An interesting drama company that performs at various venues – the address listed here is their base, not a theatre.

THEATRE

Peacock Theatre

Map 4, E3. Lower Abbey St ℡878 7222.
The *Abbey's* smaller sister theatre, in the basement, shows lesser-known plays and can often be a goldmine for great entertainment and new talent.

Project Arts Centre

Map 6, D4. 39 East Sussex St ℡671 2321.
Renowned for its experimental and often controversial theatre by the *Rough Magic* company, the Project is currently staging its productions at the *Mint Theatre* on Henry Place, off Henry Street (near the GPO), owing to building work at the Project Arts Centre in Temple Bar – although the booking office (and Project Gallery) remain open here.

Samuel Beckett Theatre

Map 4, E6. Trinity College ℡608 1239.
A venue for Trinity College's dramatic society, fringe theatre and for companies without a base of their own.

Tivoli Theatre

Map 5, E9. Francis St ℡454 4472.
A modern theatre in the Liberties, with hard seats on three sides of a raised stage. It acts as a rock venue between theatrical performances.

CINEMAS

Apart from the two art-house cinemas listed here, Dublin has numerous mainstream cinemas – see the *Evening Herald* or *In Dublin* for up-to-date screening times.

The Irish Film Centre

Map 6, E4. 6 Eustace St, Temple Bar ☎679 5744.

Art-house cinema with two screens and an excellent restaurant (see pp.195 & 221), as well as a film-related bookshop and dance-club nights on Fridays and Saturdays. Films include new, low-budget Irish works plus seasons of world, gay and children's cinema; an interesting survey of Irish film-making is shown every afternoon.

Light House Cinema

Map 6, G3. 107 Fleet St ☎873 0438.

Tiny cinema with two screens showing art-house films, mostly continental European.

GAY DUBLIN

Gay life in Ireland is essentially confined to Dublin and Cork, where attitudes are most liberal. However, there's still a risk of homophobia on a day-to-day level, so it's wise to be cautious about kissing and cuddling on the streets.

Visitors can easily get involved in Dublin's gay scene. The first thing to do is get a copy of the free monthly *Gay Community News*, which has detailed listings of upcoming **events** and all the vital info you need to enjoy yourself. You can pick one up in the gay-friendly *Books Upstairs* opposite the main gate of Trinity College, *The Winding Stair Bookshop* on Bachelors Walk, or the Temple Bar information centre on Eustace Street. Otherwise, the best sources of **information** and advice are *Gay Switchboard Dublin* (Mon–Fri & Sun 8–10pm, Sat 3.30–6pm; ✆872 1055) or the 24-hour info and events line (✆1550 122 345) of *Lesbians Organizing Together*, which has a drop-in centre at 5 Capel Street (Mon–Thurs 10am–6pm, Fri 10am–4pm; ✆872 7770).

The number of permanent fixtures on the scene is tiny, and most of the real action happens at the gay nights in the straight venues. Most **pubs** around Temple Bar and South Great George's Street have a mixed clientele and a keen eye on the pink pound, while several mainstream **clubs** have theme nights and gay events. Other gay and mixed **meet-**

ing places include *Bewley's* (see p.191) and the *Well Fed Café* (see p.197).

PUBS

The Front Lounge

Map 6, C4. Parliament St.
Not "officially" gay, but many gay men and lesbians relish its classy, bouffant hair-styled atmosphere.

The George

Map 4, C6. 89 South Great George's St.
Ireland's first gay pub when it opened fourteen years ago, *The George* remains as popular as ever. Its original bar (known as Jurassic Park due to its older clientele) is quite dowdy but full of character; the newer half is bright and breezy, serving good meals during the day. Besides *The Block* (see overleaf) upstairs, it has a weekly men-only leather/denim/uniform club on Fridays.

Hogans

Map 4, C6. 11 South Great George's St.
Just up the road from *The George*, this cool, dark modern bar caters to a stylish mixed crowd. Lively and noisy, but not the best place to make friends.

Out on the Liffey

Map 6, B3. 27 Upper Ormond Quay.
Dublin's other gay pub is a nice relaxed place for a midweek drink or to warm up for a weekend session. Equally popular with gays and lesbians, with late hours and events (quizzes, etc) advertised in *GCN*. Just beware of your safety in the backstreets.

CLUBS

The Block

Map 4, C6. 89 South Great George's St.

Wed–Sun 11pm–2am. Wed & Thurs, free before 11.30pm, £3 after;
Fri & Sat £3 till 11.30pm, £5 after.

The George's swinging alter ego. Has four sections linked by *Gone
with the Wind* stairways and a small dance floor. Wednesday night
is karaoke. Thursday's Seventies. On Fridays & Saturdays there's a
dance club with full bar. Heavy-handed security.

Freedom at the Mission

Map 6, E4. Eustace St, Temple Bar.

Mon 11pm–2am; £4.

This is the place to go if you want to meet people. Good
commercial dance music in a no-nonsense nightclub setting.
Roomy chill-out area upstairs.

Furnace: getOUT!

Map 6, G3. 1–2 Aston Quay.

Every second Sat, 9pm–1am; £4, £3 unemployed.

Monthly dance club catering to all tastes, with a young crowd.
The venue is owned by the Union of Students of Ireland. Come
early to get an elevated seat for a good view of the dance floor.

H.A.M. (Homo Action Movies)

Map 4, D10. *POD*, 35 Harcourt St.

Fri 11pm–3am; £5.

Gay night at Dublin's trendiest club. The main dance floor
looks like a Duran Duran video shoot, and the Art Deco
anteroom is for chilling out and watching the movie. Dress up,

as it's like the Grooming Olympics (though some of the staff dress like butchers). Totally queer door policy; mostly males.

The Playground

Map 6, B3. Ormond Hotel, Ormond Quay.

Sun 10.30pm till late; £5.

A cruisy dance-oriented club for those who've still got some energy left by Sunday night. Good music but bland surroundings. You can buy hot snacks or partake of the free bowls of fruit.

Powderbubble

Map 4, D10. at _Red Box_, above _The POD_.

11pm–3am; £12–15.

Monthly club that's very nearly a fullblown rave; the balcony is for those who prefer talking. Special features include exotic-looking creatures waving sparklers, complimentary candy-floss, and a false nail and eyelash implant service. The Alternative Miss Ireland is held here. Pricey but brilliant.

StoneWallz

Map 3, E8. Griffith College, South Circular Rd.

Sat 9pm–12.30am; £4 (£3 before 11.30pm).

Very friendly women-only club in unusual surroundings. Extremely popular, so get here early (bus #16 from Dame Street or Georges Street).

Wonder Bar

Map 6, E4. Temple Bar Music Centre, Curved St.

First and third Sat each month; 9.30pm–2.45am; £7, £5 with concession.

The spiritual home of the pleasuredome kids, with a stage for acts ranging from standard drag to bizarre passion plays on the life of Alison Moyet. Open door policy, mixed crowd.

SHOPPING

Dublin's recent prosperity is reflected in the development of the city centre's shops, but north and south of the Liffey are two distinct areas. The southside, focusing on Grafton Street's swish stores and the boutiques of Temple Bar, is fashion and form incarnate, while the north, based on O'Connell Street and the grid of surrounding streets, is all function. You buy what you need north of the river and what you want on the south.

....

Our listings are grouped into the following categories: antiques (p.245); art and design (p.245); books (p.246); clothing and fashion (p.248); food (p.250); jewellery (p.250); markets (p.251); records (p.252); shopping centres and department stores (p.253).

....

Dublin shops generally open from 9.30am to 5.30pm Monday to Friday, with late shopping until 7pm or 8pm on Thursday evenings, and many places are open on Sunday from around noon to 4pm or 5pm. The exception is Temple Bar, where businesses may not open until at least an hour later. Any variance to this pattern is noted in the listings that follow. Most shops, except small food stores, market stalls and secondhand shops, accept credit cards.

ANTIQUES

Francis Street in the Liberties is the place for the budget-con-
scious antiques collector. In addition to the down-at-heel
Iveagh Flea Market there's a spread of shops dispensing everything from old beer trays to expensive oriental rugs and *objets
d'art*. In the centre of town, Molesworth Street, South Anne
Street and Kildare Street are all well worth a browse, as is the
Antiques Gallery on the first floor of the Powerscourt
Townhouse. An Antiques and Collectors Fair takes place fortnightly in Dublin Castle on Sundays from 10.30am to 6pm.

ART AND DESIGN

In addition to the places listed here, there are plenty of commercial galleries in the city centre, details of which are contained in the free *Dublin Gallery Guide,* available at Dublin's
tourist offices and the Temple Bar Information Centre.

Crafts Council Design Gallery

Map 4, D6. Second floor, Powerscourt Townhouse.
Mon–Sat 9.30am–5.30pm.
This store serves as both a retail gallery and a small exhibition
centre for the Crafts Council of Ireland. Stock constantly
changes, but normally includes glassware and mirrors, ceramics,
lighting, wooden articles, such as hand-made clocks and beech
tables, rugs and knitwear.

DesignYARD

Map 6, D4. 12 East Essex St, Temple Bar ℂ677 8453.
Mon–Sat 11am–6pm.
A showcase for contemporary jewellery, ceramics, glass and
furnishings, by Irish and international designers.

ANTIQUES, ART AND DESIGN

245

Merrion Square

Map 4, G7.

On Sundays throughout the year the iron railings of Merrion Square are transformed into an art gallery as Dublin's artists stake out their claim to be the new Jack Yeats. The work on show ranges from the adroit to the diabolical, but whatever the quality you can chat about techniques with the artists themselves or haggle over prices. Cash is the preferred mode of transaction.

People's Art Hall

Map 4, D7. Second floor, Powerscourt Townhouse.
Mon–Sat 9.30am–5.30pm.

As a more cramped, but equally rewarding alternative to Merrion Square, this store is well worth a visit. Again, quality ranges across the whole spectrum and prices tend to be a little higher than purchasing from the artist directly. The shop features John Woodfull's often droll and very reasonably priced depictions of Dublin pub life.

BOOKS

Dublin's literary life is well-supported by its numerous new and secondhand bookshops, ranging from large stores such as *Eason's* to specialist outfits such as *Connolly Books*.

Cathach Books

Map 4, D6. 10 Duke St ✆ 671 8676.
Mon–Sat 9.30am–6pm.

Cathach specializes in rare first editions and antique maps, and its window alone is well worth the visit. Here you might find signed first editions of Yeats's poetry, a 1935 edition of *Ulysses*, illustrated by Matisse, or limited edition copies of the author's death mask. A bargain basement downstairs offers solace to the more impecunious book lover.

Connolly Books

Map 6, D4. 43 East Essex St ✆671 1943.
Mon–Sat 9.30am–5.30pm, Sun 2–5pm.
The red frontage and its title give the game away about the nature of this excellent political bookshop situated on the edge of Temple Bar. Its shelves are filled by works on Irish political history, including a number by James Connolly himself plus modern fiction, music and the arts. New books are often discounted.

Eason's

Map 4, D2. 40 Upper O'Connell St ✆873 3811.
Mon–Wed, Sat & Sun 8.30am–6.15pm, Thurs 8.30am–8pm.
The best bookshop north of the Liffey, *Eason's* stocks a wide range of books, cards and stationery, as well as having one of the biggest magazine sections in the country.

Greene's

Map 4, G7. 16 Clare St ✆ 676 2554.
Mon–Fri 9am–5.30pm, Sat 9am–5pm.
A long-standing Dublin bookshop just around the corner from the National Gallery, selling new and secondhand books. The barrows under its distinctive wrought-iron canopy hold all sorts of treasures. Also contains a small post office.

Fred Hanna's

Map 5, I8. 27–29 Nassau St ✆ 677 1255.
Mon–Sat 9am–6pm (Thurs open till 8pm).
Excellent general and academic shop, selling new and secondhand books; especially good for books on Ireland.

BOOKS

Hodges Figgis

Map 4, E7. 56–58 Dawson St ☎677 4754.
Mon–Wed & Fri 9am–7pm, Thurs 9am–8pm, Sat 9am–6pm, Sun noon–6pm.
Founded in 1768, *Hodges Figgis* is a Dublin institution.
Although the breadth of its coverage is huge, its emphasis is
instantly apparent – directly opposite the door is a
comprehensive Irish fiction section, while other shelves are
dedicated to contemporary and historical Ireland, its language,
art and culture. Upstairs there are book bargains and a café.

CLOTHING AND FASHION

Though department stores, small boutiques and shoe shops
fill the grid of streets on each side of O'Connell Street, you
should head for the southside if designer labels, Aran
sweaters or Donegal tweed are what you're looking for.

An Táin

Map 6, E4. 13 Temple Bar ☎ 679 0523.
Mon–Sat 10.30am–5.30pm and Sunday afternoons.
The speciality of this small shop is innovative Celtic style and
fashion, and its racks contain some startling examples by
designers such as Andrea Cleary and Pat McCarthy. The stock
ranges from t-shirts at £13 to linen dresses at £300.

Design Centre

Map 4, D7. First floor, Powerscourt Townhouse.
Mon–Sat 9.30am–5.30pm, Thurs till 7pm.
The *Design Centre*'s ever-changing panoply of stalls represents the
cream of young Irish designers of women's fashion. Designers
include Louise Kennedy, Lyn-Mor, Deirdre Fitzgerald and
Vivien Walsh, who also has her own store next door.

The Eager Beaver

Map 6, F4. 17 Crown Alley ✆677 3342.
Mon–Sat 9.30am–5.30pm.
This two-storied shop claims to stock the largest selection of next-to-new clothing in Ireland and offers special discounts to students, the unemployed and senior citizens.

The Hat Stand

Map 6, E4. 5 Temple Bar ✆671 0805.
Mon–Sat 10.30am–5.30pm.
This tiny corner store somehow manages to cram an enormous and sometimes bizarre range of women's headgear into its windows and shelves. Styles range from simple straw hats and woollen caps to Mad Hatter's concoctions which even Noddy Holder might think twice about sporting.

Kevin & Howlin

Map 4, E6. 31 Nassau St ✆677 0257.
Mon–Sat 9.30am–5.30pm.
Tweed heaven – jackets, caps, waistcoats, hats, ties, suits, all expertly tailored in Donegal tweed. Does men's and women's clothing.

The Kilkenny Shop

Map 4, E6. 6 Nassau St ✆677 7066.
Mon–Sat 9am–6pm, Sun 11am–5pm.
Once state-owned, now independent, this bright and well laid-out store plays host to a horde of Irish designed clothes, pottery, ornaments and gifts. Designers represented include the wonderfully named Kilkenny Art of Dressing. If the spectacle (and prices) are overpowering, you can recover in the café upstairs (see p.195).

CLOTHING AND FASHION

FOOD

If you fancy creating your own picnic lunch, try *Magill's Delicatessen* at 14 Clarendon St; *The Big Cheese Co*, 14–15 Trinity St; and *Byrne's*, 26/27 Temple Bar. *Down to Earth*, 73 South Great George's St, and *Harvest*, 6 South William Street are the best options for wholefoods. Temple Bar's Meeting House Square hosts an outdoor food market during the summer (Sat 9am–5pm). On the northside, there are bakers on North Earl Street and Henry Street, and you could stock up with all your needs on Moore Street alone.

JEWELLERY

In addition to the places listed below, for jewellery you should check out Johnsons Court (off Grafton Street), a little alley that has half a dozen or so jewellery shops, with a couple more in Westbury Shopping Mall next door. The *DeSIGNYARD* (see p.245) is a showcase for classy contemporary work.

Angles

Map 4, E7. 10 Westbury Shopping Mall, off Grafton St
⊘**679 1964.**
Mon–Sat 10am–6pm, Thurs till 7pm.
This tiny store sells some of the most intriguing contemporary jewellery, including work by Irish designers and samples from the collections of Europeans such as Alejandro Toussier. Most pieces are in silver, some with inset semi-precious stones or gold detailing. The emphasis is art rather than adornment and prices tend to match. *Angles* has its own workshop, producing unique pieces.

Crown Jewels

Map 6, F4. 5a Crown Alley ✆671 3452.
Mon–Sat 10.30am–6pm.
In complete contrast, the tongue-in-cheek *Crown Jewels* offers
the opportunity to construct your own designs on the spot.
Make your own jewellery from metal, wood, plastic, glass,
ceramic, plastic and pearl components from as little as 25p per
piece.

MARKETS

Dublin's once-thriving street markets have all but disappeared and the few that remain have moved into adopted
homes under cover. Despite this, there's still much pleasure
to be found on a visit to one of the following three.

The Liberty Market

Map 3, E5. Meath St.
Thurs–Sat, 10am–5pm.
The Liberty's stalls are crammed, maze-like, into a small indoor
hall halfway along a vibrant local shopping street. You can buy
anything here from Boyzone bangles to WD40, but most
people come for the cheap clothing and footwear.

Moore Street Market

Map 5, H5. Moore St, just off Henry St.
Mon–Sat 9am or earlier to 4pm or 5pm.
Locals may tell you that this is not what it used to be but on a
good day, when the sun is shining, stalls fill the length of the
street, selling vegetables and flowers, fresh fish, and cheap
electrical goods.

MARKETS

Mother Redcap's Market

Map 6, A6. Back Lane off High St.
Fri, Sat & Sun 11am–5.30pm.

Mother Redcap's packs around fifty stalls and small shops into its indoor setting. Things on offer range from the mundane (valve radio repairs, ironmongery, wholefoods and second-hand books) to the arcane (African carvings, nail-biting and cuticle problem-solvers, Thai goods, the Reptile Shop, tarot readings and numerology). There's a cheap café in the centre and, of course, the pub next door.

RECORDS

For a town of its size, Dublin possesses an astonishing array of record and CD shops. There are branches of the chain stores *HMV* in Grafton Street and Henry Street, *Tower Records* in Wicklow Street, and *Virgin* on Aston Quay and Henry Street, together with branches of Dublin's own *Golden Discs* in Grafton Street and St Stephen's Green Shopping Centre. For something more esoteric try those listed below.

Claddagh Records

Map 6, E4. 2 Cecilia St ℡677 0262.
Mon–Sat noon–5.30pm.

Offers an incredibly comprehensive range of Irish traditional and contemporary recordings, together with racks filled with world music, country, blues and bluegrass.

Comet Records

Map 6, F4. 5 Cope St ℡671 8592
Mon–Sat 10am–6pm.

Wide-ranging stock of indie and dance and a good place to collar the latest releases by up-and-coming Irish bands and to chat about their gigs with the store's owner.

Freebird Records

Map 6, H1. 1 Eden Quay ℂ873 1270.
Mon–Wed & Sat 10.30am–6pm, Thurs & Fri 10.30am–7.30pm.
This basement store, just by O'Connell Bridge, crams an enormous range of new and used indie, rock and metal CDs into its small surroundings. Prices are very reasonable.

Secret Book and Record Store

Map G, G6. 15a Wicklow St ℂ679 7272.
Daily 11am–6.30pm.
Probably the best selection of rare vinyl in Dublin, with collector items from the Fifties onwards. Mainly rock, folk and blues. Also has a comprehensive secondhand books section.

SHOPPING CENTRES AND DEPARTMENT STORES

Dublin's redeveloped centre contains the usual ration of shopping centres and malls. The majority, like the gargantuan St Stephen's Green Centre or the Jervis Centre on Mary Street, house little that is unexpected – they'll make you think you might as well be in Derby or Dorking. However, there are a couple of intriguing exceptions.

Clery's

Map 5, I5. Lower O'Connell St ℂ878 6000.
Mon–Sat 9.30am–5.30pm, Thurs 8pm.
Clery's large, traditional store is particularly good for Irish-manufactured clothing. Tweeds and woollens, especially Aran sweaters, are at the forefront in the ground-floor clothing departments and often of better quality and at lower prices than some of the specialist Irish shops.

Powerscourt Townhouse

Map 4, D6. Clarendon St.
Mon–Sat 9am–6pm, Thurs till 7pm.

The *Townhouse* is a bright and airy grade A listed building, it was constructed in 1774 for Lord Powerscourt and is well worth a visit in its own right. Its three floors have been artfully redesigned to contain a wealth of stores specializing in antiques and art, stylish fashions, hand-made jewellery and traditional crafts. There are nine restaurants, and the courtyard is often the centre of attention as the setting for lunchtime recitals, jazz concerts, fashion shows and exhibitions.

Royal Hibernian Way

Map 4, E7. Dawson St.
Mon–Sat 9.30am–6pm,Thurs till 8pm.

For those with impeccable credit, the *RHB* offers a host of tasteful and highly priced shopping opportunities. *Monaghans* displays chic menswear by designers such as Jasper Conran and Karl Lagerfeld. *Via Veneto* specializes in shoes produced by the top Milanese. You can slaver over Leonidas Belgian chocolates or estimate the weight of the smoked salmon in the window of *McConnells and Nelson's*.

SHOPPING CENTRES AND DEPARTMENT STORES

FESTIVALS AND EVENTS

Dublin has **festivals and events** for sports fans, music, drama and cinema lovers, gardeners, devotees of *Ulysses* or *Dracula* – to name only some of the enthusiasms catered for. Though sports events are the only thing happening in the winter months, there's something for everyone at almost any time of year. For most events, tickets can be obtained at short notice through the booking service at Dublin Tourism or the venue concerned. What follows is a calendar of the regular major events. For one-offs, consult *In Dublin* and the tourist offices. Sports events are covered separately in the *Sports* chapter.

MARCH

Dublin Film Festival

Now in its twelfth year, this ten-day showcase for the best in homegrown and international cinema is held at the *Irish Film Centre* in Temple Bar, the *Savoy* and *Screen* cinemas, and other venues around town. For details contact the organizing office, 1 Suffolk Street (©679 2937; fax 679 2939), or see any listings.

St Patrick's Day

March 17. "Paddy's Day" sees a parade of floats and marching bands through the centre of Dublin, watched by an average of 250,000 people, with music and jollity in pubs around the city until the wee hours.

APRIL

Easter Rising

Commemorations on Easter Sunday, with a Republican march from the GPO to Glasnevin Cemetery.

Handel's Messiah

April 13. Excerpts from Handel's *Messiah* performed at the site of the old Musick Hall on Fishamble Street.

MAY

RTÉ Proms

At the Royal Dublin Society in Ballsbridge. The RTÉ and National Symphony orchestras combine with visiting stars. Tickets from *HMV* Grafton St/Henry St; credit-card bookings ©709 0111.

Wicklow Gardens Festival

Mid–May to late June. Open days at private gardens throughout County Wicklow, the "Garden of Ireland". Some are easily accessible from Dublin (©0404 66058).

JUNE

Bloomsday

June 16. Devotees of *Ulysses* retrace the steps of characters in the novel (see overleaf), together with other events celebrating Joyce's life and times, organized by the James Joyce Centre (✆878 8547).

Festival of Music in Great Irish Houses

Classical concerts at stately homes all over Ireland, including several in the vicinity of Dublin, over two weeks in June (✆278 1528).

JULY

James Joyce Summer School

Annual event dedicated to Joyce and his works, with lectures, seminars and social events at Newman House (✆706 8480) and the James Joyce Centre (✆878 8547).

Temple Bar Blues Festival

Hours of music, talks, workshops and films on Temple Bar and Meetinghouse squares, plus lots of gigs in pubs day and night (✆677 2255).

AUGUST

Bray International Festival of Music and Dance

Street and indoor entertainment in the seaside resort of Bray, with Irish dancing and musicians, mummers, Morris dancers and international visiting groups (✆286 0080).

Bloomsday

Bloomsday, on June 16, is a unique celebration of a novel in the city that it so brilliantly evokes. Joyce's *Ulysses* relates the events of a single day in 1904 with obsessive fidelity to the localities, characters and speech of his native Dublin. As Joyce wrote, "If I can get to the heart of Dublin, I can get to the heart of every city in the world. In the particular is contained the universal." Every year, hundreds of admirers re-enact the Bloomsday "pilgrimage", retracing the steps of Stephen Dedalus, Leopold Bloom or lesser characters such as Father Conmee. Many of the pilgrims wear period costume, like the actors stationed at strategic points along the itinerary, including:

The Martello Tower at Sandycove. The starting point of the pilgrimage, where Joyce himself spent six tense days with Oliver St John Gogarty, who later noted, "He is planning some sort of novel that will show us all up and the country as well: all will be fatuous except James Joyce."

Sandymount Strand. A walk on the mudflats in Dublin Bay gave Stephen Dedalus pause for reflection, as it does for Dubliners today.

7 Eccles Street. The starting point for Bloom's odyssey and the site of Molly's climactic soliloquy; though the house has gone, its front door is preserved in the Joyce Centre on North Great George's Street.

St Andrew's and *Sweny's Chemist Shop*. On his way into the centre, Bloom drops into Mass at All Hallows Church, now St Andrew's on Westland Row, and carries on to *Sweny's* on Lincoln Place (which still exists), where he buys a bar of lemon soap (as one still can).

Glasnevin Cemetery. Paddy Dignam's funeral wends its way via Trinity, Parnell Square and Mountjoy Prison, passing the noblest and grimmest institutions in Dublin. The Joyce Centre lays on a Victorian hearse, drawn by plumed black horses.

The Oval and **Mooney's**. As the *Freeman's Journal* and *Evening Telegraph* offices no longer exist, pilgrims settle for visiting two pubs mentioned in Chapter 5. *The Oval* on Middle Abbey Street hasn't changed much, unlike *Mooney's* on Lower Abbey Street (now the *Abbey Mooney*). In 1988, a series of fourteen pavement plaques tracing Bloom's route from Abbey Street to the National Library was installed.

Davy Byrne's. Joyce wouldn't recognize this Duke Street pub, which now caters to yuppies and tourists. Nonetheless, it's a fitting place for pilgrims to consume a mustard-and-gorgonzola sandwich and a glass of Burgundy, in emulation of Bloom.

The National Library. Its great reading room was the setting for Stephen's impassioned speech on Shakespeare, extracts from which are read aloud on Bloomsday.

The Ormond Hotel. A plaque celebrates the hotel's role in the Sirens chapter at the end of Bloom's walk along Wellington Quay, and the bartenders wear period costume on Bloomsday.

Olhausen's. Since the brothel quarter vanished long ago, pilgrims content themselves with a visit to *Olhausen's* the butchers at 72 Talbot Street, where Bloom bought a pig's trotter and a sheep's hoof as a snack.

SEPTEMBER

Dublin Theatre Festival

2–3 weeks late Sept/mid-Oct. The best time to catch fringe theatre, new productions and visiting acts. Book well in advance. Centralized booking ℂ874 8525; information ℂ677 8439.

OCTOBER

Oscar Wilde Autumn School

An annual celebration of Wilde's life, works and times, with talks, screenings and performances in Bray (ℂ286 5245).

SPORTS

____

ublin offers a wide range of participation sports activities for visitors to enjoy, but its real forte is spectator sports (and betting on the outcome): rugby, soccer, hurling, Gaelic football and horse racing are avidly followed.

The following guide doesn't pretend to be exhaustive, but should give an idea of what's on offer and point you in the right direction for more detailed information.

EQUESTRIAN SPORTS

Equestrian sports are extremely popular in Ireland, with less of the snobbery attached in Britain. **Horse racing** is an Irish passion, as you'll find out if you visit Dublin's nearest large racecourse, **Leopardstown** in the southern suburb of Foxrock (bus #63 or #68). Races are held at weekends throughout the year, the main events being the Dennys Goldmedal Chase in late December, the Ladbroke and Champion Hurdle races on successive weekends in January, and the Hennessy Gold Cup in February. The **Irish Grand National** is held on Easter Monday at Fairyhouse, 25km north of Dublin. Flat racing classics are held at the Curragh, 50km southwest of Dublin (the Goffs Irish 1000 Guineas in May, the Budweiser Irish Derby in June, the Irish St Leger in September). For current information on race meetings call the 24-hr premium-rate line ©1550 11 22 18.

Show jumping has more of an élitist image, and the **Dublin Horse Show** at the Royal Dublin Society in August was once the highlight of Anglo-Irish social life. While no longer the focus of diplomatic receptions it is still a prestigious international event, with top riders competing for the Aga Khan Trophy and Nations Cup, and prizes in 88 different classes of jumping and dressage. More than 1500 horses compete, before an audience of 100,000. Though day-tickets might be available, you'd be wise to book ahead (©688 0866). The RDS pavilion in Ballsbridge is accessible by bus #5, #6, #8 or #45.

Polo has a limited following, but visitors to Phoenix Park enjoy watching matches on the Nine Acres polo grounds on Wednesday, Saturday & Sunday during the summer months.

If you'd like to go **riding**, there are plenty of opportunities in the rolling countryside to the south of Dublin. One of the most accessible places is *Brennanstown Riding School* (©286 3778; fax 282 9590), 3km south of Bray off the Dublin–Wexford road, which offers all levels of tuition and cross-country rides in the glorious Wicklow Hills.

FISHING

Ireland is renowned for its fishing, as you can read for yourself in several leaflets published by the *Bord Fáilte*. The River Liffey has **trout** fishing between Celbridge and Millicent Bridge, 20km from the centre, and there are **salmon** in other stretches of the river. **Sea fishing** is popular off Howth, Dún Laoghaire and Dalkey; it can be arranged at the harbour or through local hotels. Dublin's tackle shops can supply permits, rods, bait and advice.

GAELIC FOOTBALL AND HURLING

Gaelic football and hurling occupy a special place in Ireland, as ancient sports whose renaissance was entwined with the Celtic revival movement and the struggle for independence. The Gaelic Athletic Association (GAA) fostered a network of local clubs that are still the heart and soul of many communities, with political clout in the provinces.

Although Dubliners are less keen on both sports (especially hurling), the national stadium for Gaelic games (hurling, Gaelic football, handball and camogie, a version of hurling for women) is at **Croke Park** (✆836 3222), near the Royal Canal. Named after Archbishop Croke, an advocate of athletics and teetotalism, it is hallowed by sporting triumphs and the "Bloody Sunday" massacre of 1920, where the Black and Tans shot dead a dozen spectators and a player at a match. While the stadium may not be used for any sport not played by the ancient Gaels, the GAA have permitted U2 and Live Aid concerts to be held there.

Hurling is said to have descended from a game played by the legendary warrior Cuchulainn. The ball may be hit in the air or along the ground, and caught or carried on the flattened end of the player's hurley stick. It's a game of constant movement and aggression that doesn't permit a defensive, reactive style of play. Dublin is nowhere in the league (whose big boys are Cork and Kilkenny), so the crowd at the **All-Ireland Final** on the first Sunday in September mainly consists of out-of-towners.

To the uninitiated, **Gaelic football** resembles a cross between soccer and rugby. Cork and Kerry are the titans of the National Football League (NFL). The **All-Ireland Final** occurs on the third Sunday in September and has been won by Dubliners on 22 occasions (a record beaten only by Kerry); more people watch the game than any other event in Ireland. Like hurling, it's played right through the year.

GOLF

Golf is Ireland's fastest growing sport and a major tourist activity. There are more than twenty private golf courses in and around Dublin, and as many public ones, the majority of them affiliated to the *Golfing Union of Ireland*. Typical green fees are around £25–30 (more at weekends), usually based on a per day rather than a per round basis. It's wise to check in advance with the club, as fees and the availability of tee time vary. Mid-week is generally the best time for visitors. The *Deer Park* at Howth (☎832 2624; fax 839 2405) is Ireland's largest public golf complex, with five courses ranging from an 18-hole pitch and putt course to a challenging par-72, 6678-yard, 18-hole course, and a hotel offering B&B and golf packages. Though non-residents can't book time on the links, it's worth phoning ahead to check how busy they are. Other courses worth trying are the 18-hole *Dún Laoghaire Golf Club* in Eglinton Park (☎280 1694), or the 9-hole course at Bray (☎286 2484). In addition, there are many short pitch and putt courses. For information, contact the Pitch & Putt Union of Ireland, House of Sport, Long Mile Road, Dublin 12 (☎450 9299).

Tournaments occur all over Ireland for much of the year; the biggest is the **Irish Golf Open Championship** in late June/early July.

GREYHOUND RACING

If you fancy a flutter or just a fun evening out, **greyhound racing** requires little experience of betting and draws a lively crowd of Dubliners from all walks of life. There are races most nights of the week throughout the year; admission £4 (children free). The **Shelbourne Park Greyhound Stadium** on South Lotts Road, Ringsend, is easily accessible by bus #3 from Pearse Street, and has a comfortable enclosure for watching the races (Feb–early Dec Mon & Wed 8pm, Sat 7.30pm; rest of year Mon & Sat only). The other venue is **Harold's Cross Stadium**, off Harold's Cross Road, which can be reached by bus #16, #16A & #16B (Feb–early Dec Tues, Thurs & Fri 8pm; rest of year Tues & Fri 8pm).

RUGBY

Lansdowne Road (℡668 4601; fax 660 5640) in Ballsbridge is Irish Rugby Union's holy of holies, where national and international championships take place from January to March. The **All-Ireland Finals** is the climax of the club season, while the **Five Nations Championship** is the showcase for international rugby. All of these matches happen between January and March. Lansdowne Road is also sometimes "borrowed" for international soccer matches.

SOCCER

Although the fortunes of Ireland's national football team are a matter of keen concern for almost everyone, Dublin **soccer** fans are less enthusiastic about local teams. Ireland's national league can hardly compete with the money, allure and success of English football, where Dublin-born players like Liam Brady have achieved international stardom. This explains why the most popular teams among Dubliners are Liverpool and Manchester United (both from cities with a large Irish community), a state of affairs acknowledged by RTÉ, which relays live coverage of top English matches far more often than Irish ones. The city currently has five teams in the league of Ireland's premier division – Bohemians, Shamrock Rovers, St Patrick's Athletic, Shelbourne and UCD.

SWIMMING AND WATERSPORTS

The coastline north and south of Dublin offers ample opportunities for watersports. Though the water seldom rises above chilly even on hot days, Dubliners enjoy **swimming** in the sea in summertime, when sunbathers pack the shingle **beaches** at Killiney and Bray, and the sandy ones at Sutton, Malahide and Donabate (all accessible by DART or suburban train). Though the beach at Sandymount is small, it's only 5km from the centre, and near the famous **Forty Foot Pool**.

The other great activity along the coast is **sailing**, with long-established yacht clubs in Dún Laoghaire, Howth, Malahide and Clontarf. Unfortunately, many are members-only, so you won't be able to use the facilities unless you belong to a club with reciprocal membership. Contact the **Irish Sailing Association**, 3 Park Road, Dún Laoghaire (℃280 0239), for details. The **National Sailing School** (℃284 4195) by Dún Laoghaire's West Pier offers courses (from £99) at all levels.

Though the west coast is more rewarding, there are some fine spots to the south of Dublin, like **Dalkey Island**. Qualified divers can hire gear (£12–£25) or book a half-day's boat diving (£25 all-inclusive) at *Oceantec*, 10 Marine Terrace (Tues–Sat 9.30am–6pm; ℃280 1083).

Windsurfing is equally popular around Dalkey and Dún Laoghaire, where *Wind & Wave*, at 16A The Crescent in Monkstown (℃284 4177), rents gear and offers tuition. If you're less bothered about the setting, you can go windsurfing in the Grand Canal Dock basin at Ringsend (bus #3 from Pearse Street), where *Surf Dock* (℗668 3945; fax 668 1215) runs courses and rents sailboards by the hour.

DIRECTORY

AIRLINES *Aer Lingus*, 41 Upper O'Connell St/42 Grafton St (✆844 4777 for UK enquiries, ✆844 4747 for Europe and transatlantic); *British Airways*, 12 Duke Lane (✆0800 626747); *British Midland*, Nutley, Merrion Rd (✆283 0700); *Ryanair*, 3 Dawson St (✆677 4422).

BANKS Banks are open Mon–Fri 10am–4pm (5pm Thurs). The two major Irish banks are *Allied Irish* and the *Bank of Ireland*, with many branches around town. Others include the *National Irish* and *Ulster* banks. Most banks have automatic teller machines (ATMs), accepting a variety of cash, credit and debit cards.

BICYCLES Bicycles can be hired from: *Bike Store*, 58 Lower Gardiner St (✆872 5399); *Dublin Bike Hire*, 27 North Great George's St (✆878 8473); *C. Harding*, 30 Bachelor Walk (✆873 2455); *McDonald's Cycles*, 38 Wexford St (✆475 2586) and 1 Orwell Rd (✆497 9636); *The Old School House*, Eblana Avenue, Dún Laoghaire (✆280 8777).

CARRIAGE TOURS From St Stephen's Green, £20, lasting 30 minutes or longer by arrangement.

DISABILITY Dublin Tourism Centre can provide information on accessibility, and the National Rehabilitation Board, 44 North Great George's St, Dublin 1 (©874 7503), can offer advice and information and produces a number of free publications. *Be Our Guest*, the Irish Hotels Federation's annual accommodation guide, details hotels and guesthouses that are wheelchair accessible or suitable for people with disabilities with the assistance of a helper.

ELECTRICITY 220 volts, 50hz AC is standard, with three square pin plugs the norm. All British devices should function normally, though North American ones will require both a transformer and a plug adaptor. Australian and New Zealand appliances will only need an adaptor.

EMBASSIES Australia, Fitzwilton House, Wilton Terrace (©676 1517); **Belgium**, Shrewsbury Rd (©269 2082); **Canada**, 65-68 St Stephen's Green (©478 1988); **Denmark**, 121 St Stephen's Green (©475 6404); **France**, 36 Ailesbury Rd (©269 4777); **Germany**, 31 Trimlestown Avenue, Booterstown (©269 3011); **Italy**, 63 Northumberland Rd (©660 1744); **Netherlands**, 160 Merrion Rd (©269 3444); **Norway**, 69 St Stephen's Green (©478 3133); **Portugal**, Knocksinna House, Knocksinna, Foxrock (©289 4416); **Spain**, 17a Merlyn Park (©269 1640); **Sweden**, Sun Alliance House, Dawson St (©671 5822); **Switzerland**, 6 Ailesbury Rd (©269 2515); **UK**, 31 Merrion Rd (©269 5211); **US**, 42 Elgin Rd (©668 8777).

EMERGENCIES Ring ©999 for emergency medical aid, fire services or police.

EXCHANGE There are foreign exchange desks at the airport and Dún Laoghaire ferry port. In town, try *American Express Foreign Exchange*, Dublin Tourism Centre, Suffolk St (same hours as the Dublin Tourism Centre; see p.6) and *Thomas Cook*, 118 Grafton St (Mon–Sat 9am–5.30pm); all give fair exchange rates, although the best are usually offered by banks. Account holders with British banks may find that their own cashpoint card is accepted by ATMs. Otherwise, major credit cards, Eurocheques and cards and travellers' cheques are almost universally accepted.

HEALTH Residents of European Union countries are entitled to free medical treatment and prescribed medicines under the EU Reciprocal Medical Treatment arrangement, provided that a completed E111 form is held (available from Post Offices in Britain and Social Security offices elsewhere). Citizens of most non-EU countries are charged for all medical services except those provided by hospital accident and emergency departments. In all cases, it's advisable to take out medical insurance before travelling. Reciprocal medical agreements may apply between other countries, eg Medicare in Australia has such an agreement with Ireland and Britain, but check this before departure.

HOSPITALS Baggot Street Hospital, 18 Upper Baggot St (℡668 1577; Mater Misericordiae, Eccles St (℡803 2000); Rotunda, Parnell Square (℡873 0700); Meath, Heytesbury St (℡453 6555).

LAUNDRIES Most self-service launderettes are open Mon–Fri 8am–8pm, with earlier closing on Sat. Central ones include the *All American Launderette*, Wicklow Court, South Georges Street; *Nova*, 2 Belvedere Rd; *Powder Launderette*, 42a South Richmond St; *Wash to Iron*, 45 Francis St. *The Bridge Laundry and Dry Cleaning*, 37 Lower Ormond Quay (Mon–Fri 8.30am–6pm, Sat 8.30am–2.30pm), is the most central place for leaving laundry and items for dry cleaning.

LEFT LUGGAGE There are left luggage offices at Busarás (Mon–Sat 8am–8pm, Sun 10am–6pm), Heuston Station (Mon–Sat 7.15am–8.35pm, Sun 8am–3pm & 5–9pm) and Connolly Station (Mon–Sat 7.40am–9.30pm, Sun 9.15am–1pm & 5–9pm).

LOST PROPERTY For items lost on Dublin Bus (℡703 3055), or left on trains, Connolly Station/DART lines (℡703 2587), Heuston Station (℡703 2102).

NEWSPAPERS AND MAGAZINES The two heavyweight national daily newspapers, the *Irish Times* and the *Irish Independent*, are produced in Dublin. Its one evening paper, the *Evening Herald*, is part of the Independent group. Sundays see the production of the *Sunday Independent* and *Sunday Tribune* broadsheets and the more salacious tabloid *Sunday World*. English daily, Sunday, and tabloid papers are widely available – *The Mirror, The Sun* and *The Star* have their own Irish editions. Other European newspapers are available at larger newsagents, such as the O'Connell St branch of *Eason's*. Dublin's listings magazines are the fortnightly *In Dublin* (£1.50) and the free *Event Guide*. Other magazines to look out for include *Magill,* which focuses on political and economic analysis; *The Phoenix*, political satire; *The Big Issue,* which supports Dublin's homeless; and *Hot Press*, Ireland's left-field and iconoclastic music magazine.

PARKING On-street parking spaces may be hard to find in the city centre. The majority have coin-operated meters, but an increasing number are covered by disc display schemes, with discs available from nearby shops.

PHARMACIES *O'Connell's*, 55 Lower O'Connell St (℡873 0427), is open until 10pm daily.

PHOTOGRAPHY Most types of film are readily available from pharmacies and specialist camera shops. For rapid developing try *One Hour Photo*, 110 Lower Grafton St (✆677 4472), 5 St Stephen's Green (✆671 8578) and the ILAC Centre, Henry St (✆872 8824).

POLICE The main Metropolitan Garda station is in Harcourt St (✆475 5555). Central stations include Pearse St (✆677 3481) and Store St (✆874 2761).

POST OFFICES The General Post Office is on Lower O'Connell St (✆705 7000) and is open Mon–Sat 8am–8pm, Sun 10am–6.30pm. Another handy Post Office is situated at the rear of *Greene's Bookshop*, 16 Clare St (✆676 2554), Mon–Fri 8.30am–5.30pm, Sat 9am–1pm. Stamps may also be purchased at many newsagents. Current costs are: 28p for postcards and 32p for letters to addresses within Ireland and the EU; 38p for postcards to the rest of the world; 44p for letters to non-EU European countries and 52p for the rest of the world. Aerograms cost 45p.

PUBLIC HOLIDAYS New Year's Day; St Patrick's Day (March 17); Good Friday; Easter Monday; First Monday in May; First Monday in June; First Monday in August; Last Monday in October; Christmas Day; St Stephen's Day (December 26).

PUBLIC TOILETS Public toilets are few and far between and often require a 10p coin for entry. Key locations include St Stephen's Green (west side), most large shopping centres, and railway and bus stations.

TAXIS To order a taxi by phone call *National Radio Cabs Citywide* ✆677 2222, or *City Cabs* (✆872 7272), who run a fleet of wheelchair-accessible cabs.

TELEPHONES Local calls cost a minimum of 20p. Many phones also accept prepaid cards purchasable from newsagents, post offices and from the Telecom Éireann Telecentres situated at Upper O'Connell St and South King St (Mon–Thurs 9am–5pm, Fri 9am–4.45pm). These also have several pay phones and provide directories, including Yellow Pages. For emergencies phone ℂ999; operator services, including reverse-charge calls ℂ10; directory enquiries ℂ1190 for numbers in Ireland, ℂ1197 for Great Britain; telemessages ℂ196; international operator service ℂ114. The area code for calls to Dublin from outside the city is ℂ01. If dialling from the UK, prefix ℂ00 353 1 to Dublin numbers. To call the UK prefix ℂ0044 plus the area code (minus the initial 0).

TELEVISION AND RADIO Radio Telefis Éireann (RTÉ) is the national broadcasting company and provides two television channels, RTÉ1 and Network 2. In addition to a host of cable and satellite channels, Dublin's geographical position means that British television channels (BBC1 & 2, ITV and Channels 4 & 5) are also available. Similarly, there are three state radio channels, RTÉ 1 & 2 and the classical station RTÉ FM3, together with a national commercial station, Radio Ireland. Dublin also has a number of independent stations, including 98FM, 104FM and Anna Livia.

TIME Ireland follows UK Time. Clocks are moved forward one hour in March and back again at the end of October for daylight saving.

TRAVEL AGENTS USIT, 19-21 Aston Quay (ℂ679 8833), experts in youth/student travel; Thomas Cook, 118 Grafton St (ℂ677 1721), for general services; CIE Tours, 35 Lower Abbey St (ℂ830 0777), the largest Irish tour organizer; Trailfinders, 4/5 Dawson St (ℂ677 7888), for long-haul flights.

DIRECTORY

CONTEXTS

History

The Vikings

When Dublin Bay was first settled can never be determined, though it may have been as long as five thousand years ago. Although the Egyptian astrologer Ptolemy marked a place called Eblana in his map of 140 AD, major habitation of the area began when **Viking raiders** arrived from Norway in the first half of the ninth century. The invaders laid waste to an existing small settlement and founded their own trading post on the Liffey's southern bank, adopting the Gaelic name **Dubh Linn** ("dark pool"). This soon amalgamated with a Celtic settlement on the opposite shore, Baile Átha Cliath ("town of the hurdle ford", still retained today as the Irish name for Dublin). Though the exact date of its foundation is still questioned in some quarters, the city celebrated its millennium in 1988.

The raiders stayed and prospered, exploiting the fertility of the surrounding land, though attempts to conquer the inhabited remainder of the island stuttered, especially after their defeat in the Battle of Clontarf in 1014. Dublin was firmly set, and a largely localized Hiberno-Norse culture developed.

The Normans

Towards the end of the twelfth century, feuding in the rest of Ireland led to **Dermot MacMurrough**, the Ard-rí of Leinster, fleeing to the court of the Norman king Henry II to request assistance in regaining power. In return for his fealty, Henry dispatched a band of mainly Welsh knights under the leadership of **Strongbow**. Dublin was rapidly

THE VIKINGS & THE NORMANS

conquered in 1170 and the following year Henry granted the town a charter and established a court there. This opened the way for further migration, mainly from Bristol.

The new invaders circumscribed the town with walls, erected a castle and the cathedrals of Christ Church and St Patrick, along with other churches, such as St Audoen's. Unfortunately, most of their constructions were wooden and, consequently, little has survived for us to see today.

The Irish rose against subjugation in the early fourteenth century, and Dublin suffered during **Edward II**'s abortive attempt to reconstitute English control. The town was under constant threat, and the limited part of Ireland still under English rule became known as **the Pale**, with major restrictions placed on the movement and entry of Gaels. Dublin's isolation was exacerbated by bubonic plague, and the town's population dwindled.

The Tudors and the Stuarts

Further Irish rebellion led to forceful reconquest after **Henry VIII**'s assumption of the throne in 1536. Dublin became the focus for recolonization, and the town grew once again as a new wave of migrants swarmed in. Henry's Reformation of the Church resulted in an attempt to convert Ireland to Protestantism, and the dissolution of the monasteries led to much rebuilding on confiscated land, including the establishment of Trinity College. Irish resistance was quelled at the **Battle of Kinsale** in 1601 and the resulting **Act of Supremacy** established power firmly in London, with legal and official appointments going solely to the English Protestant migrants.

Dublin and Ireland became pawns in the **English Civil War** as various forces sought to gain control. The town was half-destroyed and its population was again decimated by plague. Rebuilding took place during **Cromwell's Commonwealth**, but the restoration of the monarchy in 1660 led to the appointment of the **duke of Ormonde** as Lord Deputy of Ireland and to the resurgence of Dublin. A rapid building programme began, including the Royal Hospital in Kilmainham, and the town again became a self-sustaining and prosperous trading entity. The arts flourished and the theatre, first established before the war, was revived.

King James and King Billy

However, another reversal came when James II fled to Dublin in 1690 and was defeated by William of Orange at the **Battle of the Boyne** two years later. Religious tolerance under the "popish" James was replaced by bigoted zealotry under the new king William III. The Roman Catholic majority of the Irish population was denied all political rights. Three-quarters of the Irish soil belonged to Anglo-Irish Protestants or absentee English landlords, a draining effect which would lead to disastrous famines in 1726–29 and 1739–41.

Dublin prospered during the eighteenth century while the rest of Ireland, with few exceptions, sank into extreme poverty. Architects were hired to build the **Royal Exchange**, the **Four Courts**, the **Custom House** and the west front of **Trinity**. Plutocrats commissioned their own extravagant town houses, like **Leinster House** and **Powerscourt House**, and the Georgian squares which so characterize Dublin today came into being. While Dublin's Protestant upper middle classes patronized craftsmen and virtuosi in the written and musical arts (Handel's *Messiah* was premiered by the composer himself in 1742), the aspirations of a rising Catholic middle class were denied.

KING JAMES AND KING BILLY

The Act of Union

Henry Grattan's Declaration of Rights during the parliament of 1782 came close to declaring Irish (or, at least, Protestant Anglo-Irish) independence. The following years saw the establishment of the United Irishmen, a movement inspired by a combination of the ideas of the patriot Wolf Tone and the success of the French Revolution. Seeking social reform and justice, they were driven underground by the government's declaration of their illegality in 1794. The subsequent revolt of 1797 was violently suppressed, leading to the 1801 **Act of Union**, which abolished the Irish parliament and instigated direct rule from London.

The impact on Dublin of this withdrawal of power was enormous. Although the social whirl continued to revolve around the new vice-regent's lodge in **Phoenix Park**, it was with the participation of a rapidly diminishing upper class. With Dublin's economic decline the town became the stage for political ferment and agitation for **Catholic emancipation**. **Daniel O'Connell** became the first Catholic MP of modern times, and ten years later he was Dublin's first Catholic Lord Mayor. O'Connell's attempts at securing the repeal of the Union resulted in his eventual trial and imprisonment for sedition.

The Famine, Parnell and Home Rule

The **great famine** of 1845–49 had a disastrous effect on Ireland. Almost 1.5 million out of a population of 8.5 million starved to death and nearly another 1.5 million emigrated, mainly to North America. Dublin's slums were already bulging at the seams when the Irish potato crop first failed in 1845 and thousands of refugees fleeing starvation began to arrive. The workhouses closed their doors, and diseases of deprivation reaped further havoc among those left on the streets. Resentment focused on the failure of the British government to intervene and on the absentee land-lords who had continued to profit while remaining indifferent to the suffering of their tenants. There was an attempted rebellion in 1848, the failure of which led to an increase in the number of soldiers garrisoned in Dublin Castle. A subsequent abortive rebellion by the Irish Republican Brotherhood in 1868 led to calls for Irish home rule.

The driving force behind home rule became Charles Stewart Parnell, MP for Meath and president of the Irish Land League, which aimed to secure Irish land for Irish people. A breakthrough appeared to be imminent until two officials of the British government were killed in 1882 in Phoenix Park by an obscure organization called The Invincibles. Attempts to implicate Parnell in the crime failed, but when his own long-standing affair with a married woman, Kitty O'Shea, became public knowledge, the Home Rule Party split bitterly and Parnell died not long afterwards in 1891. A year later yet another Irish Home Rule Bill was voted down by the British Parliament, stimulating pressure for reform from all quarters of Ireland.

In 1893, **Douglas Hyde** co-founded the **Gaelic League** in Dublin, using as his model the Gaelic Athletic Association, established eight years previously. Its aim was the preservation of Irish as a spoken language and its success prefigured the Celtic literary revival pioneered by **W.B. Yeats** and **Lady Gregory** and the establishment of the **Abbey Theatre** in 1904. Simultaneously, there was an expansion in the impact of political groups such as **Sinn Féin** and a revival of the **IRB** (Irish Republican Brotherhood). The focus for political struggle, however, became the establishment of trade unionism in Ireland, which was brought to a head by the **great lock-out** of

THE FAMINE, PARNELL AND HOME RULE

1913. The resultant heightening of political activity led to the formation in Dublin of the **Irish Citizens' Army** as a worker's defence force by socialists **James Larkin** and **James Connolly**.

The Easter Rising and independence

Promises of home rule in return for support in the war against Germany were wearing thin by the time the IRB and the ICA seized the **General Post Office** and thirteen other key buildings on **Easter Monday, 1916**. It took twenty thousand British troops and six days of bitter fighting before the fifteen hundred or so rebels surrendered.

Reaction to the execution of the leaders was followed by a revival of Sinn Féin and overwhelming success in the election of 1918. Instead of taking their seats at Westminster, the newly elected MPs met as the Dáil Éireann in Dublin and declared independence under the leadership of **Eamonn de Valera**. The killing of two members of the Royal Irish Constabulary marked the beginning of two years of war against the British, eventually leading to a truce in 1921 and the establishment of the **Irish Free State**. Disputes over the extent to which this incorporated the true Republican ideal, however, caused a ferocious civil war, eventually won by the new Free State forces. As a result of this internal strife, much of Dublin had to be rebuilt.

Since independence, the history of Dublin has become almost indistinguishable from that of its country, a new yet old nation endeavouring to overcome its colonial past. Much of the old **Georgian** city, especially north of the Liffey, has been bulldozed, and areas of the inner city, in particular on the northside, remain fractured and decaying, despite the mass decanting of people to suburban estates in the 1960s and 1970s. On the southside, especially around the Grand Canal, Georgian streets have been subsumed by rows of "tastefully designed" pseudo-Georgian offices.

One of the real successes, however, has been the revival and renovation of **Temple Bar**, which has done much to enhance the image and atmosphere of the city. Indeed Dublin has a vibrant feel nowadays, the colonial past is dead and buried, and the city is forging a cosmopolitan future within the European Union.

Music

Irish traditional music is alive and well in Dublin, and on any night of the week you'll find a session in full swing, impromptu or organized.

Though the west of Ireland continues to produce the best-known exponents of traditional music, Dublin has its own virtuosi of the whistle, the fiddle and the mandolin, and the city has played a major part in the continuation of the folk ballad, notably through **The Dubliners**, who have maintained their impetus for the last thirty years. The Dubliners have been blessed with two powerful singers – Luke Kelly (who died in 1984) and Ronnie Drew – and excellent instrumentalists in Johnny Sheehan (fiddle) and Barney McKenna (banjo). Their spirited and often bawdy performances were to directly influence the London Irish band **The Pogues**, with whom they recorded a wildly explosive version of *The Wild Rover*.

Dublin has had greatest success as a rock city. While showbands roamed the rest of Ireland, pounding out cover versions in shiny suits and with variable accuracy, Dublin experienced its own beat boom in the 1960s. Maybe it was the proximity to Liverpool or perhaps it was all down to an American studying at Trinity College, Ian Whitcomb, whose band Bluesville had a top-ten USA hit in 1965 with

You Turn Me On. Or maybe it was envy at the success of **Van Morrison**'s Belfast band Them. Whatever the reason, Dublin's music scene began to follow in the tracks of the land across the water. While bands like The Greenbeats and Purple Pussycat are long (and perhaps best) forgotten, there is no doubt that the beat groups formed a fecund spawning ground for Ireland's later success, fuelled by increasing access to pirate radio and the UK's Radio One.

While Donegal-born **Rory Gallagher** was blasting out the blues with Taste, the first Irish rock band to have a real impact, Dublin's own Skid Row set the template for others to follow. The original band featured Brush Shiels on bass (still a luminary of the contemporary scene) and an incredibly young Gary Moore on guitar, later to be replaced by Eric Bell. One of the band's lead singers was Phil Lynott and, while bands like Dr Strangely Strange and Granny's Intentions were twiddling with psychedelia and others like Horslips and Spud were beginning the experiment of amalgamating traditional music with rock, it was the black Dubliner who led the first Irish band to dominate the rock world. Thin Lizzie's first major success was a proto-metal version of *Whiskey in the Jar* (1973), but for many their finest hour was *Jailbreak* (1976), featuring *The Boys are Back in Town,* and a then unique twin lead guitar sound.

Punk hit Dublin in the mid-1970s as visiting British bands played *Moran's Hotel* and other local venues. One local r & b band took special notice and transformed both its image and its music. "We were the first neighbourhood rock heroes to happen in ten years", the singer **Bob Geldof** noted, with typical modesty. His band, The Boomtown Rats, had considerable success with singles such as *Rat Trap* and *I Don't Like Mondays*, before Geldof achieved worldwide fame through his co-organization of Live Aid. But Dublin's punk scene produced a horde of bands like Radiators from Space (with Phil Chevron, later of

The Pogues), the Virgin Prunes (with Gavin Friday), the Blades and the Vipers, all of whose influence would be long-lasting, and a certain Larry Mullen stuck a note on his school notice-board looking for co-pupils with whom to form a band.

That band, **U2**, released its first album, *Boy*, in 1980. Spin it now, almost twenty years later, and it's possible to discern how this then young band might later become the biggest thing since sliced soda bread. For, despite the recent critical backlash, U2 are, in 1997, the biggest rock band in the world. Their 1987 album *The Joshua Tree* broke them world-wide and also begat one-time popular Dublin parodists, **The Joshua Trio**. Since then, a series of albums (*Rattle and Hum*, *Achtung Baby*, *Zooropa* and *Pop*) have cemented the band's success, which they have fed back into the city through such initiatives as their own Mother label for new Irish acts.

In the wake of U2's success, a number of other Dublin bands (In Tua Nua, Aslan, Light a Big Fire) were signed to major labels, but though producing stimulating and often innovative music, none achieved lasting success. One which failed even to get signed up was Ton Ton Macoute, amongst whose ranks was a certain **Sinead O'Connor**. Her Prince-composed solo single *Nothing Compares 2 U* was a massive international hit, bringing a degree of fame which did not always sit pretty on her shoulders.

Other Dublin bands to make an impact in recent years include **Hothouse Flowers**, fronted by *sean nós* singer Liam O'Maonlai – who, since the band's split, has recorded with Tim Finn (Split Enz/Crowded House) and Belfast singer Andy White. **Something Happens**, probably the best buskers ever to appear on Grafton Street, produced some wonderful pop, but eventually faded. The quirky **A House**, fronted by singer Dave Couse, have struggled with the perversity of record labels. Both the mellifluous **Stars of Heaven** and the soulful, if unfortunately named, **Fat**

Lady Sings are no more, but the latter's singer/guitarist Nick Kelly has recently released his own solo album. Gavin Friday continues to appear in a variety of incarnations, and Lesley Dowdall of **In Tua Nua** has recently revamped her solo career. For a while, the success of Alan Parker's film *The Commitments* seemed likely to spawn a whole new era of Irish soul bands; the film's young singer, Andrew Strong, who enjoyed a brief spell in the spotlight and a band bearing the film's name, but few originals, continues to tour. The film's bass player, Glen Hansard, has experienced some degree of success with his band **The Frames**.

Today, you'll still find plenty of young hopefuls plying their trade in **Bad Bobs** or **Eamonn Dorans** (see *Live Music and Clubs*), but the dominant music in Dublin is undoubtedly dance, and there are more venues playing recorded than live music.

Books

Most of the books listed below are in print and in paperback – those that are out of print (o/p) should be easy to track down in secondhand bookshops. Publishers follow each title; first the UK publisher, then the US. Only one publisher is listed if the UK and US publishers are the same. Where books are published in only one of these countries, UK or US follows the publisher's name.

Fiction

John Banville, *The Book of Evidence* (Mandarin; Warner), *Ghosts* (Mandarin; Random House), *Athena* (Minerva; Random House). A selection of novels from the most important Irish novelist since McGahern. His 1989 Booker Prize nomination, *The Book of Evidence*, tells a sleazy tale of a weird Dublin murder.

Samuel Beckett, *More Pricks Than Kicks* (Calder; Grove-Atlantic), *Molly/Malone Dies/The Unnamable* (Calder/Riverrun). The former, Beckett's earliest publication, consists of ten tales describing the grotesque existence, marriages and accidental death of his Dublin eccentric, Belacqua Shuah. The latter is a wonderful trilogy of breakdown and glum humour.

Brendan Behan, *The Scarperer* (o/p). Originally serialized in the *Irish Times* in 1953 under the pseudonym Emmet Street, this slight crime tale, by the author of *Borstal Boy*, roams the bars and police stations of North Dublin.

Maeve Binchy, *Dublin 4* (Arrow, UK). Ireland's (and often Britain's) most popular author's four tales of Dublin life feature flat-hunting in Ringsend and disastrous dinner parties in Donnybrook.

Dermot Bolger, *The Journey Home* (Penguin, UK). One of the most powerful of contemporary Irish writers, Bolger set his third novel around the bleak lives of young people in his own native Finglas. *A Second Life* (Penguin) is an assured novel about a man who, miraculously given a second chance at life, sets out to find the truth about his adoption.

Christy Brown, *Down All the Days* (Minerva; Heinemann). The author of *My Left Foot* later wrote this flamboyantly styled but hugely enjoyable tale of working-class life in Crumlin in the 1940s and 1950s.

Ita Daly, *A Singular Attraction* (Poolbeg, UK). A woman approaching middle age seeks freedom in the post-abortion and divorce referenda Dublin of the 1980s.

J.P. Donleavy, *The Ginger Man* (Abacus; Grove-Atlantic). A raucous, rambunctious romp of a book tracing the exploits of Donleavy's semi-autobiographical and dangerously cynical law student, Sebastian Dangerfield, in postwar Dublin; banned for some years in Ireland.

Emma Donoghue, *Stir Fry (*Penguin, UK). A finely crafted lesbian love story from a young Dubliner.

FICTION

Roddy Doyle, *The Commitments* (Minerva; Vintage), *The Snapper* (Minerva; Penguin*)*, *The Van* (Minerva; Penguin), *Paddy Clarke Ha Ha Ha* (Minerva; Penguin), *The Woman Who Walked into Doors* (Minerva; Penguin). Doyle drew upon his experiences as a teacher in his native Kilbarrack to pen his initial hilarious trilogy centred around the exploits of the north Dublin Rabbitte family and written in his own vernacular style. *Paddy Clarke* is an amusing and moving account of working-class family life which won the Booker Prize in 1993, and Doyle's latest novel is a sensitive tale of a woman trying to escape a life of domestic violence.

Anne Enright, *The Portable Virgin* (Secker & Warburg, UK). Intelligent, witty, yet sometimes disquieting tales in a Dublin setting.

Bartholomew Gill, *McGarr and the P.M. of Belgrave Square* (Penguin). Irish detective novels are something of a rarity, and this is the best of US exile Gill's series featuring Dublin's Inspector Peter McGarr.

Hugo Hamilton, *Dublin Where the Palm Trees Grow* (Faber). A fine collection of stories set with equal assurance in Berlin and middle-class Dublin.

Neil Jordan, *The Past* (Vintage; Braziller o/p). Film-maker Jordan's first full-length work is an ambitious account of the troubled first years of the Irish Free State.

James Joyce, *Dubliners* (Penguin), *A Portrait of the Artist As a Young Man* (Penguin), *Ulysses* (Penguin; Random House) *Finnegans Wake* (Faber; Penguin). *Ulysses* is Joyce's masterwork, a sublimely evocative account of 24 hours in the intertwining lives of Dublin, Stephen Dedalus and Leopold and Molly Bloom. The story and its characters are loosely drawn from Homer's *Odyssey*, but the style is a breathtaking melange of parody, fantasy, realism and (Joyce's major innovation) stream of consciousness. Following its completion, Joyce strove for sixteen years to construct

Finnegans Wake, a cyclical concoction, following the Vicoesque concept of history as inevitable repetition. Often profoundly obscure, there are passages of great lyricism and humour in its account of the Earwicker family: Humphrey Chimpden Earwicker, his wife Anna Livia Plurabelle, and their two sons and pub in Chapelizod.

J. Sheridan Le Fanu, *Madam Crowl's Ghost and Other Tales of Mystery* (Wordsworth). Victorian ghost stories set in Aungier Street and Chapelizod.

Hugh Leonard, *Parnell and the Englishwoman* (Deutsch; Atheneum o/p). Fictional biography of the later years of Charles Parnell and his affair with Kitty O'Shea.

John McGahern, *The Leavetaking* (Faber). A spare and stark tale of a teacher in a Clontarf national school reviewing his life on the day he expects to be sacked for marrying an American divorcée.

Mary Morrissey, *A Lazy Eye* (Vintage; Simon & Schuster). Sensitively crafted short stories by a young Dublin writer.

Iris Murdoch, *The Red and the Green* (Penguin). Dubliner Murdoch rarely writes about Ireland – this fictional account of the time leading up to the Easter Rising is somewhat of an exception.

Flann O'Brien, *At Swim-Two-Birds* (Penguin; NAL-Dutton). A surreal and fantastically funny concoction of books within books, where characters rebel against their author, Gaelic folk heroes roam and Dublin bars are visited where "A pint of plain is your only man"; O'Brien's later works include *The Dalkey Archive*, featuring St Augustine and Joyce working behind a bar, and *The Third Policeman*, where a man imagines himself to be turning into a bicycle as a consequence of De Selby's theory of molecular transference.

Joseph O'Connor, *Cowboys and Indians* (Flamingo; Sinclair-Stevenson o/p). "Dublin at Christmas was a dangerous town. Too many familiar people, all waiting to jump out of the shadows and wave their latest attitude in your face." Life on the peripheries of Dublin and London with Eddie Virago.

FICTION |

Julia O'Faolain, *No Country for Young Men* (Penguin; Carroll & Graf). Republican politics and its repercussions seen through the eyes of four generations of the O'Malley family.

Liam O'Flaherty, *The Informer* (Harcourt Brace, US), *The Assassin* (Wolfhound Press, UK), *Insurrection* (Wolfhound Press, UK). *The Informer* is probably his best-known work, a racy tale of Gypo Nolan, a former Republican, who betrays a colleague to the Garda and is hunted down amongst the slums around Custom House by his erstwhile associates.

James Plunkett, *Strumpet City* (Arrow). A hefty and well-written account of Edwardian Dublin, extremely popular when it was first published in 1969.

James Stephens, *The Charwoman's Daughter* (o/p). Known best for *The Crock of Gold*, Stephens set this whimsical fairy tale, real rags-to-riches stuff, in turn-of-the-century-Dublin.

Bram Stoker, *Dracula* (Oxford University Press; Penguin). Stoker woke up after a nightmare brought on by a hefty lobster supper, and proceeded to write his way into the nightmares of the twentieth century.

Francis Stuart, *Black List: Section H* (Penguin). Although mainly focusing on Stuart's experiences in wartime Germany, the early chapters are set amongst the literary salons of 1920s Dublin.

Jonathan Swift, *Gulliver's Travels* (Penguin/Oxford University Press); *The Tale of a Tub and Other Stories* (Oxford University Press). Surrealism and satire from the only writer in the English language with as sharp a pen as Voltaire.

Colm Tóibín, *The South* (o/p). A woman turns her back on Ireland for Spain and returns thirty years later to resolve her life, and to die. *The Heather Blazing* (Picador/Penguin) is a powerfully understated novel of personal and political loss.

William Trevor, *Mrs Eckdorf in O'Neill's Hotel* (Penguin). A barmy American photographer flies to Dublin to undertake a study of the said hotel and encounters a bunch of bizarre characters staying there.

FICTION

Books on Dublin

Peter Costello, *Dublin Churches* (Gill & MacMillan). More than 150 churches are described and photographed in this detailed study.

Maurice Craig, *Dublin 1660–1860* (Penguin, UK). Revised since its original publication in 1952, this is a classic account of the Dublin of Ormonde, Swift and Grattan and the three great eras of the city's development.

Mary E. Daly, *Dublin: the Deposed Capital* (Cork University Press; University of Notre Dame Press o/p). A comprehensive social and economic anatomy of Dublin's development and decay between 1860 and 1914.

John Graby and Deirdre O'Connor (eds) *Dublin (*Phaidon). Detailed written and pictorial information on all the city's major and many less well-known buildings.

Desmond Guinness, *Georgian Dublin* (Batsford o/p). A photographic celebration of Dublin's Georgian houses and squares.

Vivien Igoe, *A Literary Guide to Dublin* (Methuen). Dublin's authors, literary society and fictional depictions.

Kevin C. Kearns, *Dublin Tenement Life: An Oral History* and *Dublin Pub Life and Lore* (Gill & MacMillan). Two vibrant and stimulating accounts based entirely on the reminiscences of Dubliners.

Niall McCullough, *Dublin: An Urban History* (o/p). The changing shape and texture of the city.

Frederick O'Dwyer, *Lost Dublin* (Gill & MacMillan; Salem House o/p). A paean to the city's former glories that contains many photographs of long-demolished buildings and monuments.

Peter Somerville-Large, *Dublin* (Sinclair-Stevenson; Academy Chicago). A populist history of Dublin from the Vikings to the twentieth century.

Peter Zöller and John McArdle, *Dublin: Portrait of a City* (Gill & MacMillan). Zöller's award-winning photo-journalism is teamed up with McArdle's caustic prose in an attempt to capture the essence of Dublin city.

Irish history, politics and society

John Ardagh, *Ireland and the Irish: Portrait of a Changing Society* (Penguin). A comprehensive and lively anatomy of contemporary Irish society and its attempts to come to terms with a changing world.

J.C. Beckett, *The Making of Modern Ireland 1603–1923* (Faber, UK). A classic account of the complexities of Irish history.

Douglas Bennett, *An Encyclopaedia of Dublin* (Gill & MacMillan, UK). An assiduously compiled reference book detailing everything you might ever wish to know about Dublin and then some.

Terence Brown, *Ireland: A Social and Cultural History 1922–1985* (Fontana; Cornell University Press). A brilliantly perceptive survey of writers' responses to the dog's breakfast made of post-revolutionary Ireland by its leaders.

Max Caulfield, *The Easter Rebellion* (Gill & MacMillan; Roberts Rinehart). This essential account of the events of 1916, originally published in 1963, has recently been revised and reissued.

Michael Collins, *In His Own Words* (Gill & MacMillan, UK). Extracts from the Irish revolutionary's writings and speeches.

John Cowell, *Dublin's Famous People: Where They Lived* (O'Brien Press, UK). Brief biographies of literati and glitterati.

Liam Fay, *Beyond Belief* (Hot Press, UK). An irreverent and often hysterically funny investigation into the state of religion in modern Ireland, written by a *Hot Press* regular.

Roy Foster, *Modern Ireland 1600–1972* (Penguin). Superb and provocative book, generally reckoned to be unrivalled in its scholarship and acuity, although it has been criticized for what some feel to be an excessive sympathy towards the Anglo-Irish. Not recommended for beginners.

Robert Kee, *The Green Flag* (Penguin). Awesomely assiduous history and masterful analysis of Ireland from the first Plantations to the creation of the Free State. Three volumes.

Fintan O'Toole, *The Ex-Isle of Erin: Ireland in the Modern World* (o/p). *Irish Times* journalist O'Toole examines the impact of globalism upon Irish society.

Cecil Woodham-Smith, *The Great Hunger* (Penguin). A classic and often agonizing account of the Famine and its aftermath.

Biography and autobiography

Stuart Baillie, *The Ballad of a Thin Man* (Boxtree). *Hot Press* contributor's excellent biography of Thin Lizzy's Phil Lynott.

Christy Brown, *My Left Foot* (Faber). Born with cerebral palsy, Brown painstakingly typed out this unsentimental autobiography, published in 1954 when he was 22, focusing on his upbringing in a huge southside family, dominated by the remarkable endurance and character of his mother.

Tony Clayton-Lea and Richie Taylor, *Irish Rock* (Gill & MacMillan). Now five years old, this is still the only decent book available on the subject and much of it is an account of the development of the Dublin music scene.

Antony Cronin, *Dead as Doornails: A Chronicle of Life* (Dolmen Press/Oxford University Press), *No Laughing Matter: The Life and Times of Flann O'Brien* (Paladin), *Samuel Beckett: The Last Modernist* (Flamingo). Cronin's work ranges from his sparkling account of literary bohemia in the 1950s and 1960s via an illuminating biography of Brian O'Nolan (alias Flann O'Brien) to his 1997 analysis of Beckett's life and work.

Richard Ellmann, *James Joyce* (Oxford University Press), *Oscar Wilde* (Penguin). Ellmann's wonderful biography of

Joyce is a literary masterpiece in its own right. His work on Wilde was, unfortunately, unfinished when he died, but is still an excellent insight into the work of this often misunderstood writer.

Oliver St John Gogarty, *As I Was Going Down Sackville Street* and *Intimations* (Sphere). Two of the poet and surgeon's accounts, once considered racy, of Dublin in the 1920s and 1930s; the author, much to his own disgust, was believed to be the model for Joyce's Buck Mulligan.

Michael Holroyd, *The Search for Love*, *The Pursuit of Power*, *The Lure of Fantasy* (Penguin). A massive and controversial three-part biography of Shaw.

James Knowlson, *Damned to Fame: The Life of Samuel Beckett* (Bloomsbury; Touchstone Books). This biography, by one of the world's pre-eminent Beckett scholars, makes a good complement to the more anecdotal and gossipy style of Cronin's book (see p.291), which came out at the same time.

Brenda Maddox, *Nora: A Biography of Nora Joyce* (Minerva). This is a hugely enjoyable account of the life of Nora Barnacle, wife of JJ and an absolute treasure in her own right.

Ulick O'Connor, *Brendan Behan* (Granada). An absorbing and sometimes pathetically touching account of the life of probably Dublin's most provocative dramatist and drinker.

INDEX

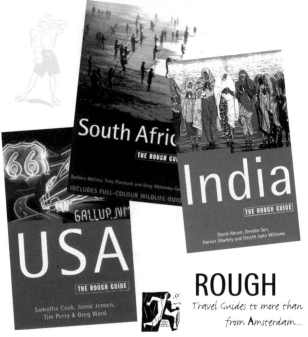

Backpacking through **Europe**?
Cruising across the **US of A**?
Clubbing in **London**?
Trekking through **Costa Rica**?

South Afric

THE ROUGH GUI

Barbara McCrea, Tony Pinchuck and Greg Mthembu-Sa

INCLUDES FULL-COLOUR WILDLIFE GUID

66

GALLUP, N

USA

THE ROUGH GUIDE

Samatha Cook, Jamie Jensen,
Tim Perry & Greg Ward

India

THE ROUGH GUIDE

David Abram, Devdan Sen,
Harriet Sharkey and Gareth John Williams

ROUGH
Travel Guides to more than
from Amsterdam...

AT GOOD BOOKSHOPS

Wherever you're headed, **Rough Guides** tell you what's happening – the history, the people, the politics, the best beaches, nightlife and entertainment on your budget

Malaysia
Singapore & Brunei
THE ROUGH GUIDE

Australia
THE ROUGH GUIDE

Europe
THE ROUGH GUIDE
1998 EDITION
30 Countries • 100 Maps •
Includes Turkey, Morocco & the Baltic States

GUIDES
100 destinations worldwide
...to Zimbabwe.

DISTRIBUTED BY PENGUIN

Stay in touch with us!

ROUGH*NEWS* **is Rough Guides' free
newsletter.**
**In three issues a year we give you
news, travel issues, music reviews,
readers' letters and the latest
dispatches from authors on the road.**

I would like to receive ROUGH*NEWS*: please put me on your free mailing list.

NAME . . . .

ADDRESS . . . .

Please clip or photocopy and send to: Rough Guides, 1 Mercer Street, London
WC2H 9QJ, England

or Rough Guides, 375 Hudson Street, New York, NY 10014, USA.

Good Vibrations!

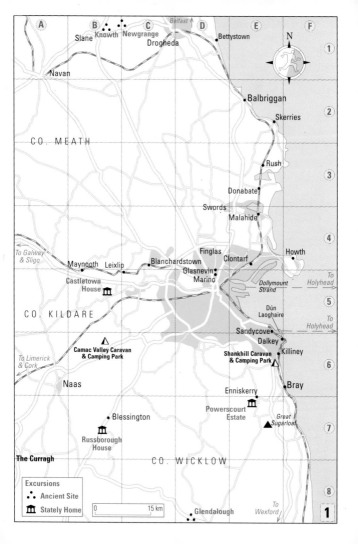

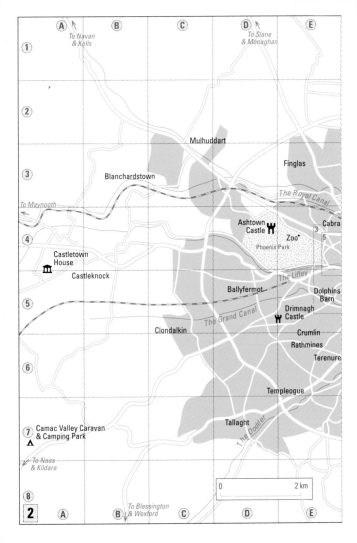

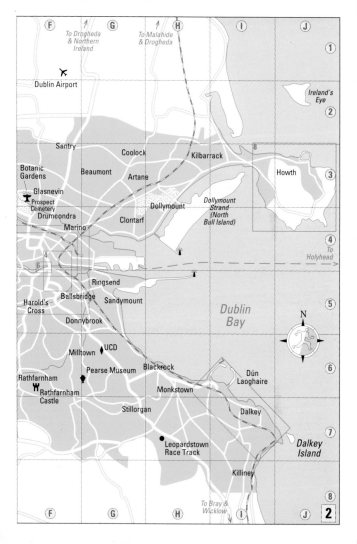

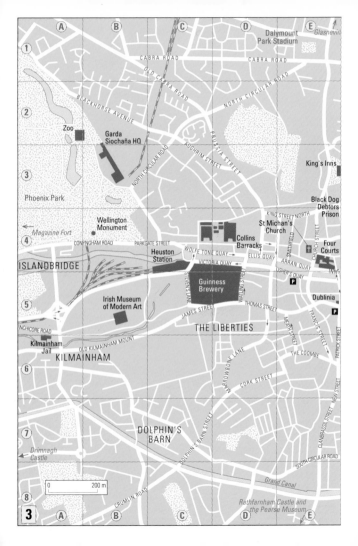

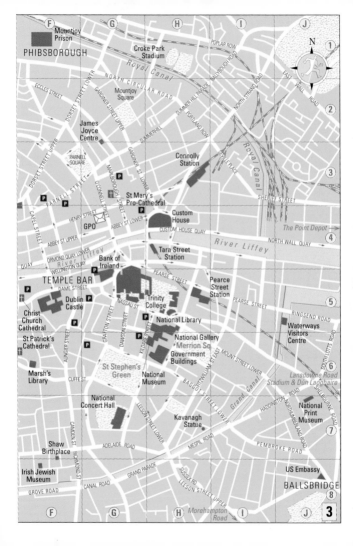

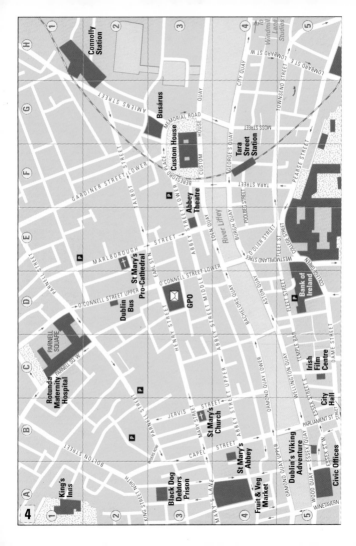

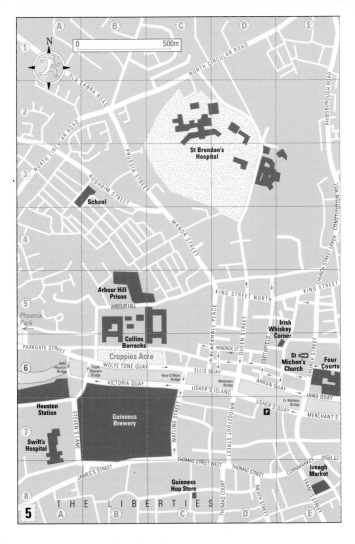

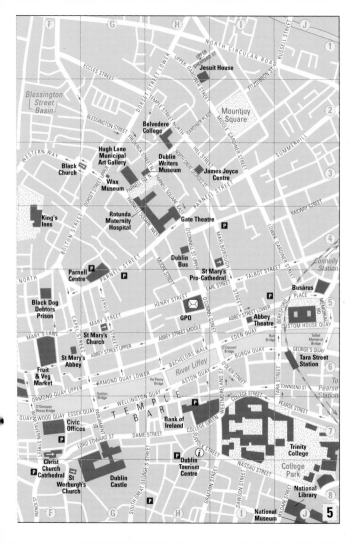

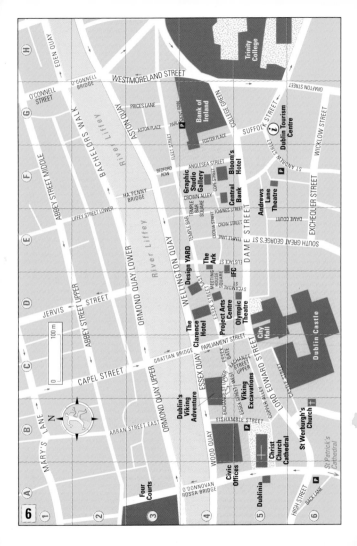

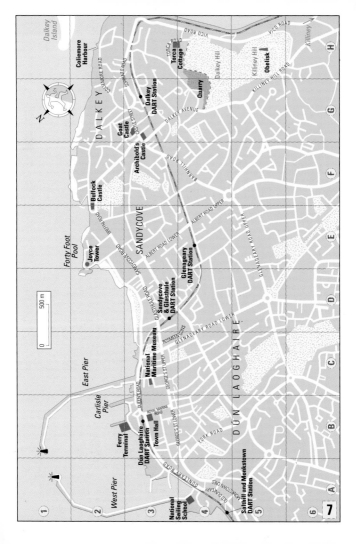

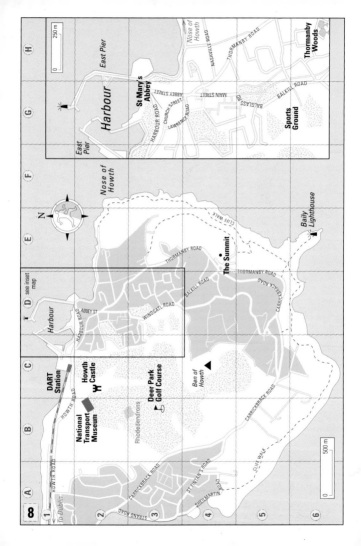